Julia Kris

transitions
General Editor: Julian Wolfreys

Published titles
TERRY EAGLETON David Alderson
JULIA KRISTEVA AND LITERARY THEORY Megan Becker-Leckrone
BATAILLE Fred Botting and Scott Wilson
NEW HISTORICISM AND CULTURAL MATERIALISM John Brannigan
HÉLÈNE CIXOUS Abigail Bray
GENDER Claire Colebrook
POSTMODERN NARRATIVE THEORY Mark Currie
FORMALIST CRITICISM AND READER-RESPONSE THEORY Todd F. Davis and Kenneth Womack
IDEOLOGY James M. Decker
QUEER THEORIES Donald E. Hall
MARXIST LITERARY AND CULTURAL THEORIES Moyra Haslett
LOUIS ALTHUSSER Warren Montag
RACE Brian Niro
JACQUES LACAN Jean-Michael Rabaté
LITERARY FEMINISMS Ruth Robbins
DECONSTRUCTION • DERRIDA Julian Wolfreys

ORWELL TO THE PRESENT: LITERATURE IN ENGLAND, 1945–2000 John Brannigan
CHAUCER TO SHAKESPEARE, 1337–1580 SunHee Kim Gertz
MODERNISM, 1910–1945 Jane Goldman
POPE TO BURNEY, 1714–1779 Moyra Haslett
PATER TO FORSTER, 1873–1924 Ruth Robbins
BURKE TO BYRON, BARBULD TO BAILLIE, 1790–1830 Jane Stabler
MILTON TO POPE, 1650–1720 Kay Gilliland Stevenson
SIDNEY TO MILTON, 1580–1660 Marion Wynne-Davies

Forthcoming titles
NATIONAL IDENTITY John Brannigan
HOMI BHABHA Eleanor Byrne
POSTMODERNISM • POSTMODERNITY Martin McQuillan
ROLAND BARTHES Martin McQuillan
MODERNITY David Punter
PSYCHOANALYSIS AND LITERATURE Nicholas Rand
SUBJECTIVITY Ruth Robbins
POSTCOLONIAL THEORY Malini Johan Schueller
TRANSGRESSION Julian Wolfreys
DICKENS TO HARDY, 1837–1884 Julian Wolfreys

---

transitions Series
Series Standing Order ISBN 0–333–73684–6
(*outside North America only*)

You can receive future titles in this series as they are published by placing a standing order. Please contact your bookseller or, in case of difficulty, write to us at the address below with your name and address, the title of the series and the ISBN quoted above.

Customer Services Department, Macmillan Distribution Ltd
Houndmills, Basingstoke, Hampshire RG21 6XS, England

---

transitions

Julia Kristeva and Literary Theory

Megan Becker-Leckrone

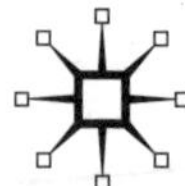

First published 2005 by
PALGRAVE MACMILLAN
Houndmills, Basingstoke, Hampshire, England RG21 6XS and
175 Fifth Avenue, New York, N.Y. 10010
Companies and representatives throughout the world.

PALGRAVE MACMILLAN is the global academic imprint of the Palgrave Macmillan division of St. Martin's Press, LLC and of Palgrave Macmillan Ltd. Macmillan® is a registered trademark in the United States, United Kingdom and other countries. Palgrave is a registered trademark in the European Union and other countries.

ISBN 0–333–78193–7 hardback
ISBN 0–333–78194–5 paperback

This book is printed on paper suitable for recycling and made from fully managed and sustained forest sources.

A catalogue record for this book is available from the British Library.

Library of Congress Cataloging-in-Publication Data
Becker-Leckrone, Megan, 1968–
Julia Kristeva and literary theory / Megan Becker-Leckrone.
p. cm.–(Transitions)
Includes bibliographical references and index.
ISBN 0–333–78193–7—ISBN 0–333–78194–5 (pbk.)
1. Kristeva, Julia, 1941 – Criticism and interpretation. 2. Literature, Modern – History and criticism. I. Title. II. Transitions (Palgrave Macmillan (Firm))

PN81.B3916 2004 2004052827

10 9 8 7 6 5 4 3 2 1
14 13 12 11 10 09 08 07 06 05

Printed and bound in China.

For Rick, for everything

Contents

General Editor's Preface

> Transitions: *transition* –, n. of action. 1. A passing or passage from one condition, action or (rarely) place, to another. 2. Passage in thought, speech, or writing, from one subject to another. 3. a. The passing from one note to another. b. The passing from one key to another, modulation. 4. The passage from an earlier to a later stage of development of formation . . . change from an earlier style to a later; a style of intermediate or mixed character . . . the historical passage of language from one well-defined stage to another.

The aim of *transitions* is to explore passages, movements and the development of significant voices in critical thought, as these voices determine and are mediated by acts of literary and cultural interpretation. This series also seeks to examine the possibilities for reading, analysis and other critical engagements which the very idea of transition – such as the transition effected by the reception of a thinker's *oeuvre* and the heritage entailed – makes possible. The writers in this series unfold the movements and modulation of critical thinking over the last generation, from the first emergences of what is now recognized as literary theory. They examine as well how the transitional nature of theoretical and critical thinking is still very much in operation, guaranteed by the hybridity and heterogeneity of the field of literary studies. The authors in the series share the common understanding that, now more than ever, critical thought is both in a state of transition and can best be defined by developing for the student reader an understanding of this protean quality. As this *tranche* of the series, dealing with particular critical voices, addresses, it is of great significance, if not urgency, that the texts of particular figures be reconsidered anew.

This series desires, then, to enable the reader to transform her/his own reading and writing transactions by comprehending past developments as well as the internal transitions worked through by particular literary and cultural critics, analysts, and philosophers. Each book in this series offers a guide to the poetics and politics of such thinkers, as well as interpretative paradigms, schools, bodies of thought, historical and cultural periods, and the genealogy of particular concepts, while transforming these, if not into tools or methodologies, then into conduits for directing and channeling thought. As well as transforming the critical past by interpreting it from the perspective of the present day, each study enacts transitional readings of critical voices and well-known literary texts, which are themselves, conceivable as having been transitional and influential at the moments of their first appearance. The readings offered in these books seek, through close critical reading and theoretical engagement, to demonstrate certain possibilities in critical thinking to the student reader.

It is hoped that the student will find this series liberating because rigid methodologies are not being put into place. As all the dictionary definitions of the idea of transition above suggest, what is important is the action, the passage: of thought, of analysis, of critical response, such as are to be found, for example, in the texts of critics whose work has irrevocably transformed the critical landscape. Rather than seeking to help you locate yourself in relation to any particular school or discipline, this series aims to put you into action, as readers and writers, travelers between positions, where the movement between poles comes to be seen as of more importance than the locations themselves.

Julian Wolfreys

Preface

The purpose of this book is to introduce students of literature to what I would argue are the most pertinently "literary theoretical" aspects of Julia Kristeva's work. As the organization of the book bears out, I examine these aspects in two different ways. First, I attempt to offer the theoretical foundations on which Kristeva makes claims about and readings of literary texts. Second, I put Kristeva's theory in close conversation with specific literary texts and figures. In Part I, I divide these foundations (though their division is by no means absolute) into two categories: her radical effort to redefine "textuality" and the new interpretation required to grapple with it; and her highly influential effort to describe the earliest workings of subject formation, which turn out to be themselves highly "textual" in their own right. In Part II, I explore the way those theoretical commitments inform her treatment of two literary figures: Louis-Ferdinand Céline and James Joyce. My final chapter in Part II looks at the way other critics have put Kristeva in conversation with a literary figure she never has, and probably never would, examine directly: William Wordsworth. In focusing on the way two good critics have juxtaposed Kristeva's theories with Wordsworth's poetry, I hope to offer a model of what other, future encounters between Julia Kristeva and literary theory might best look like.

In each of these "reading" chapters, I attempt what Clifford Geertz famously calls "thick description." That is, I work slowly through the argument Kristeva makes about Céline's peculiar, disturbing prose, aiming to demonstrate that this superb critical analysis does not merely *apply* her theoretical ideas about subjectivity and abjection to Céline's fiction, but indeed allows those ideas to come to startling fruition by putting her theoretical discourse into an intricate conversation with Céline. That is, if Kristeva's theory helps "explain" Céline's rhetorical strategies and their effects, so does that very rhetoric, his style, insinuate itself into the way Kristeva makes her analysis, implicating her pronouncements, even shaping the contours of her sentences. While English-speaking readers may be relatively unfamiliar with Céline's work, Kristeva's discussion of him offers a meticulous stylistic analysis of the affective significance at work in even the most elemental features of a prose sentence. This analysis is genuinely persuasively and carefully wrought, though perhaps lost on those who have not read Céline for themselves. In my discussion, therefore, I highlight her literary critical observations and put them in the larger context of her theory of abjection by explaining the larger context as well as the narrative particulars of Céline's works, the coordinates of which (plot, character, and so on) Kristeva rarely deigns to provide. Again, I discover that, in quite practical but also significant ways, reading Céline helps us understand Kristeva just as much as reading Kristeva helps us understand Céline.

In the case of James Joyce, Kristeva's engagement is considerably different, and my study is necessarily different as well. While her analysis of Céline is painstaking and comprehensive, her treatment of Joyce (someone she refers to in more than two decades of her work) also constitutes a "literary" analysis, but not one born of close reading. Rather, Joyce serves as an emblem for Kristeva of a certain literary tradition (of otherness, radicality, linguistic revolution) that she has variously, but persistently turned to in more than three decades of theoretical work. Here, I am interested in Kristeva's "reading of" Joyce, but also in the way "Joyce" functions as an example for her theory. I study her one substantial, extended reading of Joyce's *Ulysses* not only for what it says about Joyce but also for what, in turn, the passages from Joyce she chooses to discuss say about Kristeva's theory itself.

In my final chapter, on Wordsworth, I explore the arguments of two critics who read Wordsworth by way of Kristeva in ways that I believe transcend the mere "application" model of theory-and-literature that I, throughout the book, caution against. In a sense, what I explore in this final chapter brings us back around to Part I, indeed to what I see as the very purpose of the book as a whole. For to some extent, the two sections of the book belie its very thesis: "theory" and "reading" are *not* separate activities. In Kristeva's work in particular, they have always been deeply interconnected, mutually generating. For example, Kristeva points out emphatically and often that it was in reading certain literary texts that she came to rethink the idea of subjectivity, as much as the other way around. In Part I of the book, especially, I lay out the important ways in which Kristeva's own most penetrating theoretical arguments militate against the assumption that "theory" can serve as a masterful key for unlocking a subservient "work" of literature or anything else (the unconscious, for example). And in Part II, I try to demonstrate what reading Kristeva and reading literature would look like if we proceed not by the application of the former to the latter, but rather by seeing how they are indeed implicated by one another.

The supplementary matter in the book – its glossary and annotated bibliography – aims to follow the principles I lay out above. The glossary does not merely "define" key terms in pithy sentences; instead, it identifies the context in which Kristeva used those terms in the first place, the role they serve in the argument in which they appear. In the case of terms she has used throughout her career, I have attempted to map their multiple appearances and, when necessary, account for the ways in which the terms change with Kristeva's evolving theoretical investments. The annotated bibliography serves a similar purpose and was produced with similar imperatives in mind.

Again, the book's organizational divisions might be somewhat misleading. In every part of the book, I try not only to "explain" her terms, her theoretical concepts, her interpretations, but to "experience" them. In other words, I have tried to model the difficult but necessary process of really *reading* Kristeva, which is not the same as reading *about* Kristeva or reading distilled *summaries* of what her concepts mean. In this sense, I suppose, this book aims to tell you that this book is not good enough on its own. Its final thesis, then, would be, as Kristeva herself says of Céline: you will not just understand Kristeva's work, but get it, feel it, understand how and why it unfolds so strangely only once you read it for yourself.

Acknowledgments

I want to extend my thanks to my editor Julian Wolfreys for his ever-cheerful support, encouragement, patience, feedback, and advice as I wrote this book. My utterly peerless research assistant, Nick Myklebust, did far more than fetch books and check references; indeed, he spent long hours discussing the project with me at every stage, read drafts, read and synthesized mountains of secondary materials, and provided invaluable background in poetics and rhetoric. I would like to thank all of my colleagues in the Department of English at the University of Nevada, Las Vegas for their unwavering collegiality and support of my work. Special thanks extend to colleague Kelly Mays for her eagle-eyed proofreading. And the impressive skill and careful attention of Valery Rose, my copy-editor at Palgrave, improved my manuscript considerably. I am profoundly thankful not just for the constancy and generosity of my dear friend, Brigitte Sandquist, but also for her intellectual support. She was my perpetual cheerleader, but also my most indispensable interlocutor and reader. I give my deepest thanks to my family - my mother, father, and sister, Lauren - for their unconditional faith in my abilities and for taking care of me, in the midst of this project, when I needed it most. Finally, my greatest debt is to my husband, Rick, who has been with me since the beginning, across many states and many more cramped apartments; without his enduring love and support, this book would not exist.

Part I

Theoretical Grounds

1 The Objects, Objectives, and Objectivity of Textual Analysis

Kristeva in the English Department

In his 1984 introduction to the Columbia University Press edition of *Revolution in Poetic Language*, Margaret Waller's partial translation of the massive 664-page work that earned Julia Kristeva her doctorate, Léon Roudiez makes an announcement that, in its mixture of urgency and provocation, resembles some of Kristeva's own most memorable assertions. He maintains that: "Julia Kristeva is a compelling presence that critics and scholars can ignore only at the risk of intellectual sclerosis" (1).[1] This call to notice is implicitly directed to readers of English, particularly those in the United States, who have perhaps "been slow in recognizing the importance of her work, for it has not been translated [here] as promptly as it has been elsewhere" (1). Since that time, the warning has been duly heeded, in the United States and throughout the world. Indeed, more than thirty years of writing, psychoanalytic practice, and teaching on two continents have secured Kristeva's status as one of the most formidable figures in twentieth-century critical theory. To date, her work has been translated into ten languages.

A number of excellent resources are available to those who set out to explore Kristeva's prolific *oeuvre*. In English specifically, translations by Roudiez and others, Toril Moi's and Kelly Oliver's readers (as well as their scholarly work), Ross Mitchell Guberman's recent collection of interviews, John Lechte's critical introduction, and John Fletcher and Andrew Benjamin's collection of critical essays are only the most prominent among them. Such navigational tools, however, do not necessarily answer the crucial, though often unspoken, question of why Kristeva's work belongs in the context in which most people first encounter it, or why it might enrich that context. For despite the fact that most readers are introduced to Julia Kristeva in courses offered by literature departments, her precise relevance to the study of literature – the extent to which her theory is specifically a *literary* theory, if it is one – has yet to be articulated fully. The fact that Kristeva has sparked so much debate among feminist, political, and psychoanalytic thinkers can make her place in literary studies especially hard for new readers to fathom. In his recent *Literary Theory: A Very Short Introduction,* Jonathan Culler addresses this very problem when he outlines the general difficulty of understanding the relation between "*literary theory,* the systematic account of the nature of literature and of the methods for analyzing it" and "theory – not theory of literature, mind you; just plain 'theory.' "[2] He acknowledges that, for many, the latter represents "too much debate about general questions whose relation to literature is scarcely evident, too much reading of difficult psychoanalytical, political, and philosophical texts" (1–2). Approaching Kristeva's best-known work or that of her critics for the first time, a reader would likely place her in the "just plain 'theory' " category, with perhaps the same negative assessment. Just how her work might represent the former as well – a "systematic account of the nature of literature and the methods for analyzing it" – poses a more difficult, but similarly important, question, which this volume aims to address.

Certainly one obvious answer is that Kristeva herself often writes about literature, not only in presenting her theory of poetic language, but also in offering compelling accounts of abjection, melancholia, love, and other "borderline cases" of subjectivity. Kristeva's discussions of literature and her use of literary examples, however, rarely offer up clear models of how another reader might produce a sustained literary criticism in her spirit. Nor do they explicitly indicate *whether* and *why* one should. In some ways, this lack of clarity has not seemed to pose a problem at all, for readings of literary texts "using" Kristeva have become a fairly regular occurrence in scholarly journals and academic books. Yet while acknowledging the contributions of excellent critics whose subtlety transcends this characterization, I would also suggest that literary commentators who invoke Kristeva tend to *apply* her formulations without giving rigorous attention to what is at stake in doing so.[3] And though it is inviting to do so, reading Kristeva's accounts of signification and subjective crises primarily as *concepts* or *themes* to identify in literary or cultural texts limits – in fact, misreads – her theoretical contribution. We might see application as a readerly strategy, a critical stage, that is indeed a "resistance to theory," if an eager and well-intentioned one.[4] Its next stage – determining how one might properly produce an informed critical reading of literary texts that contends with the genuine implications of Kristeva's wide-ranging speculations – could not be more crucial to think through deliberately and self-consciously.

This question about Kristeva is a version of the vexed and much contested question of theory's relation to literature and literary study more generally. A voluminous body of discourse exists on this subject, and it is not the express domain of this book to survey it. As the title of this volume indicates, it is, instead, an effort to consider this general question by means of a particular case, one valuable for very common and practical reasons: although initiated readers may find the need to justify reading "theory" naïve or obsolete, for new readers it can be a formidable and prohibitive problem. In the case of a theorist like Kristeva – prolific, eclectic, rigorous, difficult, and occasionally outrageous – the problem has had significant effects, involving not just how her work gets used, but also how it has been situated within the academy at large. As Lechte, Moi, and even Kristeva herself have argued, prevailing Anglo-American assumptions that her work is essentially feminist, psychoanalytic, or political – assumptions at times used to condemn her – deny much of its full force, its full potential, as well as much of its intellectual context.[5] Not often enough do critics acknowledge that Kristeva presupposes and deploys a specific understanding of literary language and representation that speaks more directly to students of literature than her wide-ranging, multi-disciplinary studies might at times seem to do.

The project here will be to identify in Kristeva's work, in its sprawling "superdisciplinary" ambition, a workably coherent theory of both literary *production* and literary *criticism*.[6] On the former issue, Kristeva is fairly explicit, and on the latter, rarely so. But it is valuable to recognize that they are actually inextricable. To understand Kristeva's account of the way signification takes place in a literary work or a cultural phenomenon necessarily involves asking how that text is to be read, how it is to be interpreted. Her work persistently engages existing debate about critical discourse itself, most specifically by challenging two key assumptions: first, that language generates stable textual objects, clear referents of the world or experience, perspicuously open to critical understanding; and, second, that criticism may ever stand as an authoritative meta-discourse on such texts.

"Archivists, archaeologists, and necrophiliacs"

Articulating what is typically considered a poststructuralist critique of those assumptions, Kristeva's work reconceives both the object and the objective of literary analysis, as well as the objectivity earlier literary critics sought as an interpretive ideal. Roudiez's introduction to *Revolution in Poetic Language* not only situates this theoretical insistence, but also pointedly argues that Kristeva "has something to say to those whose principal affiliation is with 'literary' research," and even that "she, perhaps more than others, has provided a conceptual foundation for significantly changing one's approach to whatever he or she chooses to include under that vague heading" (6). To understand, however, just how her work would provide such a foundation, it helps first to recognize that Kristeva herself was working from – and seeking to dismantle – the broad foundations of a linguistic theory whose domain always included, but also extended beyond, the concerns of scholars interested in the particular forms of literary language.

While Kristeva everywhere acknowledges her debt to linguistic theory (Ferdinand de Saussure, Charles S. Peirce, Emile Benveniste) and indeed rigorously works from its precepts, she also, as Roudiez stresses, puts pressure on its "tendency [. . .] to 'eliminate from its field of inquiry everything that cannot be systematized, structured, or logicized into a formal entity' " (4). This claim is not original to Kristeva, of course. Her early articulations of it are contemporary with analogous critiques by Roland Barthes, Michel Foucault, Jacques Lacan, and Jacques Derrida. Whereas Derrida's *Of Grammatology*, for example, famously explores the simultaneous orthodoxy and radicalism of Saussure's structural linguistics, Kristeva identifies similar fissures, similar possibilities in the work of Benveniste. She argues that Benveniste, although caught up in the formalizing trend, "nevertheless opened this object called language to practices in which it realizes itself, which go beyond it, and on the basis of which its very existence as monolithic object is either made relative or appears as problematic."[7] Questioning the vision of language or signification as a static, "monolithic object," Kristeva seeks to develop a theoretical discourse equipped to regard it, rather, as a complex set of "practices" – not as signification per se, but as a "signifying process." Even more emphatically, she argues that a linguistic theory that supposes its object to be static overlooks the crucial instrumentality of the *subject* – embodied, historical, ideological – in the processes that perpetually generate this supposed object. She aims, instead, for a "theory of the speaking subject."[8]

Kristeva's "Prolegomenon" to *Revolution in Poetic Language* deals a rhetorically dramatic blow to linguistic theory's faith in the stability of its object of study and, in so doing, ushers in a new mode of inquiry:

> The archivistic, archaeological, and necrophilic methods on which the scientific imperative was founded – the building of arguments on the basis of empirical evidence, a systematizable given, and *an observable object* – in this case *language* – are an embarrassment when applied to modern or contemporary phenomena. (13; emphasis mine)

These scientists of the dead, she implies, can regard their object as such only by anaesthetizing it, by denying the living, material dynamism that her own theory aims to examine. In a calculated critical performance, the metaphorical shock of Kristeva's "Prolegomenon" revives formalism's patient etherized upon a table, by arguing that the "speaking subject" emphatically involves, in fact, a *body* that speaks language. Her project thus becomes "to perceive a signifying practice which [. . .] refuses to identify with the recumbent body" of the linguistic sciences – that is, to study the signifying practices perceptible in certain kinds of literature and other liminal discourses which existing philosophies of language have "repressed" (15).[9] Those philosophies "persist in seeking the truth of language by formalizing utterances that hang in midair, and the truth of the subject by listening to the narrative of a sleeping body – a body in repose, withdrawn from direct experience" (13). Drawing with deliberate unorthodoxy from Freudian psychoanalysis, Hegelian dialectics, and Marxian materialism, Kristeva seeks instead a "theory of signification based on the subject, his formation, and his corporeal, linguistic, and social dialectic" (15).[10] This critique of the formalist method of linguistic analysis – a method Kristeva attributes to those "archivists, archaeologists, and necrophiliacs" who are "[f]ascinated by the remains of a process" rather than by the dynamic process itself – together with the proposal she offers in its place indicate what Roudiez might have in mind when he suggests that Kristeva's work offers literary studies a shift in conceptual foundation. And indeed, such profound shifts have already taken place within literary studies itself: linguistics' "sleeping" or anaesthetized body is perhaps literary study's well-wrought urn.[11]

Formalist machines, New Critical puddings, and the "text"

The need to re-imagine literary analysis follows from Kristeva's critique of linguistic theory. For if the definition of language as a static and disembodied object is no longer tenable, neither are the influential modes of literary criticism that authorized and, in many cases, institutionalized themselves with the formal "objectivity" linguistics supposedly offered.[12] Together with the linguistic emphasis she retains are at least three key, interrelated components that distinguish Kristeva's approach to literature from those of her predecessors:

1 a commitment to rigorous and plural interdisciplinarity;
2 an understanding of texts as dynamic "processes" involving forces previously deemed outside the boundaries of the literary work; and
3 a self-consciousness that acknowledges the implication of critical discourse in that which it studies.

A number of her early works lay out these theoretical premises in lucid detail; see, for instance, "Semiotics: A Critical Science and/or a Critique of Science" (from *Séméiotiké,* 1969), "How Does One Speak to Literature?" (1971), "The System and the Speaking Subject" (1973), "The Ethics of Linguistics" (1974), and "From One Identity to Another" (1975).

She does so in the "Prolegomenon," if somewhat telescopically, through a telling shift in terminology. "If there exists a 'discourse,' " she writes,

> which is not a mere depository of thin linguistic layers, an archive of structures, or the testimony of a withdrawn body, and is, instead, the essential element of a practice involving the sum of unconscious, subjective, and social relations in gestures of confrontation and appropriation, destruction and construction [. . .] it is "literature," or, more specifically, the *text.* (16; emphasis Kristeva's)

As she stresses, bracketing the term "literature" presents a methodological challenge to "the efforts of aestheticizing esoterism and repressive sociologizing or formalist dogmatics" to treat literary analysis as a discrete exercise, separate from ideological or material concerns, which include for her the materiality of language as well as the body and its unconscious drives (17). More broadly, the brackets signal an ambition to transcend the established disciplinary boundaries of literary analysis or the formalist investment in the distinctively "literary," with all the aesthetic hierarchies that designation can imply. One consequence of this proposal, at once practical and theoretical, is that it expands the domain of literary analysis – or more properly, *textual* analysis – so that it may include the "poetic" dimension of discourses of all kinds.[13] Kristeva had begun to chart this domain by the late 1960s. For if, as she argues in *Séméiotiké*, a linguistically oriented "literary" study provides useful models of reading, "the new semiotic models then turn to the social text, to those social practices of which 'literature' is only one unvalorized variant, in order to conceive of them as so many ongoing transformations and/or productions."[14]

In the immediate context of the "Prolegomenon," Kristeva posits attention to the social or political dimensions of literary practice as one new objective of textual analysis (an objective some commentators accuse her of abandoning in later work). "Hence, the questions we will ask about literary practice," she announces, "will be aimed at the political horizon from which this practice is inseparable" (17). Thus, in *Revolution in Poetic Language*, moving from "literature" to "text" means practicing a textual analysis that resists the paradoxically "totalizing fragmentation characteristic of positivist discourse," a discourse in which literary criticism could still presume its aims and objects to be distinct from those of other disciplinary "islands" (such as economics or psychoanalysis or anthropology) (15). But the methodology she calls for aims in the other direction as well. Kristeva suggests that from such a vantage point, for example, we might notice that Deleuze and Guattari, in their theoretically groundbreaking *Anti-Oedipus: Capitalism and Schizophrenia* (1972), draw many of their examples of "schizophrenic flow" from modern literature, "in which the 'flow' itself exists only through language" (17). At once praising Deleuze and Guattari for their attention to the "de-structuring and a-signifying machine of the unconscious" and stressing, perhaps more than they do themselves, the linguistic and literary dimensions of their object of study, Kristeva makes a subtle point about method (17). Ideological and political concerns must inform critical examinations of literary texts. But so must insistent attention to the forces that generate non-normative "*signifiance*" ("this unceasing operation of the drives toward, in, and through language") inform properly rigorous examinations of social systems (17).

As the Russian formalists first argued, linguistics aims to account for the structures of "practical language," but is inadequate to describe the distinctive workings of "poetic language," which functions as more than "merely a *means* of communication."[15] Like the Russian formalists,

Kristeva's chief criticism of linguistics is that it is equipped only to study the kinds of language that serve "practical," institutional social structures, and not discourses that exist at the margins. Yet she does not hold to the relatively simple opposition Russian formalists propose; for Kristeva, elements of "poetic language" crop up in discourses of all kinds. Nor does she proceed as if the laws of "poetic language" can be explained by a formalized theory that presumes an objectivity and normativity analogous to, if distinct from, that of linguistics. By contrast, Kristeva's broad yet specialized concept of "poetic language" – which includes particular modes of literary language as well as other discursive domains – provides a way to attend to forces that at once gird normative structures of meaning *and* pose a threat to them. Kristeva's early work especially focuses on defining "poetic language" in this way, as a "kind of language, [which] through the particularity of its signifying operations [. . .] accompanies crises within social structures and institutions – the moments of their mutation, evolution, revolution, or disarray."[16] On the premise that "such crises, far from being accidents, are inherent in the signifying function and, consequently, in sociality," she commits herself to producing a "*theory* in the sense of an *analytical discourse* on signifying systems [. . .] that would search within the signifying phenomenon for the *crisis* or the *unsettling process* of meaning and subject rather than for the coherence or identity of either *one* or a *multiplicity* of structures" (125; emphasis Kristeva's). For this reason, literary or textual analysis, as Kristeva understands it, must be a necessary component of the genuinely interdisciplinary theoretical project she proposes. Analysis of "poetic language" in any of its manifestations, literary or otherwise, generates a specific kind of theoretical knowledge Kristeva distinguishes from what formalistic and humanistic sciences claimed to know.

Kristeva's 1971 review essay on the work of her mentor and colleague Roland Barthes, "How Does One Speak to Literature?," explains the basis of this very different knowledge. Both the essay's title and its approach cannily ask the obverse rhetorical question as well, the very question Kristeva implicitly poses elsewhere with regard to Deleuze and Guattari. Asking how one speaks to literature means simultaneously asking how literature speaks to us – that is, what it demands from a critical discourse genuinely responsive or responsible to it. For Kristeva, Barthes's originality lies in his self-conscious attentiveness to such a demand, in both his enactment of a true interdisciplinarity in defining "the key role of literature in the system of discourses" and his understanding that the new methods developed from shifting disciplinary boundaries engender an altogether different object of study.[17] Like Kristeva, Barthes dwells most insistently on a historical moment that seems on the verge of upheavals at once linguistic, aesthetic, political, and intellectual. His importance derives, she argues, from his being among the first to recognize that

> The investigation of these contemporary ideological upheavals hinges on a knowledge of the literary "machine." [. . .] He is the precursor and founder of modern literary studies precisely because he located literary practice at the intersection of subject and history; because he studied this practice as symptom of the ideological tearings in the social fabric; and because he sought, within texts, the precise mechanism that symbolically (semiotically) controls this tearing. He thus attempted to constitute the concrete object of a learning whose variety, multiplicity, and mobility allow him to ward off the saturation of old discourses. This knowledge is in a way already a writing, a text. (93)

Here, as throughout this essay, Kristeva highlights Barthes's studious regard for the "literary 'machine' " as something demanding a critical inquiry that is specialized without being disciplinarily discrete. In consequence, this approach produces a "knowledge" that is never as absolute as the presumptive knowledge gained by a positivist science or even a literary criticism with scientific pretensions. Along with questioning the borders between disciplines, in other words, comes an important challenge to assumptions about what delimits the literary "object" itself and about just what sort of operations it involves. In this regard, Kristeva's specific terminology here offers a felicitous contrast: Barthes's understanding of the "literary 'machine' " and its "precise mechanisms" differs fundamentally, for example, from that which informs Wimsatt and Beardsley's New Critical effort to isolate the "knowledge" offered by literature's so-called "verbal icon." In "The Intentional Fallacy," they polemically assert the need to establish literary criticism as a scientific discipline free from subjective or contextual concerns – such as authorial "intention" or readerly associations – by famously proposing that "Judging a poem is like judging a pudding or a machine. One demands that it work." According to this formulation, the literary object pre-exists interpretation ("A poem should not mean but be") and "works" or doesn't work because "it *is*, simply *is*" – the product of a "complex of meaning [. . .] handled all at once."[18] Barthes and Kristeva, by contrast, emphasize not what literature "is," but rather what it *does*; they regard it not as a product, but instead as a production, "always in the process of becoming."[19]

For Kristeva, Barthes's contribution to literary study stems primarily from his premise that any given literary work is indeed, in some sense, always a work in progress or in process, subject to a complex of forces that were, for Wimsatt and Beardsley, discernibly either "internal" or "external" to the literary object. The theories of both Barthes and Kristeva, by contrast, insist on a dynamic rather than a static vision of the literary work and its workings; it can never be "handled all at once."[20] And indeed "work" is perhaps a misleading term altogether, unless we persistently approach this "work" as a work*ing* that includes the critic's work as well.

On this issue, Barthes's essay "From Work to Text" helpfully illuminates what is at stake in the "Prolegomenon" when Kristeva shifts from "literature" to "text," or when she observes that with Barthes, " 'Literature' becomes *writing*" (94). As does Kristeva's "Prolegomenon," "From Work to Text" asserts that a "certain change has taken place (or is taking place) in our conception of language and, consequently, of the literary work," a change Barthes attributes both to the epistemological "break" brought about by Marx and Freud and to more recent interdisciplinary engagements among Marxism, psychoanalysis, linguistics, and anthropology (154, 155).[21] Likening this break in the human sciences to that wrought by Einstein's theory of relativity in the physical sciences, Barthes argues that

> the combined action of Marxism, Freudianism and structuralism demands, in literature, the relativization of the relations of the writer, reader and observer (critic). Over against the traditional notion of the *work*, for long – and still – conceived of in a, so to speak, Newtonian way, there is now the requirement of a new object [. . .] That object is the *Text*. (156)[22]

The distinction between "work" and "text" is not meant to privilege certain novels or poems, authors, genres, or periods of literary production over others. It is not, Barthes says, a matter of "declaring certain literary productions 'in' and others 'out.' " Instead, distinguishing the "work" from the "text" says as much about a specific methodological approach to literature as it does about the object it would study.[23] In the first of the seven propositions through which he defines this idea of the "text," Barthes writes:

> The difference is this: the work is a fragment of substance, occupying a part of the space of books (in a library for example), the Text is a methodological field. [. . .] the one is displayed, the other demonstrated.

> Likewise, the work can be seen (in bookshops, in catalogues, in exam syllabuses), the text is a process of demonstration, speaks according to certain rules (or against certain rules); the work can be held in the hand, the text is held in language, only exists in the movement of a discourse (or rather, it is Text for the very reason that it knows itself as text); the text is not the decomposition of the work, it is the work that is the imaginary tail of the Text; or again, *the Text is experienced only as an activity of production.* (156–7; emphasis Barthes's)

Along with other influential theorists, Kristeva has spent decades outlining and elaborating what such an activity entails, but like Barthes, she regards it as a complicated, "heterogeneous practice" that puts old texts in dialogue with new and involves the reader as well as the "writing subject," a subject shaped jointly by the forces of history, ideology, the unconscious, and the body.

Barthes subsequently builds upon a textual dynamism key to post-structuralist theory and goes on to highlight other premises on which Kristeva also depends. In the second proposition he argues that "the Text does not stop at (good) Literature; it cannot be contained in a hierarchy, even in a simple division of genres," and he proposes instead that the function of the text is to subvert these traditional divisions (157). George Bataille, whom Kristeva studies as well, serves as Barthes's example of someone writing at the limits of discourse and discursive boundaries. Particularly hard to classify generically – is he a "Novelist, poet, essayist, economist, philosopher, [or] mystic?" – Bataille is typically left out of "the literary manuals" of work-centered critics (157).

Barthes asserts, further, that the text is "plural. Which is not simply to say that it has several meanings, but that it accomplishes the very plural of meaning: an irreducible (and not merely an acceptable) plural" (159). This plurality always involves an interaction of reader with author and of texts with other texts, a condition of "intertextuality" whose dynamics also challenge assumptions about what is intrinsic or extrinsic to the literary "object," and which Kristeva first adumbrated in a 1966 presentation on the Russian theorist Mikhail Bakhtin, while she was a student in Barthes's seminar.[24]

Barthes's emphasis on the text's "plurality" follows from the crucial proposal, also central to Kristeva's approach to language and meaning, that the text engages signification differently than does the work: "The work closes on a signified. [. . .] The Text, on the contrary, practices the infinite deferment of the signified [. . .]; its field is that of the signifier" (158). This idea of signification as a series of relations among signifiers, of the text as "a playing; the generation of the perpetual signifier," is a prominent feature of the French theoretical context in which both Barthes and Kristeva elaborate their approach to literature (158). It draws from, but extends, Saussure's semiological formulation of the sign as a relation between a signifier and a signified, seeing in his model – as Kristeva suggests – "heretofore unrecognized possibilities of envisioning language as a free play, forever without closure."[25] And just as Saussure's theory informs Jacques Lacan's description of the unconscious as an endless "signifying chain" of metonymic associations in which signifiers refer to other signifiers, so does it offer a vision of literary or textual signification in which referential meaning is potentially "infinite" (158).[26]

Barthes suggests that a text so conceived necessarily changes the kind of interpretative operations one could perform upon it. For if signifiers in a text do not refer to a single, identifiable signified, then the process of determining "the meaning" of that text becomes equally open-ended. The *work* offers itself as an object that "falls under the scope of an interpretation, of a hermeneutics." But the *text* – because it is "metonymic; the activity of associations, contiguities" – demands an analysis that proceeds "according to a serial movement of disconnections, overlappings, variations" (158). One could look to *S/Z*, Barthes's book-length essay on Balzac's *Sarrasine*, as a particularly dazzling demonstration of the analytic activity he calls for here. Richard Howard, in the preface to the English edition, calls *S/Z* "the most sustained yet pulverized meditation on *reading* I know in all of Western critical literature."[27]

By defining Barthes's project as *reading*, Howard in fact highlights another way Barthes insists that the work/text distinction implicates critical discourse itself. He himself does so by pointing to the sense in which reading a text is a form of "playing," or indeed "writing," in its own right. In "How Does One Speak to Literature?" Kristeva everywhere stresses the importance of Barthes's definition of "writing" – primarily in his *Writing Degree Zero* – when she observes that his critical work is "in a way already a writing, a text" (94). In "From Work to Text," he affirms that recent experiments in music demand a new creative agency on the part of the listener that one could call "writing" (163). He similarly asserts such a shift in "The Death of the Author," concluding that "the true place of writing [. . .] is reading" (147). And in a section of *S/Z* entitled "Interpretation," he envisions a "writerly text" that "is *ourselves writing*, before the infinite play of the world" (5; emphasis

Barthes's). So the shift from work to text corresponds to a shift from "reading" to "writing," a process we may still call interpretation, but in a self-consciously specific sense. The dynamic, plural definition of the text – "a galaxy of signifiers, not a structure of signifieds" – extends to an analogously dynamic definition of textual analysis:

> To interpret a text is not to give it a (more or less justified, more or less free) meaning, but on the contrary to appreciate the plural that constitutes it. [. . . W]e gain access to it by several entrances, none of which can be authoritatively declared to be the main one; the codes that mobilize it extend *as far as the eye can reach*, they are indeterminable (meaning here is never subject to a principle of determination, unless by throwing dice); the systems of meaning can take over this absolutely plural text, but their number is never closed, based as it is on the infinity of language. (5–6; emphasis Barthes's)

Barthes carefully adds that such a vision of interpretation does not give us license to make the text mean anything we want it to mean; it does *not* usher in the unbounded critical "relativism" of which theory is often accused. Rather, "the interpretation demanded by a specific text" calls for something more like humility and rigor, an obligation to remember that "[t]o read, in fact, is a labor of language" (4, 11). In other words, reading means recognizing that both the interpretive process and the "literary" process are produced by the same material – language. "From Work to Text" concludes that the "theory of the Text can coincide only with a practice of writing" (164). Though Barthes's syntax is perhaps ambiguous enough to reference the ideological, intellectual, and historical "coincide[nces]" with which his essay begins, the discursive overlap resonates as well. Both theoretical and literary discourse, in this sense, are "writing" – not identical, but similarly implicated in the dynamics of language and the production of meaning.

From application to implication

This insight helps illuminate each of the three features I argue distinguish Kristeva's own intervention upon literary analysis, for it joins a rethinking of critical discourse with a rethinking of its object of study. Even more so, it underscores an imperative that extends as much to the task of "using" Kristeva's work as it does to her own endeavors. In fact, it renders that task unworkable and puts in its place another. Throughout "From Work to Text," calling for a newly interdisciplinary method of textual analysis and a new conception of the text confounds assumptions about what borders mark the "inside" and "outside" of each. It is easy to cite Barthes's and (even more) Kristeva's stylistic idiosyncrasies – the "literary" qualities of their theoretical writings – as merely clever performances of this insight. Defending Barthes against the possible charge that the "writerly" aspect of his essays betrays an "admission of weak theoretical discourse," Kristeva deems it instead "a methodological exigency of the most serious kind" ("How Does One Speak to Literature?" p. 95). For, importantly, Barthes makes clear that not only do *both* our mode of inquiry *and* that about which we inquire radically change when we shift "from work to text," *so does the very relation between them.* Part of this claim follows from the dynamic definition of textuality itself. If we take seriously its implications, we must recognize that critical discourse is itself a "text." As "literature" becomes "text," so does "theory" itself. As Barthes suggests, a textual theory genuinely attentive to language must recognize that it is itself made up of language. And a new objective of textual analysis is an awareness of what one's own critical procedures involve.

The practice of merely *applying* theory to literature becomes untenable in the face of such a shift from work to text, from reading to writing. Kristeva suggests that Barthes forces us to regard the relationship between theory and literature as one not of *application,* but of *implication,* "their interrelationship implicating both the 'literary' person and the quibbling 'scientific' specialist, thus setting the stakes where the subject is" (94). The co-implication of criticism and the very thing it studies begins with the linguistic "sciences" and remains the burden of any theory similarly devoted to studying the dynamics of language and signification, literary or otherwise. With that recognition, it becomes impossible to presume, responsibly, that critical discourse could remain in a masterful relation to that which it examines, that criticism could be a meta-discourse upon other kinds of texts. In "From Work to Text," Barthes reflects on a critical horizon that throws into doubt the idea of an absolutely authoritative analytic discourse:

> a Theory of the Text cannot be satisfied by a metalinguistic exposition: the destruction of meta-language, or at least (since it may be necessary provisionally to resort to meta-language) its calling into doubt, is part of the theory itself: the discourse on the Text should itself be nothing other than text, research, textual activity, since the Text is that social space which leaves no language safe, outside, nor any subject of the enunciation in position as judge, master, analyst, confessor, decoder. (164)

Kristeva credits Barthes with establishing a literary criticism attentive to this dynamic interrelationship and highlights the new aims he establishes for literary criticism: "The *objective* of this search is to make *manifest* the very *procedure* through which this 'science,' its 'object,' and their relationship are brought about, rather than to apply empirically such and such a technique to an indifferent object" ("How Does One Speak to Literature?" p. 95; emphasis Kristeva's). Not only is the theoretical claim to authority radically qualified in this description of textual criticism, but so also are the parameters of what criticism may claim to discover. The aim is no longer to uncover "the meaning" of a text, as hermeneutic models of interpretation set out to do, but rather to find the workings of a poetics ("to make manifest the very procedure") that includes at once the object of study, the instruments of study, and the interaction between them.[28]

Kristeva strongly attests to the importance of Barthes, the "precursor and founder of modern literary studies," for her own work, and subsequent chapters of this book will explore just how these methodological premises and definitions inform her specific investigations of literature. More broadly speaking, the theoretical context in which he and she established many of these ideas have influenced contemporary literary theory in ways, of course, that both overlap their efforts and draw from other influences. While linguistics serves as an undeniably central foundation for challenging prevailing models of literary criticism in the 1960s, 1970s, and beyond, so has psychoanalysis. Indeed, her deep grounding in psychoanalytic theory shapes Kristeva's understanding of textual analysis just as much as linguistics does, in ways we will explore in the next chapter.

In concluding here, it might be instructive to see how similarly another theorist presents the relationship between literature and psychoanalyis. Shoshana Felman's eloquent call for a shift from theoretical application to discursive implication highlights just what is at stake in reconceiving this discursive encounter. In her introduction to *Literature and Psychoanalysis: The Question of Reading: Otherwise* (1977), she describes the collection of critical essays that follow in a way that aptly defines what we might call Julia Kristeva's "literary theory." Reminding us that "implication" means, etymologically, "being folded within," Felman writes that the encounter between psychoanalytic and literary discourse is interdisciplinary in itself:

> The notion of application would be replaced by the radically different notion of implication: [. . .] the interpreter's role would here be, not to

> apply to the text an acquired science, a preconceived knowledge, but to act as a go-between, to generate implications between literature and psychoanalysis – to explore, bring to light and articulate the various (indirect) ways in which the two domains do indeed implicate each other, each one finding itself enlightened, informed, but also affected, displaced, by the other.[29]

As this book will suggest, Kristeva's theoretical engagements with literature operate from precisely this imperative. Just as she seeks instances in which signification at once establishes and undoes itself, so does she pursue such upheavals, such displacements at the margins and intersections of analytic discourse, as well. Such an endeavor perhaps succeeds most when it is risky, precarious – Kristeva's most influential propositions are also her most contested – but it makes a similar demand on readers who would draw upon her work in their own textual analysis. Bringing Kristeva's theory to our own task of reading literature requires a commitment to "reading" that involves all of the elements she argues come into play in her own analyses. The concept of application does not apply, and it cannot, properly, be otherwise. We are implicated as well.

2 The Subject, the Abject, and Psychoanalysis

From object to subject

If Kristeva's theory of literature depends on a critique of linguistics' approach to the literary *object*, it arguably depends even more on her deep investment in psychoanalysis' approach to the human *subject*. But it is unhelpful to say that Kristeva is a psychoanalytic literary theorist if we do not first consider what that label means from the inside, as it were: an intellectual commitment with a history, developed in dialogue with theorists of the past and the present. This chapter will outline what has been at stake in the psychoanalytic theory of the subject since Freud and will identify Kristeva's place in that history. In so doing, it will also show how psychoanalytic theory influences her approach to literature and how literature, in turn, gives force to her provocative vision of subjectivity.

In the previous chapter, we explored Kristeva's effort to see literature as an articulation of a *speaking subject* and considered her treatment of the voice of the critic as a speaking subject as well. We see that this view of literature and criticism emerges from her dialogue with linguistic theory and with a literary criticism indebted to linguistics. But psychoanalytic theory provides another crucial backdrop to Kristeva's understanding of the speaking subject writ large – in literary texts, in critical theory, and indeed in a broad spectrum of human discourses, from the most intimate discourse of the self to the most collective discourses of mankind (religious, political, and so on). The psychoanalytic understanding of subjectivity – in Freud, Lacan, and Kristeva – at once builds upon and reacts against the long history of philosophies of consciousness and self. In the hands of Lacan and Kristeva in particular, the critique of humanist subjectivity becomes one mode of attack (on linguistics, literature, philosophy) in the larger theoretical context of the 1960s, 1970s, and beyond.

The central importance of psychoanalysis to Kristeva's reading of literature becomes clear if we map out the shared premises and specific differences among Freud's, Lacan's, and her own discourse on subjectivity. Psychoanalysis never offers her a masterful instrument to wield in literary analysis. On the contrary, she deliberately begins with marginal or avant-garde literary texts and argues that their radical presentation of the speaking subject obligates psychoanalysis to re-evaluate the idea of the subject – not only the humanist subject, but also its own. Literature and psychoanalysis, in this sense, necessarily inform, and develop out of, one another. With these things in mind, tracing Kristeva's active role in producing a *new* theory of the subject serves three important purposes: first, it points out her role in pushing psychoanalysis to new limits; and secondly, it shows how some of her most compelling literary analyses developed – for instance, her influential reading of the avant-garde provocateur Louis-Ferdinand Céline. And not least, it also provides a somewhat reassuring intellectual ground for approaching her very least reassuring and most notoriously difficult theoretical concept: abjection.

In order to go forward, the discussion in this chapter will go back, identifying within the sprawling project of poststructuralism a specific territory, claimed by psychoanalysts and others, devoted to a theory of subjectivity. I will explore Kristeva's own contribution to such a project, stressing the important turn involved in the theory of abjection. Abjection is, for Kristeva, an experience of unmatched primordial horror, putting the subject in the most devastating kind of crisis imaginable; but ultimately, certain modes of discourse have found a way of speaking that horror instead of repressing it. Literature, she proposes, offers this possibility in an exemplary way, and may serve as abjection's "privileged signifier" (*Powers of Horror*, p. 208). The test of that proposal will follow in the subsequent chapters of the book, where we will read Kristeva reading literature in order, responsibly, to read literature by way of her.

The decentered subject and psychoanalysis

In 1996, Kristeva reflects in an initially predictable way on the aims of what her interviewer Ross Guberman calls "the 'poststructuralist' group." That is, she questions the very premise of Guberman's question, specifically its implication that a methodological unity or historical continuity defines the work of "Lacan, Foucault, Derrida, and others." Instead she maintains that the "writings of the authors you mention are unique to them alone, and they do not, in my opinion, form a group."

Yet she follows with a response that willingly defines the aims of poststructuralism in the collective terms Guberman provides, and allows that not only *could* we see among this "group" a "shared [...] belief or a conviction," but that, to understand the full intellectual force of their efforts, we *must*. On the heels of her qualification, she continues:

> Even so, it is extremely important to emphasize that these authors participated in a profound upheaval of mentalities and theories concentrated in France between the 1960s and the 1980s. This upheaval was unprecedented and met with great resistance, a resistance that lends these writings their apparent cohesiveness and that perhaps justifies the notion of a "poststructuralist group." (258–9)

Their aim was to resist the dominant interpretive models and assumptions of the time, especially the formalist or structuralist insistence that "meaning is a structure" (259). Kristeva's own work continually challenges the presupposition that such "structures" can be isolated as *positive* entities by a *positive* critical science.

So defined, Kristeva's version of poststructuralism offers a theory of the *object*. But, as she stresses to Guberman, the so-called beliefs, convictions, or ambitions that distinguish this group – and court the greatest resistance from others – emerge from a specific theory of the *subject* as well. This approach to subjectivity takes on nothing less than humanism's assumption of the essential "unity of man," that is, the notion that man is a coherently identified entity guided by consciousness, will, and rationality. She ascribes this approach to a vaguely collective poststructuralist "we" that would most obviously include Jacques Lacan, whose innovation was to juxtapose Freud's "discovery" of the unconscious with Saussure's structural linguistics.[1] But Kristeva elaborates a theoretical focus that best describes her own work:

> In the wake of Freud [...] we tried to highlight the heterogeneous, contradictory, and multifaceted nature of the psychic apparatus, and thus of human existence itself. [...] Our work fought against [humanism's unifying] tendencies, producing instead a vision of man and his discourse that is not "antihumanist" in the simplistic amoral sense that

> people have attributed to it, but it is clearly anti-identificatory. This new conception unveiled the hidden part of the iceberg, a part that proved to be quite active: a network made up of contradictions, of endless questioning, of shifts from one level of representation to another, and the like. By focusing on excesses – avant-garde writing, psychotic states, hallucinatory or oneiric states, sexualities, marginal or rebellious groups – we made passion into the unexpressed side of normalcy. (259)

From this critical perspective, subjectivity functions less as a fixed entity than as a locus of determining forces. Kristeva contributes to what she calls an "anti-identificatory" anti-humanism by seeking a kind of logic in the seemingly illogical energies of mind, language, and culture that structural analyses tend to brush aside. Both outside and within the normative structures of meaning, the "excesses" Kristeva identifies shape the contours of a human identity that is rational only if our critical gaze is trained on the tip of the iceberg and not its great "hidden" base. According to this "new conception," the subject both produces and is produced by structures of meaning that are multiple, illogical, and often at odds, matters of the body and culture as well as the mind.

Notably, Kristeva calls Freud the forebear of this critical pursuit. It is a gesture that serves as shorthand for the increasing privilege she gave to psychoanalysis over the course of the decades she describes to Guberman. Along with Lacan's famous "return to Freud," her work provides the most committed and sustained poststructuralist argument for Freud's theoretical importance.[2] She sees in Freudian psychoanalysis an unparalleled precedent for exploring a decentered subject by means of an "eccentric" method of analysis. "A return to Freud's text shows [...] the absolute coherence between his technique and his discovery," Lacan asserts, and Kristeva models her own technique accordingly.[3] While, in many ways, Freud's theory of the unconscious presents human subjectivity as the meaningful product of a set of structural relations, both Lacan and Kristeva (and, in other ways, Foucault and Derrida) emphasize that Freud never treats those structures as stable. Nor does he ever rest on the assumption that they are perspicuously open to fixed interpretation. "Meaning is a structure" for Freud, but in a highly contingent, conflictual, and overdetermined sense. Psychoanalysis, likewise, may follow certain protocols of inquiry, but it can never pretend to know its subject as such. Kristeva's polemical statement at the "Politics of Interpretation" symposium at the University of Chicago in 1981, highlights the undiminished force – both conceptual and methodological – she sees in Freud's project; while, in her view, Marxism and deconstruction have succumbed to academic discourse's

> extraordinary ability to absorb, digest and neutralize all of the key, radical or dramatic moments of thought. [...] Only one theoretical breakthrough seems consistently to *mobilize* resistances, rejections and deafness; psychoanalysis – not as the "plague" allowed by Freud to implant itself [...] as a "commerce in couches" but rather as that which, with Freud and after him, has led the psychoanalytic decentering of the speaking subject at the foundation of language.[4]

For such a relentlessly eclectic theorist as Kristeva – whose account of subjectivity owes itself in its early phases to Hegel, Husserl, Marx, Bakhtin and Barthes as much as to Freud or Lacan – this pronouncement is remarkable. The claim it makes for one kind of interpretation over others illustrates what many commentators consider Kristeva's epochal shift in the 1980s toward a more singularly psychoanalytic model for probing the depths of human subjectivity and signification.

Influenced by Lacan's popular seminars in the 1970s, but also by her teacher Emile Benveniste, "an extraordinary linguist [...] very interested in philosophy and psychoanalysis" who provided her with "an authoritative introduction to Freud and his world," Kristeva underwent analysis and, in 1979, became a practicing analyst herself (Guberman, *Interviews*, p. 8). *Powers of Horror: An Essay on Abjection* (1980, 1982) represents the first major work informed not only by her longstanding debt to psychoanalysis, but by this accomplishment in particular. Her two subsequent books continue this focus. Generally read as a trio, *Powers of Horror*, *Tales of Love* (1983, 1987), and *Black Sun* (1987, 1989) explore the dynamics of horror, love, and melancholia as three related manifestations of extreme subjective crisis. The latter two represent the most sustained attention she gives to the actual practice of analysis, but all transcend disciplinary borders because of the wide range of "borderline cases" she identifies, focusing her attention on such disparate sources as classical drama and philosophy, neoplatonism, renaissance painting, and case studies – both Freud's and her own.

Like both Freud and Lacan, Kristeva puts no faith in the unified, autonomous, sovereign, rational, conscious subject who strives onward and upward toward idealist perfection.[5] Her work persistently upholds the unsettling premise that subjectivity, developed in response to an "inaugural loss [at] the foundation of its own being," is always already divided, negative. And like Lacan, she reads Freud through the lens of structural semiology, seeing language as an irreducible element of subject formation. Kristeva's unique theoretical contribution is to insist upon analyzing the subject, always, as a speaking body that must negotiate identity in a field of signification *preceding* or *exceeding* either the symbolic order of signs Lacan calls "linguistic" or the structure of relations Freud calls "Oedipal."

Freud most famously makes the immodest proposal that the self is fundamentally *un*conscious rather than conscious, in *The Interpretation of Dreams* (1900), asserting that existing psychologies and philosophies of consciousness mistakenly locate the self in the manifest, empirically knowable here and now. In his concluding chapter, he reflects on both the nature of his subject and the difficulties it presents for the "science" he hopes to develop:

> It is essential to abandon the overvaluation of the property of being conscious before it becomes possible to form any correct view of the origin of what is mental. [...] The unconscious is the true psychical reality; *in its innermost nature it is as much unknown to us as the reality of the external world, and it is as incompletely presented by the data of consciousness as is the external world by the communications of our sense organs.* (651; emphasis Freud's)

Lacan and Kristeva always proceed from this skeptical insight. As Lacan defiantly announces at the beginning of "The Mirror Stage," Freud "leads us to oppose any philosophy directly issuing from the *Cogito*."[6] In other words, following Freud, Lacan and Kristeva reject the notion that subjectivity involves the willful and conscious *presence* of the self to itself, which is presumed by the Cartesian principle that "I think, therefore I am."[7] A subsequent essay collected in *Écrits*, "The Agency of the Letter in the Unconscious or Reason after Freud" (which Lacan irreverently tells us in a footnote was first presented as a 1957 lecture "in the Amphithéâtre Descartes of the Sorbonne [...] and continued afterwards over drinks"), expands this argument (176). Here, Lacan puts the *cogito* through the wringer, bringing Saussure's linguistic insight that signification works by means of *difference* (a word means what it means because it is *not* another word) to a psychoanalytic explanation of what "I am."[8] Lacan argues that the central concern for philosophy after Freud is "a question of the *place* man assigns to himself at the *center* of a universe" (165; emphasis mine).[9] And he maintains that Saussure and Freud converge in their understanding of meaning as structural, differential, negative. In Saussure's linguistics, language is "a system of pure values [...] *with no positive terms*."[10]

Similarly, in Freud's psychoanalysis, subjectivity is defined by a system of displacements and distortions – in other words, by an unconscious that is forever and by definition *elsewhere*. Thus the subject is, in Lacan's words, "eccentric" rather than "cocentric," defined by absence not presence (165). Lacan explains the orientation of the subject in "what might be called the Freudian universe" in a capricious (though serious) mangling of Descartes's neat formula: "I think where I am not, therefore I am where I do not think [...] I am not wherever I am the plaything of my thought; I think of what I am where I do not think to think" (165–6).

The subject, in the beginning

These pronouncements indicate the place designated for the subject by psychoanalysis, *what* "I am" and *where*. Just as important to psychoanalysis are the questions of *how* and *when* the "I" assumes that place. In other words, just how and when does the emergence of the subject, identifiable as a self and differentiated from others, *take place*?[11] Despite their general agreement on the nature of the psychoanalytic subject, Freud, Lacan, and Kristeva offer different accounts of its genesis. Comparing their theoretical "myths of origin" can help bring into focus what makes Kristeva's account unique. In fact, we might best chart the trajectory of psychoanalytic discourse from Freud to Lacan to Kristeva by describing the way each narrates the event of subjective differentiation: each theorist identifies an earlier and earlier moment at which the foundations of the self are negotiated.[12]

In *Civilization and Its Discontents*, for instance, Freud expresses skepticism about what religion calls one's spiritual connection to the infinite, the "sensation of 'eternity,' a feeling of something limitless, unbounded – as it were 'oceanic.' "[13] This idea "fits so badly with the fabric of our psychology" that it demands another explanation. Psychoanalysis, he argues, provides that explanation by seeking the source of the "oceanic feeling" not in the spiritual intimation of transcendent fullness, but in a painful instinctual memory of the founding separation between the self and the "external world" (12). This painful, necessary break marks the origin of civilization's discontent. This experience is recalled, throughout the course of life, with each new challenge to the presumed "autonomous and unitary" borders of "the self, our own ego" (12). And indeed there are "a great number of states in which the boundary lines between the ego and the external world become uncertain or in which they are actually drawn incorrectly" (13). The "pathological processes" that manifest such a crisis of borders harken back to the primal event through which the borders were erected in the first place – in which "there is for the first time set over against the ego an 'object,' in the form of something which exists 'outside' " (14–15).[14] In Freud's more familiar model of the Oedipus complex, the subject constitutes himself in the process of "discovering" castration, thus coming to recognize his place in the triad of mother–father–child. Freudian castration, as Kristeva describes it, "puts the finishing touches on the process of separation that posits the subject as signifiable, which is to say separate, always confronted by an other" (*Revolution in Poetic Language*, p. 47).

Lacan concurs with Freud and expands the Freudian discovery by pushing the moment of differentiation further back in the subject's prehistory, identifying its origins in the complex workings of the pre- or non-symbolic realm Lacan calls the *imaginary*. Here the first delineations of subjectivity – the first establishment of self and other – arise not from the fraught relations of the Oedipal triangle, but rather from a pre-Oedipal, "specular" relation between an "ideal-I" and an actual I. Prior to the Oedipal stage, and the entrance into language and the realm of the *symbolic*, the incipient subject experiences the pathos of division, a fundamental discrepancy between the self and the illusion of self. The dynamic set in motion by this initial structure defines subjectivity for Lacan and provides a key principle of his psychoanalytic theory: the self itself is by definition split, moved by desire, modulated by loss. At its foundation, "I" *is* other.[15]

In "The Mirror Stage," the child gains a first apprehension of self by seeing his figure in the mirror, which provides the optical illusion of an autonomous subject, an idealized version of the actually immature, dependent creature whom it reflects. "The startling spectacle of the infant in front of the mirror," Lacan tells us, provides a model for subject formation that goes well beyond literal, developmental explanation (1). Lacan narrates the event as follows:

> Unable as yet to walk, or even to stand up, and held tightly as he is by some support, human or artificial [... the child] nevertheless overcomes, in a flutter of jubilant activity, the obstructions of his support and, fixing his attitude in a slightly leaning-forward position, in order to hold it in his gaze, brings back an instantaneous aspect of the image. (2)

This mundane event acts out an "exemplary situation" full of theoretical import, in which the "*I* is precipitated in a primordial form, before it is objectified in the dialectic of identification with the other, and before language restores to it [...] its function as subject" (2; emphasis Lacan's). Lacan stresses that this stage produces the conditions by which the subject will relate to objects, distinguish self from other, in the realm of the symbolic: it is "primordial," "before" identification with an other, "before language" situates it in a structure. The insular, provisional (and imaginary) relation between the self and the mirror image of self posits a place for the subject in a structure that will define his relation to all others in the symbolic.

Kristeva reaches still further back to narrate an emphatically more primordial, extra-linguistic, and conflictual story of the subject "in the beginning." In fact, in keeping with her thesis that subjectivity is a perpetual work in progress, her story of subjective origin tellingly lacks definitive beginnings and endings. Like Lacan, Kristeva, too, offers a model that structurally anticipates "what will be 'me,' " that posits, positions, and makes possible what will come to be.[16] But she also suggests both that Lacan's mirror stage tells only a partial story and that the distinctions he makes among the realms of the imaginary, the symbolic, and the real in narrating it are incomplete and too rigidly demarcated.[17] The dynamics she identifies in the genesis of subjectivity move away from the father-centered structures Lacan and Freud rely on: the appropriation of the "Name of the Father" in the acquisition of language, the Oedipus complex, castration, the phallus. Her early work especially shifts the focus to the role of the maternal body in the process of the subject's coming to be.

Ironically, Kristeva derives force and authority for her critique of Lacan by following his own exhortation: she returns to Freud. She sees powerful instinctual drives and primary processes, first outlined by Freud, at work in these pre-subjective relations, which remain unexplained by the mirror stage that marks the subject's transition from the imaginary to the symbolic. Kristeva favors Freud's theory of the drives because it offers a way to understand the signifying process as bodily or biological as well as social; it provides a "bridge between the biological foundation of signifying functioning and its determination by the family and society" (*Revolution in Poetic Language*, p. 167). The Freudian drives are not merely dualistic, life drives versus death drives, but rather, radically "heterogeneous." They dynamically and contradictorily move (the subject) in several directions at once. Importantly for Kristeva, sustained theoretical attention to the drives reinforces the decenteredness and even fragmentation of the psychoanalytic subject: "Drives are [...] the repeated scission of matter that generates significance, the place where an always absent subject is produced" (167).

According to Kristeva, the infant's intimations of self emerge from a multiplicity of bodily sensations not limited to specular recognition in the mirror. She proposes the concept of the *semiotic* – an "asymbolic" realm that is also not reducible to Lacan's categories of the imaginary or the real – which *precedes* and *exceeds* the workings of the mirror stage. In "The Subject in Process," *Revolution in Poetic Language*, "Place Names," "Stabat Mater," and elsewhere, cries and laughter, sound and touch and gesture indicate for Kristeva a pre-symbolic dimension to signification that is bodily and drive-motivated and that lacks the defining structure, coherence, and spatial fixity implied by Lacan's formulations. Bodily interdependence, shared smiles, crying, and the abstract rhythms, sounds, and touches of the symbiotic mother–child interaction set up and intimate a space, without interior or exterior, that Kristeva calls the "semiotic *chora*." In "Place Names," Kristeva describes infantile laughter as an example of the "semiotic disposition." It presents the "imprint of an archaic moment, the threshold of space, the '*chora*' as primitive stability [...] simply markers of something in the process of becoming stability."[18] "Chronologically and logically long before the mirror stage," the newborn's laughter is "a joy without words," an early creation of the space (the "riant spaciousness") that will only later become the demarcated space between self and other, or between the self and the illusion of self in the mirror stage.[19]

As the example demonstrates, Kristeva's theory of subject formation claims temporal priority and also expands the dynamics of signification beyond the normal boundaries of language. She also pointedly distinguishes herself from Lacan on the question of language, arguing that Lacan's over-reliance on an "always already there of language" prevents him from attending adequately to the subtle and shadowy universe of signification that "cannot be reduced" to meaning, in a properly linguistic sense (Oliver, *Reading Kristeva*, p. 39). Kristeva makes this case in a 1983 essay included in a special volume of *Psychiatry and the Humanities* devoted to "Interpreting Lacan."[20] She cites Lacan's late interest in the notion of *lalangue*, the non-totalizable and even nonsensical language of the "mother-tongue," which he distinguishes from normative communication or dialogue and aligns more with the supposedly "impossible real" than with the imaginary. Kristeva argues that *lalangue* still leaves key questions unanswered, that the concept is still "*homogeneous* with the realm of signification," as Lacan describes it (35). She suggests that "[n]o matter how impossible the real might be" for Lacan, no matter what space he provides for aspects of signification that seem extra-linguistic, ultimately "nothing escapes" his system:

> The problem of the heterogeneous in meaning, of the unsymbolizable, the unsignifiable, which we confront in the analysand's discourse as an inhibition, a symptom, or an anxiety, characterizes the very condition of the speaking being, who is not only split, but split into an irreconcilable heterogeneity. And this problem *still* remains unresolved. (35–6; emphasis Kristeva's)[21]

It helps to note the ambiguity of that last sentence: that this "problem *still* remains unresolved" means at least two things. In the first sense, Kristeva criticizes Lacan's theory (and implicitly, existing linguistic theory as well) for giving insufficient attention to the "irreconcilable heterogeneity" of the unsymbolizable. To call the problem unresolved or irreconcilable, however, is not to say that the unsymbolizable is untheorizable. Kristeva seeks to theorize it; she insists, in fact, that she must. For that which lurks at, or is shunted to, the limits of both symbolic structures and analyses of them is, for Kristeva, key to the constitution of those structures in the first place. By tracing the shadowy preludes to Lacan's founding drama, Kristeva follows through on Lacan's own insistence that the "taking place" of the subject is always elsewhere, offstage, another scene. "I think where I am not, therefore I am where I do not think to think," Lacan says, speaking for the anti-Cartesian psychoanalytic subject. Kristeva's theory "thinks" where Lacan's does not, aiming at the unthought of psychoanalytic and linguistic theory as a way to probe still further the unthought of the subject as such. Telling the story of when and how the subject comes to be by dwelling on the receding origins of its prehistory thus signals a specific theoretical ambition: "the real stakes of a discourse on childhood within Western thought involve a confrontation between thought and what it is not, a wandering at the limits of the thinkable" ("Place Names," p. 276).

In the second sense, Kristeva's statement that the "problem of the heterogeneous in meaning [...] *still* remains unresolved" describes the condition not only of subjectivity, but also of modernity, as she understands it: a "permanent crisis."[22] Her work of the 1980s especially draws from her analytic insight that subjectivity originates in crisis and, significantly, *remains* in crisis. In her explorations of abjection, melancholia, and love – extreme conditions of the subject that nevertheless define the subject in crucial ways – Kristeva establishes an analytic position that maintains the suggestively fraught contours of that crisis in order to explore them fully. The challenge for the analyst, as she says in her next sentence, is "[t]o keep it unresolved," not to assume that theoretical exploration is mere neutralizing explanation ("Within the Microcosm," p. 36). In pursuit of this effort, *Powers of Horror*, *Tales of Love*, and *Black Sun* will focus on the most primordial and, simultaneously, the most extreme experiences of the self. As she explains in her Guberman interview, this approach sees the "excesses" of human being as the "unexpressed side of normalcy." Her work's eccentric gaze both examines existing discourses of the unexpressed and seeks to articulate its own.

"Before the beginning"

In *Powers of Horror*, Kristeva's theory of *abjection* seizes the pathos of poststructuralism's decentered subject and plays it for highest drama. In prose that unsettlingly mingles formidable theoretical difficulty with strangely inviting lyricism, she urges her audience to envision subject formation as a kind of theater of cruelty, in which intense joy, pleasure, beauty, and promise exist in uncomfortable proximity to violence and horror. Kristeva identifies pivotal instances of abjection in the earliest establishments of selfhood and in the deepest structures of cultures. The abject harkens back to the shadowy beginnings of our prehistory, both individual and collective. But it can also occur at any time, and does – all the more potently because it recalls those primal struggles. Pre-symbolic, abjection yet persists and returns in flashes, at places of strain or moments of crisis within the symbolic system. Like love and melancholy, abjection brings into relief by bringing into crisis the lines that distinguish self from other. In abjection, "I behold the breaking down of a world that has erased its borders" (4). As such, abjection offers rich territory for exploring the eccentricity of human subjectivity, giving Kristeva a further opportunity to argue that the dynamics at the margins of self and culture significantly shape – indeed serve as the foundations for – their symbolic "norms." The "abject and abjection," in this regard, "are my safeguards. The primers of my culture" (2). In the broadest sense, abjection experientially and theoretically "notifies us of the limits of the human universe" (11).

Kristeva's theory of abjection stresses, with a starkness that sets it apart from previous psychoanalytic accounts, the intense affective turmoil and visceral materiality of our earliest negotiations. As the "developmental" account it aims on one level to be, her treatment of abjection forcefully revises existing psychoanalytic narratives of subjective origins. Whereas Freud sees relative placidity in our pre-differential infancy – what he characterizes in *Civilization and Its Discontents* as the untouched pleasure of the "infant at the breast" (Freud, *Civilization and Its Discontents,* p. 11) – Kristeva presupposes no such Eden. There is an inherent pathos, of course, in Lacan's mirror stage; the discrepancy between self and the reflection of self opens up a lack and a desire that can never be fulfilled. The more suggestive figure for this dynamic becomes not Oedipus but Narcissus, and – in Lacan's account – the love of Narcissus for his reflection is turbulent from the start. But Kristeva, in both *Powers of Horror* and *Tales of Love,* exponentially heightens the precariousness of that affair. Citing Freud by name but not Lacan, Kristeva invokes the idea of "primary narcissism" both to reconsider and implicitly to revise Lacan's account:

> Narcissism then appears as a regression to a position set back from the other, a return to a self-contemplative, conservative, self-sufficient haven. Actually, such narcissism never is the wrinkleless image of the Greek youth in a quiet fountain. The conflicts of drives muddle its bed, cloud its water, and bring forth everything that, by not becoming integrated with a given system of signs, is abjection for it. (*Powers of Horror,* p. 14)

Both Lacan and Kristeva exploit the illustrative value of Ovid's myth by acknowledging the implicit absurdity of Narcissus' static, self-reflexive love. In Lacan's case, the surface of the pool in which Narcissus sees himself is stirred by Narcissus' error in reading the reflected image – the error, that is, of thinking the ideal reflection is real. This error and the discrepancy it implies generate desire, which in turn structures all the subject's subsequently fraught relations to objects and others.

Desire for Lacan, as for Kristeva, means loss, lack, want. But Kristeva locates the inaugural "experience of *want*" at a moment more "preliminary to being and object" than Lacan's mirror stage (10; emphasis Kristeva's). She sees this want as the impossible "wrinkle" within subjectivity produced by the very earliest separation of the living being: birth. Narcissus' pool is muddy for Kristeva because it has *already* been stirred by the "immemorial violence with which a body becomes separated from another body in order to be" (10). Whereas Lacan locates Narcissus' pathos in an early cognitive error, Kristeva locates it in an even earlier bodily precondition.

With a vision closer to Aeschylus than Ovid, Kristeva plumbs the depths of these turbulent waters to identify where the first, formative moments in the separation of self from other take place. These moments prepare the "structures of meaning [that] govern and condition me" and "demarcate a space out of which signs and objects arise" (5). As abjection, this violence signals a dynamic that shapes the subject not just in the beginning, but always. Again, this initial separation does not belong, properly speaking, to the order of linguistic signs. It is acted out "even before things for him *are* – hence before they are signifiable" (6; emphasis Kristeva's). Yet it is not insignificant. Kristeva's examination of this separation and the drive-motivated separations which are modeled on it follows from a thesis present in all of her work and central, especially, to *Powers of Horror*: "Significance is indeed inherent in the human body" (10).

"Neither subject nor object"

Abjection's peculiar horror involves the throes of the body and the violence of the drives. But perhaps most definitively, it involves a crisis of place, and Kristeva persistently describes this crisis as a matter of ambiguous borderlines and unmapped frontiers, of strays and exiles and outcasts. Tellingly, Louis-Ferdinand Céline's gruesomely, tragically comic *Journey to the End of the Night* serves as one of Kristeva's privileged literary examples in *Powers of Horror*. Céline's title becomes an explicit trope for the concept of abjection itself: the "one by whom the abject exists is [...] on a journey, during the night, the end of which keeps receding" (8).[23] She also, in keeping with psychoanalytic tradition, considers Oedipus at length, but focuses on the disgraced and wandering figure of *Oedipus at Colonus*, not *Oedipus Rex*. As these literary texts attest, Kristeva argues, abjection draws the subject to the limits of its own defining boundaries. This crisis of place ("Where am I?") precipitates a crisis of meaning and identification (What is that? Is that me? What am I?) (8).

This concept distinguishes itself from other psychoanalyses of fear, though at times only by subtle allusion, primarily because Kristeva's abjection concerns fear of neither objects nor other subjects, but rather the threat of indistinction between the two. This indistinction presents itself, definitively, as a crisis of place and identity. In explaining just what sort of disorientation she is talking about, Kristeva refers to abjection as a kind of "uncanniness," yet she implicitly differentiates her understanding of uncanniness from Freud's (as she will later do with existing theories of phobia, taboo, and cultural rites of defilement). Dwelling for a moment on the difference between uncanniness and abjection, however, proves instructive, even if Kristeva does not do so herself. She acknowledges the unnerving horror of Freud's uncanny, that simultaneously familiar and alien force (*heimliche* and *unheimliche*) that puts the subject "beside himself" with torment (1–2). For Freud, the uncanny can be produced by some sort of jarringly alien object; by another subject, who was once familiar, and though long forgotten, yet hauntingly returns; or worse still, by an alien force that settles in too close or even insinuates itself within the threatened subject – a *Doppelgänger* or possessing demon. Frankenstein's monster is, for example, uncanny: the return of Victor's repressed, coming back again and again to exact from his maker his due. The abject, however, registers a still more profound horror. "Neither subject nor object," "abjection" names not a thing but a potentiality, a gravitational field that summons the subject from its proper place to a no-man's land where the subject is not only "beside himself" but also almost ceases to be. Abjection's power of horror derives from the fact that the subject is ex-statically drawn from its proper domain to this "land of oblivion" at the same time that the subject is repulsed (8).

At such moments of radical displacement and disorientation, the abject manifests itself to the "straying" subject as food loathing, the shock of seeing a corpse "without God and outside science," amorally calculated crime, religious purification rites, incest taboos, war (4). All impose themselves on the delineations of life, law, and order (4). They are "death in infecting life. Abject. [...] What does not respect borders, positions, rules" (4). Abject confrontations that threaten to obliterate meaning or that utterly resist making sense "throw" (*jeter*) one violently to a place of radical ambiguity, where the structural order of subjects and objects does not hold. The abject is "[n]ot me. Not that. But not nothing, either. A weight of meaninglessness, about which there is nothing insignificant, and which crushes me. On the edge of non-existence and hallucination, of a reality that, if I acknowledge it, annihilates me" (2).

Food loathing constitutes "perhaps the most elementary and most archaic form of abjection" (2). The reflexive nausea of such loathing – invoking the infantile relation to the mother's breast, Kristeva's overdetermined example is revulsion of the "skin on the surface of milk" – expresses a drive to separate me from a not me which the "I" cannot bear to assimilate, and yet from which it cannot cleanly part. The "spasms and vomiting [...] protect me" in such instances, but at a risk. With that violent bodily reaction, one throws oneself (*se jeter*) into crisis as well. In expelling the abject, "I expel *myself*, I spit *myself* out, I abject *myself* within the same motion through which 'I' claim to establish *myself*" (3; emphasis Kristeva's). This negative dialectic between the self and the abject precipitates the "shattering violence of a convulsion that, to be sure, is inscribed in a symbolic system," but is not wholly explained by it (3). The "archaic" and emphatically bodily dynamic of food loathing illustrates Kristeva's claim that abjection involves meaning, but *not* a meaning integrated into the symbolic system of subjects and objects, signifiers and signifieds. Food loathing "expresses" itself immediately, wordlessly, from one's primal depths. In other words, the skin on the surface of milk that makes me gag does not *represent* abjection; it thrusts me into it.

In Lacan's myth of subjective origin, the relation set up by the mirror stage depends both upon a certain space between self and image and upon *enough* placidity for Narcissus' pool to render a reflection – that is, to render a *mimesis* or representation of the self, however illusory. Representation, or *mimesis*, implies distance – from the thing it signifies, from the one who beholds it. Approaching abjection, no such distance can be maintained. Kristeva's second example demonstrates this important distinction more clearly. If the food loathing example shows us the first paradigmatic encounter with the abject, her second shows us the ultimate encounter: "The corpse, seen without God and outside of science, is the utmost of abjection. It is death infecting life" (4). Yet the corpse is not a *signifier* of death – that is, the portion of the Saussurian sign that refers to or represents the *signified* (the concept) – but something else. A signifier of death would be a "flat encephalograph, for instance," for it symbolically points to a concept or signified from which it maintains an uncontaminated, unembodied distance (3). A corpse, by contrast, obliterates that distance and puts death in intolerable proximity to the subject: "as in true theater, without makeup or masks, corpses *show me* what I permanently thrust aside in order to live" (3; emphasis Kristeva's). The corpse is death – not signified but incarnate.

"Approaching abjection"

In trying to theorize this mode of representation, which is mimetic in a uniquely immediate way, incarnating what it signifies rather than merely referring to it, Kristeva deploys a discursive method that fittingly bears the traces of this very dynamic. And indeed, from its first words and its heterogeneously strange examples, *Powers of Horror* performs and inspires the crisis of place it describes, for and in her readers, for her own theoretical authority, and for theory itself.

In "Approaching Abjection," the exhilaratingly dense first chapter of the book, Kristeva introduces her topic in a style that, even more than Lacan's verbal high-wire acts, seems calculated to shock. This chapter's title promises both a critical investigation (the way, for instance, Descartes's *Meditations* "approaches" the core of human consciousness) and a description of an affective encounter. Within the chapter, her use of a first-person pronoun – notably not the conventional scholarly "we," but rather an ambiguous "I" – disorients the reader from the start. An account bearing witness to the intense experience of abjection and the theoretical exploration of it are thus implicated with one another from the beginning. The "I" on Kristeva's pages belongs to both discourses. Her critical language, in other words, acts out what it aims to describe: a radical disruption of the borders that separate the subject from its objects, the "I" from the "not-I," from the encroachment of a horrifying something that is neither subject nor object.

The first delineations of the subject come about as objects distinguish themselves as other. Abjection, however, involves the subject in a different, wholly negative relation:

> When I am beset by abjection, the twisted braid of affects and thoughts I call by such a name does not have, properly speaking, a definable object. The abject is not an ob-ject facing me, which I name or imagine. Nor is it an ob-jest, an otherness ceaselessly fleeing in a systematic quest for desire. What is abject is not my correlative, which, providing me with someone or something else as support, would allow me to be more or less detached and autonomous. The abject has only one quality of the *object* – that of being opposed to I. If the object, however, through its

> oppositions, settles me within the fragile texture of a desire for meaning, which, as a matter of fact, makes me ceaselessly and infinitely homologous to it, what is abject, on the contrary, the jettisoned object, is radically excluded and draws me to the place where meaning collapses. (1–2; emphasis Kristeva's)

Throughout her text, Kristeva explores the dynamics of the subject–object – abject relation by considering radical instances in which subjective distinction becomes most precarious. Within the abject, there "looms [...] one of those violent, dark revolts of being, directed against a threat that seems to emanate from an exorbitant outside or inside, ejected beyond the scope of the possible, the tolerable, the thinkable" (1). At once attractive and repulsive, the threat within abjection

> lies there, quite close, but it cannot be assimilated. It beseeches, worries, and fascinates desire, which, nevertheless, does not let itself be seduced. Apprehensive, desire turns aside; sickened, it rejects. [...] Unflaggingly, like an inescapable boomerang, a vortex of summons and repulsion places the one haunted by it literally beside himself. (1)

Kristeva's initial description of the abject, similarly, settles in too close at the same time that it pushes away; like the abject, it seems at once "unapproachable and intimate" (6). The vividly emotive opening suggests an intimacy, which some commentators mistake for accessibility, that the gathering opacity of her description nevertheless thwarts.[24] Through this stuttering, unsettling approach, Kristeva offers a theoretical definition of a dynamic that resists definition, gives meaning to a force that "draws me to the place where meaning collapses." The texture and accumulation of Kristeva's sentences here – nuanced with dependent clauses, riddled with oblique pronouns and allusive etymologies, layered with repeated proposals to tell us what the abject is, largely by declaring what it is not – precisely act out what they aim to describe.

Kristeva's unfamiliar critical idiom reflects the difficulty of representing the unrepresentable domain she explores. Her own theoretical point of view is no more exempt from abjection's thrilling and threatening force than is the subject in question. No mere ornament, Kristeva's style is in fact an important part of her argument. It resembles the kind of writing her study will privilege: liminal, "literary" discourses that manage to approach the abject without evasion. In *The Legend of Freud,* Samuel Weber asks a rhetorical question that

Kristeva's *Powers of Horror* answers with a resounding and principled No, No, Yes, and Yes. He wonders:

> can psychoanalytic thinking itself escape the effects of what it endeavors to think? Can the disruptive distortions of unconscious processes be simply recognized, theoretically, as an object, or must they not leave their imprint on the process of theoretical objectification itself? Must not psychoanalytic thinking itself partake of – repeat – the dislocations it seeks to describe? (x)[25]

A theoretical proposition in itself, Kristeva's style demonstrates that a discourse aiming to articulate the abject in a way that does not merely repress it must bear the imprint of its eccentric force, of its threat. Through "thoroughly poetic mimesis," she strives for a mode of representation that does not describe but rather "incarnates" abjection in its very rhythms and contours, a discourse "not of purification but of rebirth with and against abjection" (*Powers of Horror*, p. 31).

The literature her study will proceed to interpret does the same, she argues. In so doing, it provides "probably the only counterweight to abjection" (*Powers of Horror*, p. 210). That observation, as we will show in the next chapter, is meant to be neither consoling nor resigned. She sees great power in such discourses. In the hands of the properly unflinching and experimental writer, the abject is, in fact, edged by the sublime.

The sublime turn

A crucial turn thus takes place in Kristeva's argument, one readers will miss if they find themselves too taken by her examples or her strange presentation of them. More suggestive than her meticulous catalogue of horrors – which have been especially popular in critical applications of her theory – is her emphasis on the ability of certain discourses to transform the abject into something productive and promising, if not sublime. Throughout the book, Kristeva's examples model themselves on the strange *alpha* and *omega* of the "human universe" of signification established by her two initial, "phenomenological" examples of food loathing and confronting a corpse. These two experiences prove paradigmatic because they are the most visceral versions of abject crises, which always recall infantile pangs of separation or threaten "death infecting life." Thematically, it is easy to see how the eclectic set of texts and topics Kristeva explores in *Powers of Horror* would fit this model of abjection: the blind, incestuous, exiled Oedipus; or Freud's phobic Little Hans; or biblical prohibitions against menstrual blood; or cultural taboos regarding the maternal; or Céline's graphically death-obsessed, misogynistic, anti-Semitic and otherwise egregious picaresque narratives. The broadest foundations of Law, Religion, Morality – of the symbolic realm as such – are built upon and against the dynamics of abjection, after all. So its manifestations are to be found everywhere. But not all these responses to abjection are the same, and the distinctions make all the difference to Kristeva.

Just as she sets herself the task of theorizing abjection in order to think what remains unthought in existing psychoanalytic theory, so does she see power in *certain* modes of discourse that attempt, in radical ways, to speak (of) the sublime by manifesting it in the very contours of their language. Kristeva elegantly defines the sublime in terms similar to those she applies to the abject. Following the aesthetic definition of sublimity authorized by Kant, Kristeva aligns the abject and the sublime by noting that, like the abject, "the sublime has no object either" (12). In elaborating this idea, she draws more from her own poetic, critical approach to abjection than from the aesthetic tradition, though the subtle influence of Kant still echoes: "the sublime is a something added that expands us, overstrains us, and causes us to be both *here*, as dejects, and *there*, as others and sparkling. A divergence, an impossible bounding. Everything missed, joy – fascination" (12; emphasis Kristeva's). Nevertheless, sublimity and abjection are not identical terms: "The abject is edged with the sublime. It is not the same moment on the journey, but the same subject and speech bring them into being" (11). As the next chapter will reveal, Kristeva's reasons for making this distinction are complex, but the essential point is that abject discourses neither "transcend" the human horror to which they are bound nor exempt us from that horror. They articulate abjection, rather, from the place itself. The psychic, linguistic force capable of responding to abjection in this way, Kristeva calls *sublimation*, a term Freud introduces in *Civilization and Its Discontents* and which Lacan considers in his *Seminar VII: The Ethics of Psychoanalysis*. Kristeva defines sublimation as "nothing else than the possibility of naming the pre-nominal, the pre-objectal, which are in fact only a trans-nominal, a transobjectal" (11). If abjection describes an experience, or a *symptom*, sublimation names one "healthy" response to it: "In the symptom, the abject permeates me. I become abject. Through sublimation, I keep it under control" (11).

Kristeva's discursive style aims to be the sort of sublimating articulation she wishes to distinguish from the normative, repressive response to abjection. In the final pages of her book, she puts herself and her theoretical work on the side of all those discourses daring enough to situate themselves "on the fragile border [...] where identities (subject/object, etc.) do not exist or only barely so – double, fuzzy, heterogeneous, animal, metamorphosed, altered, abject" (207). She sees her work, like the "privileged" work of literature, as "represent[ing] the ultimate coding of our crises, of our most intimate and most serious apocalypses" (208). Because of the eccentric place in which it is willing, uncomfortably and at risk, to dwell, "literature may also involve not an ultimate resistance to but an unveiling of the abject" (208). Kristeva clearly hopes to create a kind of critical discourse that "unveil[s]" without explaining away or definitively situating abjection's threat or its dynamic crisis of place and meaning.

Law, religion, and morality seek to give order to horror, to push it to the margins of normative meaning and to keep it on the margins when it threatens to encroach. Prohibitions against (and punishments for) sin, taboos and defilement rites "purify" the abject. Historically and culturally, the presentable face of the abject, purified and properly repressed, we call *sacred* – "a threatening otherness – but always nameable, always totalizeable" (17). Before the emergence of the decentered subject, in other words, throughout the long history in which philosophical idealism, humanism, and monotheistic faith prevailed, such repressive strategies were at least tenable. Kristeva argues that they no longer are, and in their place emerges a different kind of discourse that responds to abjection in a new way. Art and literature, significantly, seem "destined to survive the collapse of the historical forms of religions" (17).

This proposal should not be mistaken for the consoling aesthetic privilege that Matthew Arnold, for instance, granted to literature in the midst of the nineteenth century's crisis of religious faith. Kristeva does not favor the kind of literature that would take religion's place by providing us with a secular humanism that establishes new symbolic authority in artistic articulation, the Arnoldian "best that has been thought and said." Kristeva privileges instead extreme examples that seem closer to perversion than sublimity. "The writer, fascinated by the abject, imagines its logic, projects himself into it, introjects it, and as a consequence *perverts* language – style and content" (16; emphasis mine). Stylistically radical literature in particular exerts power by "acknowledg[ing ...] the impossibility of Religion, Morality, and Law – their power play, their absurd seeming" (16).

Like (but not identical to) the rites of defilement and taboo present in most monotheistic religions, literature is among the media that make up "that catharsis par excellence called art" (17). The "artistic experience" shares with religion what Kristeva calls the "essential component of religiosity," namely the impulse to give utterance to the abject, and in doing so to "purify" it. The key difference between art and religion, she suggests, is a matter of history, for art is "destined to survive the collapse of the historical forms of religions" (17). Like many of her fellow poststructuralists, Kristeva privileges an avant-garde, stylistically experimental literature. She sees it as a survivor of the intellectual collapse – wrought by Hegel, Marx, Nietzsche, Freud, and others – of the transcendental idealism that reaches its apogee with Kant. The "catharsis" Kristeva identifies in art, therefore, is a skeptical, unsettling sort that does not "purify" abjection but seizes it, offering an "utterance that testifies to its closeness to, cohabitation with, and 'knowledge' of abjection" (30).

"Great modern literature" provides one such incarnation, and perhaps offers the only kind of transcendence available in the wake of this intellectual collapse (18). Such literature – the work of "Dostoevsky, Lautréamont, Proust, Artaud, Kafka, Céline" – variously names abjection, otherwise unnameable. Imperfect, provisional, it nevertheless produces a kind of transcendence "without consecration," sublimation rather than sublimity, which we may still consider a triumph (11–2, 26):

> In a world in which the Other has collapsed, the aesthetic task – a descent into the foundations of the symbolic construct – amounts to retracing the fragile limits of the speaking being, closest to its dawn, to the bottomless "primacy" constituted by primal repression. Through that experience [...] "subject" and "object" push each other away, confront each other, collapse, and start again – inseparable, contaminated, condemned, at the boundary of what is assimilable, thinkable, abject. Great modern literature unfolds over that terrain: Dostoevsky, Lautréamont, Proust, Artaud, Kafka, Céline. (18)

Among these writers, Kristeva suggests, none confronts the abject with more relentless audacity and power to shock than Louis-Ferdinand Céline, whose works will become the focus of the entire second half of *Powers of Horror*. Kristeva's analysis of Céline, indeed her very choice to feature him so centrally in the theoretical elaboration of abjection, is complex and overdetermined and has been the locus of much critical resistance. For like abjection itself, Céline's work fascinates and repulses, throws its reader into unsettling states in which the boundaries of life and death, the stability of meaning, seem constantly threatened. Céline himself, a documented anti-Semite and avowed misanthrope, presents unique difficulties for the literary criticism Kristeva will undertake. Her reading of Céline will be the focus of our next chapter and our opportunity not only to expand our understanding of abjection, and literary negotiations of it, but also to see in action – both in Céline's "literary" discourse and in Kristeva's own literary critical discourse upon it – what Kristeva means by modes of discourse that "speak" abjection from the inside, without diminishing its threat.

Part II

Reading Kristeva, Reading Literature

3 Céline's Pharmacy

> In the enclosed space of the pharmacy, the reverberations of the monologue are immeasurably amplified. The walled-in voice strikes against the rafters, the words come apart, bits and pieces of sentences are separated, disarticulated parts begin to circulate through the corridors, become fixed for a round or two, translate each other, become rejoined, bounce off each other, contradict each other, make trouble, tell on each other, come back like answers, organize their exchanges, protect each other, institute an internal commerce, take themselves for a dialogue. Full of meaning. A whole story. An entire history. All of philosophy.
>
> (Jacques Derrida, "Plato's Pharmacy"[1])

Taking it the wrong way

> Hey, they're putting *Journey* on the rails again.
> What a feeling it gives me. [...]
> Everything gets taken the wrong way. I've been the cause of too much evil.
> Just think of all the deaths, the hatreds around me ... the treachery ... the sewer it adds up to ... the monsters ...
> Oh, you've got to be blind and deaf!
>
> (Louis-Ferdinand Céline, Preface to *Journey to the End of the Night*, 1952)

Lacking a first-hand acquaintance with the writings of Louis-Ferdinand Céline, it is entirely possible to read the six chapters of *Powers of Horror* devoted to his work and not realize just how laugh-out-loud funny, absurd, or even mind-numbingly tedious he can be. Kristeva speaks of his "laughter" – "piercing laughter," "cheerful laughter," "apocalyptic laughter" – as a counterpart, and more importantly a counterweight, to the unremitting horrors of war, hatred, violence, disease, and death he chronicles. But the portentous seriousness with which she seems to do so may not encourage the earnest reader, painstakingly navigating Kristeva's theoretical argument, to unfurrow the brow enough to see at the outset the rather important fact that Céline is a *comic* writer. I offer this observation – while a genuine account of my own initial experience of reading Kristeva on Céline and then reading Céline – not merely to suggest that Kristeva can seem relatively humorless, as theorists go, nor to speculate that her sense of irony and playfulness fail to "translate" well. Both may be the case. More importantly, however, the discrepancy highlights the potentially diminishing returns of reading a literary theory of a literary corpus, or in the case of this very book, of reading a summarizing explanation of a literary theory of a literary corpus.

Put simply, to read Kristeva reading Céline, it helps tremendously to have read Céline. With the implicit injunction, then, that we must read for ourselves both Céline and Kristeva on Céline, this chapter will model readings of each, demonstrating at the same time the necessary *rhetorical* connection between Céline's narrative and Kristeva's critical discourse. "Rhetorical" reading, in this sense, means attending to the figures and disfigurements of speech on the level of the letter – *rhetorical* rather than *thematic*, concerned with *form* not just *content*.[2] Céline calls this distinction the difference between "ideas" and "style." For Kristeva, the distinction becomes a critical commitment to venture "beyond the themes" toward "the way one speaks," which is ultimately "where the abject lies" (*Powers of Horror*, p. 23). We will proceed on the premise that a basic readerly acquaintance with Céline's work, one Kristeva at once presumes her readers already have and on critical principle refuses to give, mitigates the risk of either author being "taken the wrong way." Understanding Céline's work on the broadest levels of narrative structure, of plot and protagonist, serves as a helpful way into the unsettling interstices of the "Célinian universe" Kristeva's microscopic stylistic analysis seeks to explore. In fact, it can highlight – on a different molecular level, as it were – the specific dimensions of Céline's discourse, its articulation of the abject, and the abject effect on its readers Kristeva powerfully, but often cryptically, critiques.

In its emphasis on the "strange state" we are "thrown into" when reading Céline, Kristeva's theory in fact demands that we read for ourselves. As she says at the outset, "the true 'miracle' of Céline resides in the very experience of one's reading" (133). This experience takes place most significantly, Kristeva insists, on the level of the sentence, as a matter of *style*. Reading Céline for ourselves significantly changes, for example, how we read this characteristically difficult description of

Céline Kristeva offers at the outset of her analysis. Céline chronicles but also imposes on his readers a very particular subjective crisis, in which

> Even your cherished abjection belongs to the realm of a puppet show's gang [*guignol's band*] and the enchantment is postponed until some other time … [*féerie pour une autre fois*]. As for jouissance, be it of language, meaning, or transcendence grasped from within, in pure literary style, you are barking up the wrong tree … All that remains is the tune, without notes … Not even worship of Death … The three dots … Less than nothing, or more … Something else … The consuming of Everything, of Nothing, through style … (*Powers of Horror*, p. 135)

The statement alludes to, without naming, the dark, uncomfortable themes of Céline's writing – "all the deaths, the hatreds, […] the treachery … the sewer, […] the monsters" he himself acknowledges in the "Preface" I cite above. But it does something else as well.

Paying attention to the "rhythm" of Kristeva's statement, we might recognize that, while indeed ponderous and maybe not all that funny, Kristeva's cryptic description is basically a joke. It is an exaggerated impersonation of Céline's own rhythms, a ventriloquism of his style. In fact, in the larger context of the paragraph in which it appears, the passage is not even Kristeva's own constative thesis about Céline's strange "effect."[3] Rather, it is indirect discourse: a paraphrase, in Céline's voice, of what his work collectively says to us. With the condensed flashiness of a movie trailer, it references Célinian titles, employs characteristic colloquialisms ("you are barking up the wrong tree") and winkingly overuses ellipsis, his signature stylistic feature ("… The three dots …"). In this instance, and indeed always, style matters for reading Kristeva as much as she says it matters in reading Céline. But as this example suggests, attentive reading involves something other than, or added to, a sheer cognitive effort to follow the argument. It requires as well an ear, so to speak, for the "tune, without notes" – that is, the tone, voice, and performance of a given statement even "without" its meaning – and a willingness to account for its effects.

Thus the specific contours, the "music," of Céline's discourse shape the reader's experience most profoundly. Not only does he report abjection to us, in the thematic content of his stories, he also imposes it upon us in the cumulative effect of his discourse. Kristeva asserts that her critical language approaches Céline in a peculiar, seemingly indirect, manner because it *must*; its otherness resists conventional critical response and "calls upon what, within us, eludes defenses, trainings, and words" (134). Utterance as such in Céline's corpus provides a rich and varied textuality of the "speaking subject" at its extreme limits, in that Barthesian sense of "text" (as we explored it in Chapter 1) that transcends discrete delineations among author, narrator, character. Accordingly, her treatment of Céline as author is idiosyncratic, shifting between seemingly biographical reference to the utterances of Louis-Ferdinand Destouches, the doctor and novelist who took "Céline" as his penname, and those of his novels' narrators and characters. This strategy itself implies a critical argument. Denying us recourse to what literary training would call irony, narrative voice, or point of view, Céline gives us no comfortable way to distinguish clearly between what "[h]e believes" and what he "has us believe," no key for deciphering what effect he intends "through the contrivance of a word" (134). By no means a feature exclusive to his writing (though Kristeva's exultant prose gives the impression it is), his works offer an ambiguous, indeterminate distinction between "Céline" the author and the quasi-biographical narrators or other characters who seem to do his talking for him.

Céline offers "delirium" as a dominant strategy for upsetting our ability to "rely" on him as a narrator, both in the simple unfolding of the plot and in the manner in which he presents it. His narrators frequently succumb to explicitly identifiable fits of delirium; at other times, the narration shifts without warning to scenes we must infer to be "unreal," hallucination, sexual fantasy, or simply logically impossible. Further complicating the stability of the narrative point of view, the characters lie to and scheme against one another. At other times, seemingly coherent "philosophical" arguments about the politics of war or the nature of human being are offered within dubious frames. In *Journey to the End of the Night,* the narrator Ferdinand Bardamu demonstrates the slippery dynamics of Célinian delirium on every level; as the narrator of *Death on the Installment Plan,* Céline's second novel, which relies heavily on memory and flashback, Ferdinand's vertiginous perspective dominates the structure of the plot even more. The Ferdinand of *Journey,* to give just a few examples, falls into war-related traumatic delirium on several occasions. After being discharged from duty in World War I, he succumbs to shell shock in a carnival shooting gallery, convinced "They're shooting at me" (48). Despite the voice of reason from his girlfriend Lola, "I fell sick. I was delirious, driven mad by fear, they said at the hospital. Maybe so. The best thing to do when you're in this world, don't you agree, is to get out of it. Crazy or not, scared or not" (49). This breakdown is Ferdinand's first among many; fevers contracted en route to Africa and America produce similar breaks with reality.

Ferdinand's pervasive mistrust of his fellow man, and his own avowed unscrupulousness, further upset the reader's ability to find his narration reliable. Because Ferdinand claims to lie to other characters in the novel and cynically suspects them of lying to him ("her answers were vague, pretentious, and manifestly unreliable, calculated to make a brilliant impression on me," he says of his American girlfriend), he conditions his readers to be similarly wary (45). On several of these occasions, seemingly in every corner of the globe, Ferdinand improbably meets up with his friend Léon Robinson, a figure he first befriends during the war. Though we are clearly meant to believe in the reality of Robinson – his schemes, illnesses, love life, and ultimate death comprise significant portions of the plot – his preposterously coincidental reappearances, calmly offered as fact, prevent us from trusting the realism of the text.

The implications of Céline's "delirious" narrative unreliability have long been noted by literary critics. Allen Thiher's book *Céline: The Novel as Delirium* (1972) makes it the focus of an entire study. Wayne Booth's *Rhetoric of Fiction* (1961) devotes a discrete section – in the midst of his influential analysis of unreliable and impersonal narration – to "The Seductive Point of View: Céline as Example," where he lays out the readerly problem of fixing the Célinian point of view with questions surprisingly similar to Kristeva's own. What distinguishes Kristeva's approach is her explicit embrace of "delirium" as a critical position as well as a narrative one.

In "Psychoanalysis and the Polis," she cogently asserts this position as a theoretical necessity not just for reading Céline (though his delirious discourse highlights the necessity), but for interpretation in general, psychoanalytic and literary. Delirium, in this context, is essentially a name for the instability of the object of study she asserts in her theory of literary analysis (explored in Chapter 1) and the decentered subjectivity that dictates her psychoanalytic theory (explored in Chapter 2). In each instance, Kristeva posits an analytic position that denies fixity in relation to or mastery over that which it examines, whether literary text or speaking subject. "Psychoanalysis and the Polis" also emphasizes the affective implications of delirium – its dizziness, giddiness, both pleasurable and unsettling, its "passion" and *jouissance* (318–19). In so doing, she points out the aspect of interpretation driven, as is the subject in general, by desire. These observations constitute acknowledgments of at once a liberty, a limitation, and a responsibility.

> If I know that my desire can make me delirious in my interpretive constructions, my return to this delirium allows me to dissolve its meaning, to displace by one or more notches the quest for meaning which I suppose to be *one* and *one only* but which I can *only* indefinitely approach. (310; emphasis Kristeva's)

With that recognition comes as well the ethical imperative for interpretive humility, so to speak, a recognition that one's interpretation can never provide hermeneutic truth, that "analytic interpretation is only, in the best of cases, *partially true*, and its truth [...] is demonstrable only by its *effects in the present*" (309; emphasis Kristeva's). As "Psychoanalysis and the Polis" outlines, reading Céline – particularly contending with the complexities of his discursive voice – serves as the specific impetus for this theory of analytic delirium.

Powers of Horror provides the elaborate illustration of her commitment to such an analytic stance, and the performative gymnastics of the example we examine at the outset of this chapter must be read in this theoretical context. The argument implied by this performance is similarly central. Accordingly, throughout the book, she contends that thematic readings of Céline, or hermeneutic interpretations that seek *the meaning* of his work, are rendered unstable, if not impossible, in the midst of utterances of ambiguous agency and muddled complicity. His narratives offer "relentless mockery" in the face of the darkest situations, of horrifying inhumanity, violence, and death (134). With this vertiginous voice, proffering reprehensible views and aggressively horrific tales, is Céline "[a]ctor or martyr"?[4] Are his texts instances of "playacting or possibly perversion"? Neither, Kristeva says, or maybe both. "Better than that," these shockingly rendered discursive performances, with their ambiguities of intention and voice, *make something happen*. They are themselves abject. In "affecting mankind's ultimate guarantee – language," Céline's texts act out abjection's threat to the symbolic order of signification (137). This produces, in turn, a readerly crisis of abjection in its own right: "When reading Céline we are seized at the fragile spot of our subjectivity" where borders seem to collapse. Kristeva contends that his texts confront us with – and *implicate* us in – a "universe of borders, seesaws, fragile and mingled identities, wanderings of the subject and its objects, fears and struggles, abjections and lyricisms" (135).

The horrible power of Céline's writing, she emphasizes throughout, stems only superficially from his lurid, morbid "themes" (137). What he achieves derives not from the narrative chronicling of such subject matter, "but through much deeper, more remote, and riskier probes." These "probings [...] tamper with vocabulary and syntax" and convey an "inhumanity that resides in his very words" (137). At the end of *Powers of Horror*, which she has said from the beginning "will not be [...] thematic," Kristeva points to a similar power, "riskier" and more "radical," in the discourse of the analyst. She means the *psycho*analyst, specifically, predisposed "to begin hearing, actually to listen to himself build up a discourse around the braided horror and fascination that bespeaks the incompleteness of the speaking being" (209). But as her discussion of Céline demonstrates throughout, she presents herself as a *literary* analyst of just this kind, rhetorically attuned to "hear" the discourse it examines and to "listen" to its own. This imperative, implicitly, urgently extends to Kristeva's readers as well.

Powers of Horror approaches "Célinian scription" on the terms Kristeva lyrically outlines: as a writing that does not merely report but actually *produces* the abjection it so relentlessly explores, a writing that disrupts normative structures of signification and thereby demands non-normative strategies for analyzing it. On the premise of this thesis, she will examine the key features she highlights in this passage – his use of ellipsis, of materially graphic description, his insistence on linking extreme emotion with syntactical deformation, his gutter-mouthed colloquialism – in exquisite detail. But, as we have already seen, Kristeva's methodological choices are themselves idiosyncratic and overdetermined. Her quotational bricolage, her seeming conflation of author and narrator and reader, her lack of contextualizing plot summary, the occasional ecstatic flights of her own critical prose, are all disorienting from the start. The readerly confusion she herself precipitates, by engaging in a literary criticism that lacks so many of the orienting markers we conventionally rely upon, corresponds to the sort of disorientation she cites in Céline. This is no accident. And therefore it makes a difference to notice, along with Céline's literary smart-bombs, Kristeva's own stylistic provocations. It is also important to speculate on the logic, and the theoretical commitment, behind them.

Kristeva's highly self-conscious performativity makes it difficult to tell, in other words, whether taking her at her word is taking it the wrong way. As she says of Céline, taking Kristeva at her word means reading her by the letter, and by the affective contours of the letter, which is no simple task. Acknowledging that risk, however, is far better than ignoring it. Approaching *Powers of Horror* (or explanatory summaries of it) in search of a merely *conceptual* understanding of abjection might mean barking up the wrong tree in more than one way. With such an approach, one is more likely to misread Kristeva's affective account of Céline's stylistic force as weakly uncritical impressionism, or to take her series of long, weirdly juxtaposed, and decontextualized quotations as an easily reproducible catalog of abject horrors. Such misreadings have at least three potential consequences, which would be unfortunate to varying degrees. It could lead a reader to give up quickly, or to reject Kristeva's reading as offering little more than the sort of thematic analysis she claims to reject. Worse still, it could encourage readers to reproduce the straightforward and easy literary analysis they might think they are getting. Our aim here, therefore, will be to respond to Kristeva's methodological recommendation that a literary criticism of Céline be at least on one level the record of a readerly encounter, and still more importantly, that it be a rhetorical analysis, where attunement to the "rhythm of a sentence" guides critical speculation on the "meaning of that sentence." And we will attune ourselves, accordingly, to Kristeva's critical rhetoric itself. Nietzsche's admonishing epigraph, which stands at the beginning of *Powers of Horror*'s chapters on Céline, in this sense should serve as a *caveat lector* for Kristeva's readers as well as Céline's.

Letter bombs: the rhythms of abjection

Aside from the subtle performative work of Kristeva's initial thesis statements, even seemingly conventional critical gestures serve to orient a careful reader. In the opening chapter of her analysis, she situates Céline within and outside of a literary tradition and, moreover, distinguishes her own project from critical work already done. Standard tropes of academic discourse, these moves are nevertheless more than perfunctory. They underline that Kristeva's discussion will not be literary critical business as usual. They announce a specific way of talking about literature theoretically that Kristeva wants to distinguish from New Critical paraphrase, formalist close reading, or structuralist narratology. Accordingly, she will *not* read Céline by those methods – or in the idiom of conventional literary criticism at all.

What she effectively announces, in other words, is an approach reflected by Robert Graves' tongue-in-cheek statement in *The Common Asphodel* (1949):

> One doesn't "listen" when reading standard prose; it is only in poetry that one looks out for metre and rhythmic variations on it. The writers of *vers libre* rely on their printers to call your attention to what is called "cadence" or "rhythmic relation" (not easy to follow) which might have escaped you if written as prose; *this* sentence, you'll find, has its thumb to its nose.

Graves' assertion expresses Kristeva's own understanding of a literary criticism that "listens" to the rhythms and cadences of prose with the kind of attention typically reserved for verse. Kristeva's performative cleverness in the process of doing so, furthermore, mirrors the gesture Graves wittily makes in the statement above. In calling for a critical stance prepared to grant prose a kind of attention conventionally reserved for verse, she simultaneously writes prose that demands such attention – as our previous section observes.[5] Like Graves', the tone of Kristeva's call is provocative and iconoclastic, a dare more than a suggestion. Kristeva's often unaccommodating prose reflects, thus, both a critical principle and a rhetorical stance. It too has its thumb to its nose, waving at a critical tradition from which she wishes to distance herself. Her sheer difficulty and seriousness, moreover, suggest that she extends that gesture, to a certain degree, to her readers as well. Put to the challenge, we are often left to discern for ourselves what Graves helpfully points out in his last sentence. Reading with attentiveness to moments where Kristeva does provide such pointers can, thus, illuminate not only her meaning but also her motivations.

Invoking Mikhail Bakhtin's studies on the novel, Kristeva provisionally aligns Céline's narratives with the "carnivalesque tradition" of Rabelais and Dostoevsky and contrasts the "Célinian universe" to the literary visions of other important figures in the French canon (or more precisely, the Kristevan canon) – Proust, Mallarmé, Lautréamont, Artaud. In spite of these authors' shared commitment, variously manifested, to revolutionize poetic language and articulate abjection, "Céline's effect is quite other" (134). She duly acknowledges that, following the "black lineage" of Lautréamont or Artaud, Céline counters the "lyrical" or romantic tradition and covers that lineage's "appropriate themes" of "death, madness, orgy, outlaws, war, the feminine threat, the horrendous delights of love, disgust, and fright" (137). And, with perceptible disdain, she briefly references the well-trod ground of a criticism of Céline's "bad form." "Obviously," she writes, "one could read [his texts] by following the meanderings of the narrative, which, similar to those of well-known storytellers, is picaresque" in early works such as *Journey to the End of the Night* and *Death on the Installment Plan*.

One could, but she will not, because style significantly supercedes narrative form in Céline's *oeuvre*. His later works especially, in which a radically disjointed narrative discourse "bursts its shell and veers towards [...] polyphony," render narrative or generic analysis inadequate. That polyphony does not allow it, which we realize if we "let Céline's text ring" and listen. "I am not a man of ideas" – he asserts in a statement Kristeva quotes both in *Powers of Horror* and "Psychoanalysis and the Polis" – "I am a man of style. Style, well, everyone stops before that, no one really reaches the thing. Because it is very hard work. It involves taking sentences, as I was saying, and having them fly off their handle" ("Psychoanalysis and the Polis," p. 188).[6] It is not the linearity, or even nonlinearity, of a narrative progression Kristeva's analysis will follow, but rather the eccentric trajectory of these "flying fragments" (202). She will not offer a narratology, therefore, because demanding more urgent analysis is the "more specifically Célinian feature" of a narrative "drown[ed] in a style" that gives writing the bodily urgency and emotion of oral speech (137). The "inhumanity" he so often expresses and bears witness to "resides in his very words" (135). Collectively Céline's texts produce the

> greatest homage to the Word that was not made flesh in order to hoist itself up into Man with a capital letter but to join, body and language being mingled, those intermediate states, those non-states, neither subject nor object where *you* is alone, singular, untouchable, unsociable, discredited, at the end of a night that is as particular as it is incommensurable. (135; emphasis Kristeva's).

Kristeva here again asserts her fundamental claim about Céline's style: it "embodies" or "incarnates" abjection. It performs syntactically and rhetorically what the visceral narrative discourse chronicles thematically as well. On the most primary, primal level – that is, on the material level of a "word made flesh" – Céline's words materially *do* what they *describe*. As the starkness of his vision repeatedly makes clear, Céline's journey through abjection does not render it sublime, per se. Writing about abjection by writing abjection does not thereby transcend it; neither is such consolation available for the reader. That is Kristeva's point in the statement above: Céline's "scription" insists, incessantly, on giving utterance to the abject, which affects the reader by throwing her into the force field of abjection as well. His language not only does what it describes, it does it *to us*. It offers an encounter with language where, as in the scenes it describes, "*you* is alone."

Kristeva clearly believes in the ultimate value, the readerly benefit, of going through the experience Céline imposes upon us; but she does not suggest it offers revelation, per se, or salvation – for Céline, his characters, or for us. His "word made flesh" is visceral, distinctly *not* on the order of a romantic faith in the power of poetic language (a faith in the analogy, that is, between the "word" and the "Word"). The poetic language of the "Célinian universe" is transformative, but untranscended, the anguished, but nevertheless *productive* utterance of psychoanalysis's decentered subject.

* * *

The correspondence between the primal, prelinguistic signification of bodily affect and its manifestations in language – that there is indeed such a correspondence – is a guiding principle of Kristeva's work. Céline offers a rich test of that hypothesis both in his avowed expressions of creative intent and in the texture of his art itself. After long explorations of the anxious – if not indefensible – roles of the feminine figure and, especially, the Jew in Céline, Kristeva devotes her penultimate chapter to the question of style on the level of the letter she calls for at the outset of her argument.[7] Whereas the explorations of these roles veer into the thematic territory she claims to move beyond, in chapter 10 Kristeva genuinely engages in the close stylistic analysis she promises and insists upon in chapter 6. Chapter 10, "In the Beginning and Without End," begins with a well-known Célinian assertion from "Louis-Ferdinand Céline vous parle": " 'In the beginning was the word.' No! In the beginning was emotion." Kristeva links the statement to his similar avowal that his primary literary aim is to approximate, in written language, the "natural" rhythms of speech, to "smuggle spoken language into writing," as she puts it (*Powers of Horror*, p. 192). For he believes that "emotion is encountered in spoken language alone" (191).

The pervasive colloquialism of Céline's texts provides the most obvious testament to this strategy. And Kristeva carefully stresses that it is indeed a stylistic strategy, not simply a literary incompetence or the deployment of an ideological position, one in keeping with the semiotic radicality he inflicts on the "Word." She writes:

> The vocabulary of slang, because of its strangeness, its very violence, and especially *because the reader does not always understand it*, is of course a radical *instrument of separation*, of rejection, and, at the limit, of hatred. Slang produces a *semantic fuzziness*, if not interruption, within the utterances that it punctuates and rhythmicizes, but above all it *draws near to that emptiness of meaning* at which Céline seems to aim. (*Powers of Horror*, p. 190; emphasis mine)

The statement is worth quoting at length, with emphasis, because it provides a particularly lucid account of the experience of reading Céline – a disorientation compounded despairingly by English-speaking readers attempting to navigate the French, or worse, trying to negotiate the significant discrepancies between the original French and the English translations. For precisely the same reasons, it also speaks to the plight of Kristeva's own readers, as we have observed. Here, she will go on to examine specific rhetorical strategies that, like slang, seem to reproduce the rhythms of spoken language and, in the process, to produce a "semantic fuzziness" with far-reaching implications. Because it offers some of the book's most concrete literary analysis and sheds light on Kristeva's own discursive strategies, her outline of Céline's "plan to smuggle spoken language into writing" warrants careful scrutiny (*Powers of Horror*, p. 192).

Kristeva identifies "two basic devices" in Céline's stylistic effort: "sentence *segmentation*" and "*syntactic ellipsis*" (192; emphasis Kristeva's). The first of these devices involves the "particular, colloquial segmentation of the Célinian sentence," which, Kristeva acknowledges, the linguist Leo Spitzer was with first to theorize. The citation is telling, if partial, for it indicates the extent to which Kristeva draws the terminology of her prose analysis from the formulations of a linguistic intonational theory that remains obscure to an English-language audience and is typically associated with verse analysis (as outlined in Clive Scott's *Poetics of French Verse*, for example). Ivan Fonágy serves as one rather buried source, supplying Kristeva with the otherwise inscrutable reference to the syntactic ordering principles of "Hungarian and classical Chinese," and with the important, but perhaps overly abstruse "theme/rheme bitartition" formula for understanding Céline's characteristic reordering of sentence structure (194, 193). On the one hand, if not bracketing the originality of Kristeva's approach, this conceptual context does highlight the fact that Kristeva's theories often depend upon putting existing work from a diversity of disciplines to new uses, in new combinations. (The superimpositions of Husserl upon Marx upon Freud in *Revolution in Poetic Language* that we observed in our first chapter, for instance; or the juxtaposition of Bakhtin and Barthes with theories of subjectivity, which we will explore in the next.) On the other hand, it offers the Kristevan critical mode that readers are likely to find most off-putting: the highly allusive, densely accreted technical discourse she inherits from formalism and largely sheds in the decade leading up to the publication of *Powers of Horror*. However, rather than taking this discursive snarl as a cue not to pay attention, or to find the true power in more felicitously challenging portions of her book, readers will find, I would argue, that doing the work of untangling the analysis from its jargon does bear fruit.

Kristeva observes that there "are countless examples" in Céline's prose, particularly the early work, of a peculiar syntactic pattern. They involve "cutting up the syntactic unit and displacing one of its constituents, postponing and preposing it" (192). What results is a sentence that does not sound or act like a typical French sentence, intonationally speaking: "the normally descending modulation of the sentence is transformed into an intonation having two centers" (192). There might seem good cause to abandon Kristeva right here. If not a linguist or a prosodist, a reader might find it difficult to grasp just what "descending modulation" would sound like in a "normal" sentence, much less in the innovative disruptions Kristeva wishes to map out in Céline; that these intonations surely differ in the French and English languages might imply further cause for disorientation. But in fact, her argument about the relationship between Céline's style and his linguistic "embodiment" of abjection has well prepared us for this claim. On the most obvious level some of Kristeva's assertions at the outset of her study, about the poetic musicality of Céline's style (his "tune, without notes"), which might read as airy lyricisms in their initial context, find concrete theoretical grounding and elaboration here.

The intonational and syntactic analyses Kristeva offers overlap in complicated ways, the particularities of which will remain beyond the scope of this discussion. Generally speaking, Kristeva's interest in *intonation* concerns the "segmented" rhythm, the "preposings, displacements, or repetitions" that create "*successive surges of the intonational curve*" within a given Célinian utterance (194; emphasis Kristeva's). These "often staccato" rhythms go beyond the dictates of punctuation and create utterances that generate a "very particular thrill" at once "musical and intimate" (195). She cites a sentence from Céline's

Journey to the End of the Night, full of breathless, self-interrupting starts and stops, vividly to illustrate this intonational peculiarity (194–5). But for the purposes of following Kristeva's argument, it suffices to focus not on *intonation*, but on the concept of *syntax* broadly understood – that is, as the order of the words within a given sentence or group of sentences.

Kristeva offers two suggestive specimen statements from Céline's *Journey to the End of the Night* that demonstrate the dynamics of "segmentation" on this syntactic level. Both examples involve words within the sentence that break up the normal subject–verb–object ordering – that is, words appearing syntactically out of place or lacking an identifiable syntactic role altogether ("desyntacized") (193). Though Kristeva's spare exposition only implies it, the examples illustrate a significant parallel: their unassimilability within the structure of the sentence corresponds precisely with the unassimilability of the ideas (war, grief) they represent. Céline "embodies" abjection, therefore, by acting it out in the very structure of the language that reports it.

The first example appears early in the novel, as the narrator, a soldier in the First World War, reflects on the disorienting horror that surrounds him. Kristeva wants to draw attention to the noun, "the filthy thing" ("la vache"), which she italicizes, and to the fact that, despite its thematic centrality to the passage in question, its actual articulation is *postponed* until the very end of the sentence:

> I had suddenly discovered, all at once, what the war was, the whole war. I'd lost my innocence. You need to be pretty well alone with it, face to face, as I was then, to see it properly, in the round, *the filthy thing*. (192; emphasis Kristeva's)

The second example appears later in the novel, and reports the reaction of Bébert's aunt, the guardian of a dying child for whom the narrator, working as a doctor in the slums of Rancy, has cultivated an uncharacteristic affection.[8] In this case, Kristeva is concerned with the appearance and reappearance of the word "grief." Whereas "the filthy thing" is postponed – or "*postposed*" – "grief" is syntactically *preposed* and then returns in displaced "reentries" (193). In other words, the term heads up the sentence, as if appearing unexpectedly and too soon, and then comes back in two repeated references:

> *Grief* had come to her, in fact, when her words came to an end; she did not seem to know what to do with it, with that *grief* of hers; she tried to wipe it away with her handkerchief, but it came back into her throat, *her*

> *grief* did, and tears came too, and she began all over again. (192; emphases Kristeva's)

Though understated within this particular discussion, Kristeva's argument in the early chapters of *Powers of Horror* motivates her reading of these statements. She wants to stress their emotive impact, their relationship to affective significations that develop logically prior to the subject's entrance into the symbolic. These syntactical displacements in Céline suggest, for her, some link to that pre-linguistic realm, and some justification for Céline's claim to represent "*spoken* language's emotion through writing" (191; emphasis Kristeva's). She means to link his writing to the "archaic structure[s]" of subjectivity, and to read their "tune" as "a token of emotivity close to the drives, [...] a syntactic organizer both very precocious and very profound" (196). Fonágy, one of the first linguists to propose such a deep-seated connection between the structures of colloquial syntax and human being, thus provides Kristeva with a theoretical foundation for testing this hypothesis. Following Fonágy, she notes that, in both these examples from Céline, the displacements of the key terms reorder the normal way in which sentences (in French and English) tend *first* to offer the topic at hand and *then* to provide information about it. The linguistic theory from which Kristeva draws calls this topic the "theme" ("in other words, that about which the speaker is talking"); distinct from the "theme" is the "rheme" ("that is, information pertaining to the theme") (193). Keeping in mind the very specific sense in which she uses the term "theme" in this portion of her analysis, we can read the Célinian sentences she offers as suggestive demonstrations of the notion that his disordered syntax works to signify affect.

The placement of "the filthy thing" in the first example provides the more obvious illustration of a rheme/theme logic rather than the more normative theme/rheme. We hear all about "it" – that the narrator has "discovered" something profound about it, seen it as a "whole," become intimate with it – before he names it; the name comes last. Remarkably, by postponing the "theme" in this way, Céline acts out on the level of the letter the very experience the narrator describes. The unnameable thing, wholly other, which the narrator studies and mulls over and becomes acquainted with only over time, gets named in the sentence (and only then with an obscenity) according to a similarly delayed temporality.[9] In other words, the "*logic of the message*" models "that of *the syntax*" (193; emphasis Kristeva's).

"Grief" would be the "theme" of the second statement and, because it comes right at the beginning, it would seem to conform to the standard theme/rheme structure. But here too the logic of the message and the syntax intimately correspond. In this case, the thing appears ("*Grief* had come to her"), name and all, before it can be understood or given a place. Moreover, it keeps popping up – within the sentence, as for the grieving subject – beyond her capacity to control it. Like "the filthy thing," "grief" is something unassimilable to the subject in question: Bébert's aunt "did not seem to know what to do with it, with *that grief* of hers." And because it does not make sense, syntactically or cognitively, it returns disruptively: "she tried to wipe it away with her handkerchief, but it came back into her throat, *her grief* did, and tears came too, and she began all over again." It is the "return of the repressed" represented as an "enunciative strategy" (197).

In keeping with the performative nature of her argument, Kristeva often highlights the effects of preposing and postposing by employing the strategy herself. Mingled with the seemingly daunting rigor of statements asking readers to "identify the true semantico-logical value of the constituents" of a given sentence in Céline are statements that demonstrate the impact of syntactical derangement by precisely acting it out. On the heels of pointing out that Céline rhythmically cuts up his sentences, staccato-like, with stops and starts that go beyond the pauses indicated by commas, and before providing an example from *Journey to the End of the Night*, she writes: "as if, with colloquial segmentation, Céline procured, in addition to punctuation, new means of shaping his sentences and imparting rhythm and music to them" (194–5). Her own sentence does what it is talking about, "shaping" its rhythm in accord with that very strategy.

In retrospect, we can see Kristeva offering one of the most compelling examples of preposing in an early thesis statement that, in its initial context, seems unremarkable. The seemingly understated observation, in the second paragraph of chapter 6, that "[w]e are thrown into a strange state when reading Céline" (133) takes on new significance when we notice, in the French, its telling syntactical logic: "Étrange état que celui dans lequel nous plonge la lecture de Céline" (157). Just as the statement reports to us that reading Céline "plunges" us into a "strange state," presumably without preparation or adequate defenses, so does Kristeva offer its "theme" ("strange state") in an awkwardly front-loaded syntactical structure. (In English, the sentence might read more literally as follows: "A strange state is the one into which we are plunged in reading Céline.") The preposed "Étrange état," like Céline's preposed "grief," functions syntactically the way the sentences tell us strangeness and grief function psychically. In Kristeva's case, the disorientation is magnified by her "postponing" until chapter 10 the theoretical explanation of an enunciative strategy she herself employs in chapter 6.

Another characteristic feature she "previews" is the highly performative statement we have already analyzed: *ellipsis*. Kristeva regards Céline's more obvious and pervasive use of ellipsis – "the famous 'three dots,' or points of suspension" – as a concentrated, radical extension of the strategy enacted by preposement and postponement (198). In this analysis, she identifies several specific ways in which "the three dots" function in his texts. Significantly, these go beyond the definition of the term in classical rhetoric (ellipsis as syntactic omission, "leaving out" a word or phrase) or, more subtly, in structuralist narratology – such as the temporal gaps and discontinuities outlined in Gérard Genette's *Narrative Discourse*.[10] Not incidentally, in fact, much of Kristeva's subtle theoretical positioning seems an effort to distinguish her emphatically *stylistic* discussion of ellipsis from Genette's well-known formulations. (As "Discours du récit," Genette's essay was published as part of *Figures III* in 1972.) Genette approaches ellipsis as a subset of "duration," the means by which a narrative renders the passage of time, the rhythm by which it dwells on certain moments, skips over others, and connects one temporal point to another. We might read Kristeva's momentary comparison here between the Proustian and Célinian sentence, and her passing Proustian allusions elsewhere, as a strategic non-reference to an influential text with which Kristeva would have been familiar. Whereas Genette's consideration of ellipsis treats it as an element of narrative structure, Kristeva insists upon it as a stylistic device, in keeping with her thesis that, in Céline, style subsumes narration.

Thus, while ellipsis traditionally involves omission, her first example concerns a kind of ellipsis that, paradoxically, omits nothing. On the contrary, in such cases, "the three dots rather point to the *overflowing of the clause*." In such instances, what Céline seems to indicate is that, while the information is complete, "the *enunciation*, on the other hand, is not; it continues, becomes displaced, concatenates other clauses" (198; all emphases Kristeva's). In one sense, the affective charge of the statement overflows the words themselves, so that the three dots suggest "we are dealing not with a 'less' but with a 'more' of syntax" (197). And they suggest an excess, an overdetermination, of meaning as well. Displaced, the clauses are freed up to join with other clauses, to produce new "chains" of signification, "to concatenate" (*enchaîner*) with them.

On the basis of this observation, Kristeva goes on to identify ellipsis as the privileged discursive mode of Céline's later novels. In works such as *Rigadoon* and *Castle to Castle*, for instance, this strategy upsets syntax and sense so much more than the theme/rheme reversals of *Journey to the End of the Night* because it not only reorders subject–verb–object sentences, but often obliterates elements of them altogether. Noun phrases are left floating without verbal connectors, without indication of the subject's relation to the "flying fragments" of object phrases that follow (202). In some instances, ellipsis produces statements that contain "themes whose rhemes are suspended. It is as if the main information that these descriptions contain were hushed up" (199).

To illustrate these various "modalities" of ellipsis, Kristeva provides an example from Céline's *Castle to Castle*. The long passage reads in part as follows:

> I've got to tell you that in addition to being a voyeur I'm a fanatic about the movement of harbors, about everything that goes on on the water ... everything that sails or floats or docks ... I was on the jetties with my father ... a week's vacation in Le Tréport ... Christ, the things we saw! ... the fishing boats' entrances and exits ... whiting at the risk of their lives! ... the widows and the kids imploring the sea! ... the emotion of those jetties! ... the suspense! ... make the Grand Guignol and the billion-dollar thrillers from Hollywood look like a kindergarten! (198)

The narrator's exclamatory enthusiasm for the topic at hand, his "fanatic[al]" interest in "everything that goes on on the water" provides the impetus for a wash of information about such things, his remembrances of them, the emotions they aroused in him and others. As Kristeva points out, he conveys the implied excitement of having too much to say about these "things on the water" by means of a proliferation of "three dots." They clearly suggest not that information is being elided, but rather that it is crowded into the utterance, dashed about like the fishing boats on the "whiting" sea.

In another sense, however, the ellipses do indicate a certain omission. What the passage lacks are the kinds of subject–verb constructions that normally tell the reader where to situate the noun phrases presented to us. Kristeva illustrates what Céline's passage would look like with the grounding of such words: " '(*there was*, or *we spent*) a week's vacation in Le Tréport'; '(*we could see, or there were*) the fishing boats' entrances and exits'; '(*they went out for*) whiting at the risk of their lives!' " (199; emphases mine). Without such constructions, these elliptical statements destabilize the position of the speaking subject who is uttering them. As a noun phrase (an object) without a subject and verb to situate it, "a week's vacation in Le Tréport" gives a semantic fuzziness to the enunciation, leaving open to question what affective valence we should give it. In other words, the phrase "*indicates* – without making clear – my place, my emotional and logical attitude as a subject who remembers, with melancholy or delight" (200; emphasis Kristeva's).

Most notably, ellipsis serves as Céline's "privileged expression" for representing the "infernal rhythm of the war" (201). Exploded sentences offer a "condensed scription" that models war's explosive violence. In *Rigadoon*, Céline noisily represents a bombing with ellipses and onomatopoeia that "score" and literally "punctuate" the utterance, tear it apart, make it reverberate (202). Kristeva quotes a long passage that reads in part as follows:

> The whole earth jumps! worse! like it had been broken in two! ... and the air ... this is it! Restif hadn't been lying ... *boom*! and another! ... further away ... we can see it! The flashes of their cannon! ... red! ... green! no! shorter! howitzers! ... all on the station! ... I can see them now ... Oddort! ... an ocean of flame, as they say ... big flames from all over, the windows, the doors, the cars ... and boom! another! ... another! [...] I won't bore you with the shelling ... dead center ... all on the station ... a furnace! ... now we can see it plainly [...] we know the sound ... *rat-tat-tat*! *rat-tat-tat*! ... in bursts ... like grinding coffee by hand ... I say to Lili ... I don't need to say, she knows ... down! flatter! And *wham*! ... *crash*! ... a bomb! and flying fragments ... the death blow! ... (201–2; emphases Céline's)[11]

Kristeva analyzes the crowded disarray of information and impressions offered by this passage, seeing in it a complicated interplay of Celine's early and later rhetorical strategies. Like the elliptical profusion wrought by enthusiasm and memory in *Castle to Castle*, here violent sensory overload strips the language of verbal markers, producing a narrative "deprived of comment." In this case, we encounter "that extreme Célinian situation where the most objectal, most sparing description is blended with the most intense affective charge" (202). Because the conceptual link between the physical violence of a bomb and the syntactical "flying fragments" of Céline's sentence is particularly self-evident, Kristeva suggests that it "is now easier to understand" one of his key assertions: "Style is a certain way of doing violence to sentences" (203).

Kristeva asks a rhetorical question at an intermediate point in the stylistic analysis of chapter 10: "Finally, what could be the psychological value of such a technique?" (195) She is referring to the strategies of preposing and postposing, but it is relevant to every Célinian device she presents. As a whole, her answer to such a question comes at the end of the chapter, reminding her readers that what Céline aims to articulate, in every case, is some version of abjection. Performative utterances, they make something happen: "an affect bursts out, in sound and outcry, bordering close on drive and abjection as well as fascination. Bordering on the unnameable" (204). He produces language that maps out the limits of language and the speaking subject "of which Freud has caught a glimpse: the gushing forth of the unconscious, the repressed" (206). Kristeva likens this "glimpse" to the revelatory vision of apocalypse, but emphasizes that what Céline witnesses and would have us see is, specifically, not transcendent, not "sublime." He writes of "an apocalypse without god. Black mysticism of transcendental collapse" (206). Céline's texts traverse the landscape of abjection, bringing readers on the same journey. But, unlike Dante's journey through the underworld, they do so without offering a guide, without implying access to some greater truth, without promising salvation. Céline's ambivalent narrators with their tortured sentences act out a "scription [...] without morality, without judgment, without hope" (206). Céline's journey takes us to the place where he says language is "in the beginning": to emotion, and to the point where it "speaks" materially, through the body and the drives. And as the title of Kristeva's chapter reminds us, this journey is "without end."

We can perhaps best understand this conclusion, that Céline brings us to a limit that is ecstatically unnameable but not *sublime*, by recognizing the uncanny similarity between her analysis and Longinus' famous first-century treatise "On Sublimity." For indeed each Célinian strategy she identifies finds a close antecedent in Longinus' own analysis. Her readings of the preposing and postposing maneuvers in *Journey to the End of the Night* remarkably resemble Longinus' consideration of *hyperbaton*, the "arrangement of words or thought which differs from the normal sequence" that he considers "a very real mark of urgent emotion."[12] For Longinus, working from a firmly grounded faith in Platonic idealism, Homer's description of shipwrecked sailors imperiled by a raging sea is sublime, while another author's presentation of the same scene is not, specifically because Homer's syntax corresponds to the affectively charged situation it describes. Through the "forced combination of naturally uncompoundable prepositions: *hupek*, 'from under.' Homer has tortured the words to correspond with the emotion of the moment." As the waves pound and the winds roar, "The sailors shudder in terror: / they are carried away from under death, but only just." Though the two writers could not be more different, Homer, like Céline, "has in effect stamped the special character of the danger on the diction" (142). But Longinus attributes this "magnificent" connection between syntax and affect, beyond its linguistic felicity, to the grandeur of the scene Homer describes, to the heroism of the men involved, and – not least – to the "noble mind" of the author who crafted it (141). Ultimately, this literary effort not only seeks "something higher than human," but brings its readers along with it: "sublimity raises us towards the spiritual greatness of god" (153, 152).

Such an affectively inscribed language – "tortured words" that materially act out the abjection they approach – produces a "transport" that carries us not onward and upward to sublime heights, in Kristeva's critical system, but back to our subjective beginnings. Literature provides, as I point out in the previous chapter, the "privileged signifier" for Kristeva, "the ultimate coding of our crises, of our most intimate and serious apocalypses" (208). Céline's "scription" does so by offering us language and nothing else, which amounts to a kind of sublimity in its own right that references no higher power than its own, an "indefinite catharsis" that unveils, discharges, elaborates abjection through "[m]usic, rhythm, rigadoon, without end, for no reason" (206). Céline thus takes the reader on a journey to the place that takes the place of the sacred, after the various intellectual, political, and religious upheavals of the nineteenth and twentieth centuries. The "Crisis of the Word" wrought by abjection brings us to the borderline, the limits of the speaking subject.

Céline most radically chronicles this "human adventure" not by unsparing storytelling but through the physical rhythms of a language that, as literally as possible, explodes on the page. Céline's journey "without end" traces the dynamics of the speaking subject itself, in permanent crisis, in perpetual battle against abjection, acted out in language and signification. The critical reader too, drawn to "the only place that is his [the analyst's], *the void*, that is, the unthinkable of metaphysics," can find in Céline an opportunity "to begin hearing" but also "actually to listen to himself build up a discourse around the braided horror and fascination that bespeaks the incompleteness of the speaking being" (209; emphasis Kristeva's). In every case – Céline's, his readers', that of the subject itself – such discursive explorations function as a continual work in progress.

Tangles and cuts: narrating abjection in Céline's *Journey to the End of the Night*

Kristeva eschews what, "after so much 'Russian formalism' " and biographical criticism, the critic typically says about Céline's narratives because she wants to regard them as privileged specimens ("the most elaborate attempt") of precisely that: utterances of the "speaking being" within abjection (140). She sees the motives of the Célinian narrator through the lens of psychoanalysis, as a decentered subject in the play of the drives, within the dynamics of abjection. Narration, in this sense, represents a reaction to the threat of death, a negotiation of it. In each of Céline's novels, his protagonists' "whole narrative stance seems controlled by the necessity of going through abjection" (140). But this necessity makes for a precarious endeavor, in which the "narrative web is a thin film constantly threatened with bursting" (141). Rather than repress or work against such threats, the very structure of Célinian narrative brings them to the surface, exploits them, and acts them out. Céline's experimental disruption of conventional narrative form "takes up where apocalypse and carnival left off" (141). According to Kristeva, his "narrative stance" marks a moment in the history of the subject and of literature when, paradoxically, genre and literary history get left behind.[13] It constitutes a break and breaking down that ushers in something else in its wake:

> For, when narrated identity is unbearable, when the boundary between subject and object is shaken, and when even the limit between inside and outside becomes uncertain, the narrative is what is challenged first. If it continues nevertheless, its makeup changes; its linearity is shattered, it proceeds by flashes, enigmas, short cuts, incompletion, tangles, and cuts. (141)

As we explored in the previous section, these tangles and cuts, flashes and shatterings are indeed what makes Céline's prose so explosive. But Kristeva's insistence that such challenges to narrative "linearity" obviate any discussion of narrative form makes her analysis especially inhospitable for readers who might need orientation, in the plainest sense, with what happens in Céline's stories and in what manner we are told about these happenings. And though Kristeva deliberately bypasses an analysis of the picaresque "meanderings of the narrative" She acknowledges in Céline's earliest work, *Journey to the End of the Night*, they in fact contribute significantly to the discursive effects she considers so radically unsettling.

The narrative's structure and logic, its use and abuse of generic narrative conventions, suggestively act out the very rhetorical drama of the "word made flesh" Kristeva traces on the level of the sentence. Momentarily acknowledging the picaresque, she conveys a degree of disdain not only for critics who would take a generic focus, but even, subtly, for the genre itself. In keeping with Bakhtin's privileged pantheon of authors – Rabelais, Dostoevsky – Kristeva prefers to align Céline with the carnivalesque and its "fundamental dialogism," asserting that the sheer ironic noise, the dizzying irreverence of his novels, which puts the "height of tragedy" side by side with "the most cavalier mockery," brings the tradition "to its paroxysmal climax" (138). The carnivalesque is quite close to the picaresque, however, with an irreverent and ironic history of its own, and Céline clearly works within – even if to wreak havoc upon – that tradition as well. While Kristeva is busy engaging in a largely unacknowledged theoretical dispute with ghostly critical forebears, her reader might be denied a generic and narrative context that would actually strengthen her acute stylistic analysis.

It helps considerably to see that, in the broadest strokes at least, the "hero" of Céline's notorious and celebrated first novel, *Journey to the End of the Night*, is a picaro. Ferdinand Bardamu lavishly falls prone to misadventures that recall Fielding's "ill-starred" Tom Jones, though Tom's impediments were never so abjectly dark. Like Thackeray's Barry Lyndon, he finds himself in wildly disparate situations he fell into by chance and often did little to earn or deserve – fighting in a regiment against an enemy he does not hate, the object of paranoid suspicion turned to patriotic worship on a ship to Africa, working on the assembly line at a Ford plant in Detroit, practicing medicine in French slums, acting a silent part in a singing and dancing stage show, an unwillingly implicated figure in a sordid murder plot, head of an insane asylum.

Also in keeping with the picaresque tradition, Ferdinand demonstrates an irrepressible staying power – a sheer, tenacious will, exasperating and monotonous as it often is, to keep telling his story. Like that of Sterne's Tristram Shandy, this staying power is conspicuously narrative or verbal. But whereas Shandy's adversities tend toward the banal (his own short attention span, a large cast of annoying relatives),

Ferdinand's tend toward the apocalyptic: chaotic warfare, political hypocrisy, imperialist tyranny, poverty, and disease. The threat implied by each is death, which lurks in the corner of every place along his journey. As he realizes early on, his struggles are in every case the struggle to save his skin, to stay alive by "defer[ring]" its threat, to grant himself a "suspended sentence" in the face of the "different ways of being condemned to death" (*Journey to the End of the Night*, pp. 43, 10). Ferdinand self-effacingly attributes his impulse to stay alive to the basest instincts of man – cowardice, cynicism, self-involvement – but the impulses manifest themselves as well in a life force not merely reducible to them. Ferdinand's, and in turn Céline's, sheer insistence on continuing to narrate horror, to utter it exuberantly and outrageously, points to the correspondence between various thematic abjections chronicled in Céline's work and his rhetorical negotiation of them. In other words, the narrator's relentlessly inventive, often just lucky, ability to escape his "death sentence" is enacted by means of literally "suspended sentences": a narrative that keeps going and going and going, in phrases bursting with expletive, exclamation, ellipsis, and strange syntax that comprise the style Kristeva sees as paramount.

In the unfolding of the plot, words repeatedly both save Ferdinand and get him into trouble. Rhetorically and stylistically, and more specifically by means of the very deviations Kristeva here describes – shattered "linearity, [...] flashes, enigmas, [...] tangles, and cuts" – Ferdinand the narrator acts out the life-and-death connection between his experiences and the way he talks about them. Exploring even some of the initial episodes in the novel, specifically the unsettling links and discontinuities among them, demonstrates vividly the abject narrative shattering Kristeva identifies. Examining these disruptions provides a helpful context for understanding Céline's radical treatment of the "word made flesh." It helps us see the violence he inflicts upon the sentence as a performance of the bodily violence Ferdinand chronicles so relentlessly.

We can look to the novel's very first scene, where mere words and picaresque impetuousness come together to precipitate disaster. Ferdinand begins his adventures in *Journey to the End of the Night* by signing up to serve in the French army during World War I, as a dare, after some pretentious political posturing in a café conversation with a friend. With an impulsiveness that characteristically plagues the picaro, he backs up his "anarchist" argument to Arthur Ganate that the French race is and has always been "[h]ateful and spineless, raped and robbed, mangled and witless," that we are all ruled by "lord and master [...] Misery," unconsoled by the ideality of love: "love is the infinite placed within the reach of poodles" (4). We are a ship of fools, and war amounts to nothing more than a standard cynical, hysterical paradigm that Ferdinand summarizes as follows, extending the metaphor: "We're at war! Those stinkers in Country No. 2! We're going to board them and cut their livers out! Let's go! Let's go! We've got everything we need on board! All together now! Let's hear you shout so the deck trembles: 'Long live Country No. 1' " (5).

Arthur actually agrees on this point, though he had opposed his own belief in "the established order" to Ferdinand's earlier "anarchist" rant. A chance coincidence compels Ferdinand nevertheless to put his ideas to the test. An army regiment marches past the café in the midst of this discussion and, moved by his own speech, "Enthusiasm lifted me to my feet [...] and off I go to enlist, on the double." Arthur reasonably warns, "Ferdinand! [...] Don't be an ass!" Ferdinand ironically supposes that Arthur's reaction stems from being "nettled by the effect my heroism was having on the people around us," and from there his path is set. When enthusiasm wanes – the admiring crowd disperses, the music stops – he comes to his senses: " 'Come to think of it,' I said to myself, when I saw what was what, 'this is no fun anymore! I'd better try something else!' " But it is too late. "When you're in, you're in" (7).

What Ferdinand is "in," he surmises, is a war that "in fact, made no sense at all" (7). His enlistment is decisive and irrevocable, however, despite his cognitive protest. Though comprising only the first few chapters of *Journey to the End of the Night,* the most affecting part of the narrative involves the brutal chaos of Ferdinand's experience in World War I. Within the structure of this novel, the war provides both a starting point and a constant frame of reference for Ferdinand's abiding assessment of human life, including his own. He observes:

> You can be a virgin in horror the same as in sex. How, when I left the Place Clichy, could I have imagined such horror? Who could have suspected, before getting really into the war, all the ingredients that go to make up the rotten, heroic, good-for-nothing soul of man? And there I was, caught up in a mass flight into the collective murder, into the fiery furnace ... Something had come up from the depths, and this is what happened. (9)

Kristeva cites the first line of this passage as the epigraph to chapter 7 of *Powers of Horror,* where she stresses the fundamental role of both

World Wars in Céline's texts, not just in this novel but in all of his writing.[14] War is his very catalyst, the speaking being's reason for being. She likens its force to a vision of the apocalypse (an "unfurling of aggressivity and death") or a descent into the underworld. But, for her, this force is not *revelatory* so much as *dynamic*, distinct because it offers not *insight* per se but rather *energy*, motive in the most fundamental sense. It is "the wound that Céline never ceases to palpate" (153).

In Kristeva's assessment, war "plays the role of Beatrice's death, which leads to the *Vita Nuova*, or of Dante's avoidance of death, which initiates the first canto of the *Divine Comedy*" (152–3). In Dante, the death (of another) precipitates the narrative drive – the narrator's drive – to avoid death. It is the primal scene that brings the narrative into being: narration as articulation of the death drive itself. Kristeva's juxtaposition of Dante and Céline offers a suggestive generic link, but again the force of her reference is eccentric to the apparent literary historical claim she makes. More obliquely, She seems to let Dante's titles alone (rather than his plots) underline her thesis on Céline's "narrative stance" toward abjection. Céline's narratives look death in the face and up close, seem perpetually to run scared from it and be motivated by it. But, crucially, this energy is generated by – and generates – life force as well as death drive. In Céline, the "comedy" is decidedly not divine, never consoling; death sets Céline's narrators on a perpetual journey, but not an epic one. Like the experience of abjection she describes in the opening pages of *Powers of Horror*, Céline's narrators face death "without God and outside of science" (4), bodily and untranscended. And nevertheless, these experiences lead to "new life" – more absurd, lurid garrulousness from a narrator who refuses, even while charting the topography of hell, to meet horror with silence.

Again, Kristeva sees this energy in Céline's texts as an issue of style rather than narrative structure, even while the peculiarities of that structure indeed highlight abjection in precisely these terms. With a basically transitionless cut from the café to the battlefield, the narrative of *Journey to the End of the Night* briskly plunges its readers into the supremely "strange state" of inhumanity on a global scale. Like Ferdinand himself, Céline's readers are caught up short and unprepared. In chapter 1, Ferdinand's existentialism and anarchism are ironically framed within the light, comic absurdity of immature rhetorical posturing. That setting shifts abruptly in chapter 2, where the picaresque comedy turns quickly black. As a number of writers chronicling World War I had begun to do, Céline conveys the callous inhumanity and existential purposelessness of war through the eyes of a disbelieving protagonist whose bewilderment and assertive cowardice represent a vestige of sanity in a world gone mad.[15] Ferdinand confronts this world in breathless contemplations, sentences stuffed with the mess and din of a chaos that thwarts synthesis and sense:

> Could I, I thought, be the last coward on earth? How terrifying! … All alone with two million stark raving heroic madmen, armed to the eyeballs? With and without helmets, without horses, on motorcycles, bellowing, in cars, screeching, shooting, plotting, flying, kneeling, digging, taking cover, bounding over trails, root-toot-tooting, shut up on earth as if it were a loony bin, ready to demolish everything on it, Germany, France, whole continents, everything that breathes, destroy, destroy, madder than mad dogs, worshipping their madness (which dogs don't), a hundred, a thousand times madder than a thousand dogs, and a lot more vicious! A pretty mess we're in! (9)

Céline's distinction, in comparison with the bitterly ironic trench poetry of Siegfried Sassoon or the memoir of Robert Graves, however, is to cast this experience as savagely comic. The sheer inappropriateness of comedy, truly funny comedy, in the midst of often literally nauseating descriptions of carnage and brutality, have an impact on the reader in a way that is difficult to account for. Céline generates a comic, "lurid glee," through the unique voice of his narrator, but also by exploiting a key convention of picaresque plot development: its episodic randomness, in which events are tied together by tenuous or illogical causality over which the protagonist exerts little, or at times wayward, control.

Two vivid episodes that follow these apocalyptic visions illustrate Céline's subversive deployment of this convention to particularly unconsoling effect. As he dodges bullets from unseen Germans and watches the intrepid movements of his colonel with bewilderment, Ferdinand asks himself, with the force of revelation, "How much longer would this madness have to go on before these monsters dropped with exhaustion?" He finds this uncertainty, this potential interminability, unbearable and decides, uncharacteristically, to act. He hatches a putatively sensible, yet practically ridiculous plan to take matters into his own hands:

> [S]eeing events were taking such a desperate turn, I decided […] to see if I couldn't stop the war, just me, all by myself! At least in this one spot where I happened to be.

> The colonel was only two steps away from me, pacing. I'd talk to him. Something I'd never done. This was a time for daring. The way things stood, there was practically nothing to lose. "What is it?" he'd ask me, startled, I imagined, at my bold interruption. Then I'd explain the situation as I saw it, and we'd see what he thought. The essential thing is to talk things over. Two heads are better than one. (10–11)

The revelatory urgency with which Ferdinand announces this decision, the dramatic tension implied by the "daring" break in command he is about to commit, and the hopeful anticipation with which he rationally rehearses his proposal are all ironically undercut in a stroke – by a chance interruption followed by a cataclysm. The arrival of the messenger, interrupting Ferdinand's plan, occurs by chance, though the very implausibility of Ferdinand's intervention fantasy, the puffed up bravado with which he imagines it (so out of keeping with the cowardice he professes just before) makes his readers wonder just how likely this meeting of minds would have been.

His description exaggerates the picaro's outlandish tendency to have his fate turned by serendipity: "I was about to take that decisive step when, at that very moment, who should arrive on the double but a dismounted cavalryman" (11). The trembling, mumbling, filthy and terrified messenger comes to tell the colonel that "Sergeant Barousse has been killed," news the colonel receives coldly (12). A brief exchange – where the colonel meets each of the messenger's details about the death with an impatient "So what?" – is itself halted abruptly, subsumed by a blast Ferdinand can only perceive as "flame and noise. The kind of noise you wouldn't have thought possible. Our eyes, ears, nose, and mouth were so full of that noise I thought it was all over and I'd turned into noise and flame myself" (12).

Of course, for everyone in this scene but Ferdinand, it is "all over." The colonel is dead, and so is the cavalryman. He narrates what he sees, once the smoke clears, with a gruesome and unsettling specificity:

> The blast had carried him up the embankment and laid him down on his side, right in the arms of the dismounted cavalryman, the courier, who was finished too. They were embracing each other for the moment and for all eternity, but the cavalryman's head was gone, all he had was an opening at the top of the neck, with blood in it bubbling and glugging like jam in a kettle. The colonel's belly was wide open, and he was making a nasty face about it. It must have hurt when it happened. Tough shit for him! If he'd beat it when the shooting started, it wouldn't have happened. (12)

The stock comic rhythms of this scene's unfolding, from Ferdinand's peace plan to the carnage on the hill, work cumulatively to produce the "strange state" Céline so often imposes on his readers. Ferdinand's self-mockery, the dramatic interruption, the miscommunication of leader and underling – all underscore the existential absurdity and randomness of the war itself. Ferdinand's cavalier tone barely changes as he goes from deriding the dishevelment and inarticulateness of the messenger to describing his mutilated corpse. The "tangled" juxtaposition of low comedy with cataclysmic horror, the abrupt "cuts" from one to the other, mirrors the causal illogic of the events themselves.

Céline's exploitation of the tone and structure of the picaresque thus lends impact to his representation of war's arbitrary horror. But what makes the randomness and jarring juxtapositions stranger and more unsettling is the fact that narrative causality – which looks like randomness – is replaced by a *rhetorical* causality, with a logic and violence of its own. Kristeva argues that Céline "embodies" abjection in the very materiality of his language. She locates Céline's discursive power in his ability to produce "[a]n inhumanity that resides in his very words." His discourse, she suggests, "is hence most radical, affecting mankind's ultimate guarantee – language" (135). Yet what does this mean for Kristeva's own argument, not as an abstract truth about "mankind," but as a specific literary critical observation? If her assertion seems somewhat cryptic in its own context, if it seems to identify little more than the assaultive vividness of his prose (which he "shows" rather than "tells"), a look at the strange rhetorical logic of the episodes we have been examining proves illuminating. In the subtle linguistic negotiations of Ferdinand's narration, we can see just how this "inhumanity" manifests itself, "in his very words." Crucially, we must understand that such assertions speak to more than Céline's unflinchingly graphic, meticulously revolting, representations of violence, war, death. Céline's representation is abject because it "embodies" violence on the level of the letter. His rhetoric of violence is "radical" precisely because he superimposes upon it the violence of rhetoric.[16]

Ferdinand's unsparing description of the two corpses, arm in arm, one beheaded, takes on an altogether stranger aspect when we see that it is not only a graphic representation of death, but also a reworking of the wishful truism with which the scene begins: "Le tout c'est qu'on s'explique dans la vie. A deux on y arrive mieux que tout seul" ("The essential thing is to talk things over. Two heads are better than one" – Manheim). In its initial context, the statement is a benign expression of faith in man's rational capacity to think, discuss, cooperate, and agree – expressing faith that life is better explained and endured "à deux," in fellowship with others, than "tout seul," alone. After the blast, that consoling utterance metamorphoses into a graphic literalism that is, significantly, no less true. The unlikely bodily arrangement of the corpses relies on a comic reversal: the hierarchically distant figures mis-communicating moments earlier are now intimately locked in an eternal embrace. But Ferdinand's rhetorical maneuvering throughout the scene represents violence through a certain violence of rhetoric itself: "Ils s'embrassaient tous les deux pour le moment et pour toujours, mais le cavalier n'avait plus sa tête" ("They were embracing each other for the moment and for all eternity, but the cavalryman's head was gone" – Manheim). He describes their joined corpses in tones that initially mimic humanistic piety, of fellowship ("tous les deux") in death as in life, of unity between this world and the next ("pour le moment et pour toujours"). But mid-sentence, he abruptly halts this lyricism with the information of the cavalryman's missing head. Ferdinand further refuses any lofty attachments we might associate with the image of a man decapitated in war – Virgil's symbolically charged, heroic image of Priam headless on the shore after the sack of Troy, by contrast – by means of a decidedly un-epic simile. In the case of Virgil's epic, the abrupt announcement of Priam's corpse carries with it the apocalyptic weight of history, of greatness reduced to nothing, of a nation's end:

> That was the end
> Of Priam's age, the doom that took him off,
> With Troy in flames before his eyes, his towers
> Headlong fallen – he that in other days
> Had ruled in pride so many lands and people,
> The power of Asia.
>
> On the distant shore
> The vast trunk headless lies without a name.[17]

Céline's sentence, in jarring contrast, offers a visceral description of the headless body, monstrously likened to an otherwise soothing domestic image of hearth and home: "comme de la confiture dans la marmite."

Invoking the fortuitously worded English cliché "Two heads are better than one," Manheim's canny translation of the French highlights the brutal logic of this scene's unfolding. His rendering, which invites readers to connect these "two heads" to the joined bodies with one missing "head" after the explosion, explicitly turns the episode into an elaborately sick joke, a linguistic trick. Just as the blast cancels the possibility of Ferdinand and the colonel putting their "heads" together and making sense of their senseless situation, so does it wrest sense from the expression representing rational communication itself: "two heads are better than one." In a way Céline would likely endorse, Manheim "unhinges" that sentence with a cognitive violence that parallels the physical violence of the deadly blast. Two heads are indeed better than one, but the explosion imposes a revision of this assertion, which shifts from philosophical abstraction to a barren literalism – a "truth" one feels in the "gut." That is how the American writer Tim O'Brien reconciles the unrepresentability of war's horror with the effort to tell about it. As O'Brien's narrator puts it in "How to Tell a True War Story," "It comes down to gut instinct. A true war story, if truly told, makes the stomach believe."[18]

As the tonal shifts demonstrate, Ferdinand's narration throughout this scene discomfits the reader simply because it refuses a stable, much less a humane, point of view. Here and throughout Céline's work, the speaker's position is ambiguous and ambivalent. Ferdinand's connection to the blast, which assaults his every sense and "stayed in [his] head," is at once intimate and detached, sympathetic and weirdly affectless, almost cruel. It affects them all – "*Our* eyes, ears, nose, and mouth were so full of that noise I thought it was all over" – but Ferdinand has the distinction of surviving it. The blast levels all the colonel's imperious bluster and the messenger's obsequious fluster in an instant, and Ferdinand only narrowly, arbitrarily escapes it himself. Observing the consequence of the blast, he implicitly proffers a "lesson" in the poignant, ironic image of the "human condition" metaphorically suggested by the death embrace; namely, that we are all equal in and therefore united by death. Ferdinand momentarily allows this interpretation, which would include himself, by implying a certain gut-level sympathy for the colonel's gaping "belly" wound ("It must have hurt when it happened"), then abruptly, cynically undercuts it ("Tough shit for him!"). In the next line, the men lose their pronominal status altogether: "All that tangled meat was bleeding profusely" (13). Shells still bursting around him, now under no-one's command, Ferdinand quickly takes off, "hum[ming] a tune" and talking to himself (14). As the rest of the novel will prove, no horror has the power to reduce him to silence.

Fairly conventional from a syntactic standpoint, the image of the men's corpses nevertheless offers a characteristic glimpse of the strange "Célinian universe" Kristeva seeks to map. Unsentimentally non-metaphorical, the phrase "tangled meat" reports the grisly transition, in death, from human subject to something horrifyingly other in tones that perfectly illustrate Kristeva's definition of abjection in the earlier chapters of *Powers of Horror*. This scene acts out chapter 1's disturbing example of the abjection of confronting a corpse, which does not "represent" death to the one who confronts it, but rather "*show*[*s*] *me* what I permanently thrust aside in order to live" (*Powers of Horror*, p. 3; emphasis Kristeva's). Ferdinand's discursive cutting loose, from sympathy to detachment, marks a common pattern throughout the novel, both in his actions and in his narrative style. It is easily readable as the very reaction to the abject that Kristeva describes. In response to this confrontation with horror up close, Ferdinand separates himself both emotionally and physically.

Rhetorically, this negotiation is just as vigorous, but more subtle: "tangled meat" becomes the logical connection to the next episode he describes, in which he goes to collect food for the regiment at a military distribution point set up behind a church. With his colonel gone, Ferdinand finds himself wandering alone. He finally meets up again with a regiment, and this time becomes a messenger himself, bringing news of the colonel's death. The response he gets mirrors the indifference the colonel himself demonstrated on learning of Sergeant Bourousse's death. "Plenty more colonels where he came from," is the "snappy comeback" of the corporal in charge (14). Curiously, both death announcements are met with inquiries about food.[19] Because, as the messenger tells us, Sergeant Barousse had died on his way to the "bread wagon," the colonel's own dying words are "[W]hat about the bread?" (12). In this instance, Corporal Pistil decides that Ferdinand should make himself useful until they find him a new leader: "you can be picking up meat with Empouille and Kerdoncuff here, take two sacks each" (15). Collecting his "two sacks" of meat, Ferdinand describes an egregiously grisly scene of blood and "pounds and pounds of guts," of greedy bad behavior and petty disputes among a "bunch of halfwits" (15, 32). At this point he reacts, either to the makeshift slaughter or to the bad behavior or both, "overcome by an enormous urge to vomit, which I did so hard that I passed out" (15).

Linking the two scenes as he does, around the metonymic connection of two scenes of tangled meat, Ferdinand also separates himself from the horror of both. In the first instance, his words dehumanize the men who die in front of him; his sentiments deny any connection but a brute bodily one. "It could as easily have been me as them" quickly shifts to "better them than me." As a narrator, he similarly offers little sympathy to his readers or their conventional expectations. In this instance, the link to the assaultively disgusting next scene not only further levels and reduces man – "tangled meat" is tangled "meat" – it also disorients any reader looking for reflection or insight offered in repose. Ferdinand offers little more narrative consolation – a summing up, an assignment of meaning or message or lesson to the cumulative set of experience – than does a messenger without a head. At its conclusion, he has gotten nowhere, and the scene ends where it began. Soldiers carry him, unconscious, back to his adoptive regiment: "I woke up to one of the corporal's harangues. The war wasn't over" (15).

Strange fruit: the rhetoric of abjection in Tim O'Brien's "How to Tell a True War Story"

> The real cannot be uttered as such.
>
> (Julia Kristeva, *Tales of Love,* p. 369)

Kristeva does not examine Céline's rhetorical negotiation on the diegetic level; that is, as a narrative dynamic by which "this and then this and then this" unfolds according to a brutal and unsparing logic. Her syntactic analysis, as we have seen, remains at the level of the sentence. Yet I would argue that on both levels Céline's writings work to inscribe abjection in just the way Kristeva outlines throughout *Powers of Horror*. There is something unspeakable, unassimilable about the episodic unfolding of Ferdinand's experiences, both within the war and without. Vomiting, Ferdinand himself "expresses" as much in his ultimate response to the grotesque food fair, and to its metonymical connection to the traumatic horror that precedes it.

On the readerly level as well, there is something profoundly, instinctively "undigestible" in what Ferdinand narrates. Analytically, I find it difficult to find the paradigm that properly captures what is so unsettling about this collection of episodes. As a critical reader, I intuitively sense that its implications are rich to the point of unfathomability, like the "navel" of the dream Freud tells us his analysis cannot conquer, the dream's point of contact with the "unknown."[20] It recalls Lacan's reworking of Freud's idea, what he calls the "tuché" or the dream's momentary unveiling of a traumatic "real" – that which is "*unassimilable* in it."[21] Freud's observation in *Beyond the Pleasure Principle* of the "fort/da" game, his grandson's rudimentary "story" about coping with the transition between his mother's being here then not here, poignantly raised to the level of life-and-death parable when his mother actually dies, offers suggestive resonance with Ferdinand's narrative negotiations. The fact that Freud offers the "fort/da" game as a logical paradigm for explaining a psychic phenomenon he newly observes among World War I survivors – "traumatic neurosis" – makes this psychoanalytic model relevant in overdetermined ways.[22] And Kristeva's theory of abjection, of course, so aptly applies that it seems, at this point in our discussion, redundant to say why.

At the same time, aiming to draw a conclusion about the meaning of Céline's violence of rhetoric, I come up short. Perhaps it is not accidental, for all of the reasons we have explored, that what this rhetorical logic most compellingly calls to mind is another example: a moment in Tim O'Brien's metanarrative short story about the Vietnam War and, more significantly, about the impossibility of narrating it "truly." This episode in "How to Tell a True War Story" specifically concerns the trauma of witnessing a deadly explosion during war, thus an obvious thematic resemblance exists. But more suggestively, an identical rhetorical logic, brutal and unnameable, comic and horrific at once, joins the two. O'Brien's story, itself an explicit meditation on narrative and narratability, articulates the skepticism toward humanistic "truth" Céline largely implies. "True war stories do not generalize. They do not indulge in abstraction or analysis," the narrator generalizes. "For example: War is hell. As a moral declaration the old truism seems perfectly true, and yet because it abstracts, because it generalizes, I can't believe it with my stomach. Nothing turns inside" (78).

O'Brien's narrator grapples with this problem, rehearsing, retelling, and attempting to reflect on a series of stories that purport to lend "meaning" to the experience of war. More than one of these stories concern the death of the narrator's comrade Curt Lemon, including an extremely chilling one that serve as an illustration of the insight about the impossibility of insight O'Brien's narrator offers above. With metanarrative circularity – where the point involves the ineluctability of articulating the point, which nevertheless urgently demands articulating – the narrator observes:

> Often in a true war story there is not even a point, or else the point doesn't hit you until twenty years later, in your sleep, and you wake up and shake your wife and start telling the story to her, except when you get to the end

> you've forgotten the point again. And then for a long time you lie there watching the story happen in your head. You listen to your wife's breathing. The war's over. You close your eyes. You smile and think, Christ, what's the point? (82)

The particular story that falls into that category (though the whole of O'Brien's piece does as well) comes back to the moment of Lemon's death with a visceral specificity that the earlier accounts of that same event lack. "This one wakes me up," the narrator begins, adumbrating a suggestive connection to the war neuroses Freud analyzes, the compulsion to repeat in dreams and flashbacks the experiences traumatized subjects seem least able to assimilate sensibly (82). This time, superadded to the representation of violence each of the story's episodes recounts is the remembrance of a specific rhetorical violence analogous to Céline's own:

> In the mountains that day, I watched Lemon turn sideways. He laughed and said something to Rat Kiley. Then he took a peculiar half-step, moving from shade into bright sunlight, and the booby-trapped 105 round blew him into a tree. The parts were just hanging there, so Norman Bowker and I were ordered to shinny up and peel him off. I remember the white bone of an arm. I remember pieces of skin and something wet and yellow that must've been the intestines. The gore was horrible, and stays with me, but what wakes me up twenty years later is Norman Bowker singing "Lemon Tree" as we threw down the parts. ("How to Tell a True War Story," pp. 82–3)[23]

As a joke, Bowker's gesture acts out the paradigmatic response, "what I permanently thrust aside in order to live," that Kristeva outlines in her definition of abjection (3). It also exerts the stylistic force Céline himself identifies as his goal: to "take sentences[...]and have them fly off their handle," literally to "unhinge" them. The unassimilable power of the "Lemon Tree" joke, a monstrously clever play on words, itself depends upon "unhinging" statements from their referential, representative meaning and doing something else instead.

Through the lens of that definition, O'Brien's example perhaps illuminates the strange effects of Céline's narrative tangles and cuts, and gives us a way to map the peculiar logic by which episodes are linked. Rhetorically speaking, the joke operates by means of *metalepsis*, which the classical rhetorician Quintilian describes as the "change from one trope to another," specifically, the use of metonymy to replace a word already used figuratively. In other words, metalepsis involves the "replacement of one image with another more remote image" generated by the logic of "a chain of auditory associations."[24] The association implied by metalepsis, when used for comic effect, often depends upon an especially far-fetched or obscure causal logic, as Bowker's very black "comedy" does here.[25]

We might also understand the joke, both tropologically and psychoanalytically, as an "apotropaic act" (to use Freud's words), a talismanic response that wards off death by literally "turning away" from it. Achilles wielding his shield against the deadly gaze of the Medusa provides the classical narrative example of apotropaia that Freud considers. He regards it as a psychic response that functions rhetorically, a reaction to the threat of castration that says, in effect, "I am not afraid of you. I defy you."[26] In this sense, Bowker's gesture performs a rhetorical equivalent, but a logically complicated one: the "Lemon Tree" trope more precisely acts as a "turning against" than a "turning away." For the joke does not obscure the literal, factual truth of what confronts them. It is comic without being euphemistic, bluntly looking straight at death, crudely addressing its sheer materiality.

But all of that terminological pinning down does not explain away what so precise a source as the *Princeton Encyclopedia of Poetry and Poetics* refers to as the "spooky sense" metalepsis produces in its readers, its haunting otherness.[27] In this regard, the psychoanalytic lens provides helpful support. Like Kristeva's privileged witnesses to the abject, Bowker *articulates* the horror he faces by means of a rhetorical trick, a linguistic felicity. The play on words, acted out in the song Bowker sings to the narrator but not the reader, temporarily mitigates its horror, suspending the humane reactions of sympathy or grief. In Kristeva's *Black Sun* (in a chapter entitled "The Life and Death of Speech"), she speculates that such discourse, uttered in the midst of a psychic crisis that "overwhelms us [and] paralyzes us [is] also a shield – sometimes the last one – against madness" (42). Kristeva specifically theorizes depressive discourse here, but her formulation allows for some relevant explanation of the logic of the joke. Working from her terminology, "Lemon Tree" presents an "ambiguous source of pleasure," albeit a "perverse" one, that "evicts death." It is a linguistic "act of severance" that removes its speaker from the source of the affective pain as it removes him from its meaning. The signifying shift of "Lemon" offers, if inadequately, "a shield against death" (48–9).

But whatever this joke does to diffuse the horror of the situation on which it is an immediate commentary, for O'Brien's narrator, it ultimately compounds it. O'Brien implies that the force of the joke, and the traumatic element within it that keeps the narrator up at night, is that it adds to the rhetoric of violence (the "war story" as such) the powerful violence of rhetoric itself. In fact, the linguistic violence seems to traumatize the narrator, to remain unassimilable, in a way even the physical violence of the dismembering blast, or the emotional violence of watching a friend die, does not. While the "gore was horrible, and stays with me," the joke itself, somehow, was more so: "but what wakes me up twenty years later is Norman Bowker singing 'Lemon Tree' as we threw down the parts." The narrator is careful to distinguish by degree between these two types of violence. The difference between what "stays with me" and "what wakes me up" seems to be, for him, the difference between memory and trauma.

By means of a logic like Ferdinand's description of World War I, Bowker's joke depends on a sheerly linguistic association between a song and a scene of carnage whose only connection is a starkly literal one, made possible only by the accident of a proper name. Calling a tree strewn with the mutilated remains of a man named Lemon a "Lemon Tree" brutally reorganizes the normal structure by which a signifier refers to a signified; and it supplies a new sign in its place. In an essay published the year before *Powers of Horror* first appeared, Kristeva speculates that there are certain "strategies of discourse" that manage to brush up against the unsayable, able to articulate something she calls the "true-real" (*le vréel*). These "strategies" negotiate the speaking subject's "abrupt passages" between the symbolic order and the impossible realm of the "real" ("The True-Real," p. 218). In the midst of such passages, "we therefore find ourselves in a border zone where the real, in order to burst on the scene as truth, leaves a hole in the subject's discourse" (228).

Both Ferdinand's narration and this moment of linguistic horror in O'Brien seem to operate in such a "border zone." Kristeva here provides a possible way to account for the specific violence of the rhetorical "strategies" each presents. In O'Brien's case, Bowker's song seems to "burst on the scene as truth" – even "truth" as O'Brien himself fruitlessly aims to define it – because it demonstrates what Kristeva calls "the fragility of the proper name when it comes to fixing a signified identity" (235). Bowker's joke seizes on that fragility by taking the "Lemon" that serves as the proper name, the signifier, of a human identity (their friend, Curt Lemon) and reassigning it as the suddenly gruesomely appropriate signifier of something else altogether (a "lemon tree").

In this instance, as in Céline's repeated deployments, rhetorical violence seems especially unassimilable or traumatic when it mirrors the physical violence, the death, it represents. As she does throughout *Powers of Horror*, in "The True-Real" Kristeva points out the powerful correspondence between the fragility of signification and the exquisite mortal fragility of its users, which is all of us: "Thus the truth of the signifier, namely its separability, otherness, death, can be seen to be exerted on the flesh itself – as on words" (236). Bowker's joke acts out that "truth" of the signifier in a way that points directly at the violence that the blast has just "exerted on the flesh" of Curt Lemon – and furthermore, at the trauma that witnessing Lemon's ineffable passage, his "peculiar half-step" from living identity to mutilated remains, has exerted on the narrator. Both Céline's and O'Brien's war narratives, in the examples I explore, suggest a keenly powerful analogy between the arbitrary nature of the signifier and that of death itself, of war's random, utterly explosive indifference.

Despite the felicity of these mutually resonating examples, Céline and O'Brien are in many ways, of course, singing different tunes. As a meditative reflection on the very nature of the "war story" – its conventionally episodic unfolding, necessarily punctuated by brutal horror, often saturated with what Kristeva calls "a meaninglessness [...] about which there is nothing insignificant" – O'Brien's story allows for a certain narrative closure, even if the conclusions drawn are contingent and circular; because O'Brien casts his narrator also in the quasi-critical position of the analyst, or the reader, wondering and worrying about the issues of narratability and rhetorical violence as he presents them. In Céline, to cite the Dante analogy Kristeva herself invokes, the reader undertakes a journey without a guide – or rather with a guide who shows as little empathy for his reader as he does for his fellow sufferers within the story of the novel.

In this sense, the examples I select from Céline and O'Brien operate on different registers. O'Brien's rhetorical violence occurs metanarratively, as an example the narrator mulls over, tries to talk about and theorize. Whether or not he ultimately admits defeat, he at least implies that the problem of linguistic, narrative, and psychic assimilability is a predicament we all share; for his more self-conscious narrator, also a narratee, suggests an elegant parallel between the characters' experience of Curt Lemon's death and the impact the story has on the reader as well. Ferdinand never allows such mutuality; even narratively speaking, he denies any fellowship between narrator and reader. As

Kristeva highlights dramatically at the end of *Powers of Horror*, Ferdinand's *Journey* and Céline's are emphatically without end. To the end, they disallow summing up.

O'Brien's narrator hears the Peter, Paul, and Mary song Bowker sings at the traumatic event of Lemon's death, whereas we as readers do not. Among its many gruesome incongruities with the scene at hand, as I have outlined, it is a love song, or rather a song of disappointed love, a bittersweet parable warning of the dangers of being seduced by something seemingly sweet that is truly bitter. The lover, of course, not heeding the wise advice, learns for himself the hard way: "One day she left without a word, she took away the sun. / And in the dark she left behind, I knew what she had done."[28] At the very end of "How to Tell a True War Story," O'Brien's narrator comes back once more to the haunting moment of Lemon's death, not to the song, but to his own ineffable impression of Lemon's passage from life to death. Like the song that still "wakes him up" at night, the vivid impression he has described to us in variously elaborated form throughout the story he recounts again:

> Twenty years later, I can still see the sunlight on Lemon's face. I can see him turning, looking back at Rat Kiley, then he laughed and took that curious half step from shade into sunlight, his face suddenly brown and shining, and when his foot touched down, in that instant, he must've thought it was the sunlight that was killing him. It was not the sunlight. It was a rigged 105 round. But if I could ever get the story right, how the sun seemed to gather around him and pick him up and lift him high into a tree, if I could somehow re-create the fatal whiteness of that light, the quick glare, the obvious cause and effect, then you would believe the last thing Curt Lemon believed, which for him must've been the final truth. (84)

Conveying Lemon's own "final truth," of course, is impossible, just as the narrator's own efforts to convey truth seem to fall short and demand, like the ancient mariner's curse, repeated retelling. Lemon's death, punctuated by sunlight, seems for the narrator to have taken away the sun, leaving the darkness of denied insight.

But the end of the story does make a crucial turn that is both subtle and telling, recuperating the initial rhetorical violence that so monstrously, so inappropriately, links the song to the moment of Lemon's death. It is the gesture implied by this recuperation that I believe distinguishes O'Brien from Céline decisively. The narrator returns obsessively to the play of light and dark that, for him, meaningfully dictate the "obvious cause and effect" of Lemon's passage from life to death.

He also focuses on Rat Kiley, the friend Lemon was laughing with at the time, the grief-stricken comrade whose own effort to tell Lemon's story, in a letter to Lemon's sister, was met with heart-breaking silence. The memory of that strange sunlight, which leads to the memory of "Rat Kiley's face, his grief," moves the narrator to conclude, in this story he cannot stop telling, that after all: "It *wasn't* a war story. It was a *love* story" (85; emphasis O'Briens'). And if it was, with all its "gore" and violence, not a war story but a love story, the jarring invocation of that bittersweet love song can be allowed a further rhetorical valence that perhaps mitigates its monstrousness.

Céline's war stories, by contrast to the ones O'Brien's narrator discusses, are about war and not something else. They are devoid of love (read most broadly as an empathy with his fellow man, an ability to connect with others in joy or sorrow), unless it is a love already so disappointed that its narrator gives no glimmer of it. Repeatedly, Céline's Ferdinand refuses to sum up, even to sum up as O'Brien does by telling us there is no way of summing up. As he does when witnessing the explosion of the men who die arm in arm, Ferdinand's narrator detaches, consistently and to the end, as if to say "better them than me – time to move on." Whereas O'Brien's narrator's effort to imagine Lemon's experience at the moment of his death conjectures a flash of "final truth," even if only a private one ("for him"), Ferdinand imagines the physical pain ("it must have hurt when it happened"), the empathetic reflection on which he drops like a hot potato ("Tough shit for him"). Ferdinand leaves the scene "humming a tune" to himself. O'Brien's narrator leaves the scene with a searing and heart-breaking collection of impressions (his own, but also those of Lemon himself and of those who loved him) he can never assimilate and which he will find himself forever bound to tell.

Once O'Brien's narrator comes to the (still narratively open) conclusion that he has been telling a love story, not a war story, "How to Tell a True War Story" gains a new level of pathos. Despite its remaining ineffability, this conclusion draws its readers into a collective human and narrative condition, albeit a condition most often characterized by pain, disappointment, and missed communication: "And in the end, of course, a true war story, of course, is never about war. It's about sunlight. [...] It's about love and memory. It's about sorrow. It's about sisters who never write back and people who never listen" (85).

If people indeed "never listen," narrating a story becomes a daring speech act, a shot in the dark. Willing to fail, it is an act of faith in narrative itself, its potential for correction, mourning, the possibility of getting at some truth. In this sense, the narrator's war story is possibly true but definitely necessary. It keeps needing to be told: "You can tell a true war story if you just keep on telling it" (85). Although the ironic frame of the story's end has the narrator encountering an admiring but misguided reader at a public reading (she doesn't seem to "get it"), the imperative remains: keep telling. "All you can do is tell it one more time, patiently, adding and subtracting, making up a few things to get at the real truth" (85). Reading O'Brien's unsparing, brutal war story, it may be the "gore" that stays with you, but it is that patience, that humble but also empathetic commitment to keep telling, that keeps you reading.

Ad nauseam

> Writing is no more valuable, says Plato, as a remedy than as a poison. [...] There is no such thing as a harmless remedy. The *pharmakon* can never be simply beneficial.
>
> (Jacques Derrida, "Plato's Pharmacy")

"And yet, in these times of dreary crisis, what is the point of emphasizing the horror of being?" Kristeva asks in the concluding chapter of *Powers of Horror* (208). The question is rhetorical because, for Kristeva, there is a profound point in "emphasizing the horror," and she is willing to follow Céline through all of his writing to find it. Kristeva clearly embraces in Céline the sort of open-endedness we consider in O'Brien's story above, laying emphasis on what his apocalyptic vision cannot illuminate. The anti-prophetic prophet of abjection takes his readers on a journey without end. He is a truth-teller without answers or empathy for those caught in the human condition he so darkly and relentlessly explores. In large part because of his poisonous cruelty – the brutally visceral descriptions of death and suffering, the relentless misanthropy – Kristeva celebrates the force of Céline's language as seductive, fascinating, and ultimately important, a triumph of style.

For Kristeva, writing is a *pharmakon* in the sense Plato proposes in the *Phaedrus:* both a poison and a cure. The language of Céline's pharmacy holds this ambivalent power. She avows to the end a critical commitment to "approach abjection" in its darkest, most difficult places, and seems willing to take the poison in order better to understand the workings of the cure. Kristeva concludes *Powers of Horror* with a searingly memorable, beautiful recourse to Céline's discourse: it represents for her not only a distinguished moment in the literary history of the avant-garde, but an enduring exemplar of the "revolutionary" power of literature itself. Quite literally, she gives him the last word. Opposed to the normative discursive forces that work, tirelessly, to repress abjection (the institutions of law, religion, cultural taboo, political ideologies), "everything else[...]is only literature: the sublime point at which the abject collapses in a burst of beauty that overwhelms us – and 'that cancels our existence' (Céline)" (210).

Other readers might be forgiven for not following Kristeva quite as far along the path of Céline's dark night. Céline's literary distinction, what he refuses to offer and the matter in which he does so, brings with it certain consequences Kristeva perhaps does not account for fully. In Céline's case in particular, the cumulative effect of his black humor "works." It is genuinely funny, in ways I think Kristeva also overlooks, and ultimately more than I can, or want, to digest. But it works with a brutality that seems at once "true" in some unflinching sense, a marvelously radical literary achievement, and also ultimately unbearable. Just as Kristeva encourages us again and again to see as deliberate writerly strategies what might, in Céline, seem like artistic weakness or ideological bad faith, I wonder if my impatience is not significant. That is, I wonder if Céline doesn't *dare* his readers, force them ultimately, to give up or turn away, and whether his radical inhospitability isn't itself – in Kristeva's very understanding of radicality – part of his point. Perhaps Céline's unwavering articulation of human horror, in the entirety of his *oeuvre*, proves too bitter: As the song says, like the fruit of the lemon tree, seductive but ultimately undigestible.

In the last of Ferdinand's picaresque stations in life, in *Journey to the End of the Night*, he finds himself as an administrator at an insane asylum, a narrative expansion of the cliché, since those in charge, for various reasons, prove little saner than the inmates. Ferdinand befriends colleague Baryton, despite regarding him as a deluded fool. As narrator, he has fun at Baryton's expense, describing the details of his enthusiastic insistence that Ferdinand tutor him (in English, incidentally), and mocking the absurdity of Baryton eagerly engaging Ferdinand at dinners, where he would earnestly "distill philosophical conclusions from our disjointed remarks" (358). Longtime friend Robinson is similarly barking up the wrong tree when, on his deathbed (that conventional novelistic site of revelation), Ferdinand once again comes up short. With Robinson about to die, he fails in precisely this way, and unflinchingly attributes his failure to a lack of both empathy and larger-than-life insight:

> I stayed with Léon to commiserate. I had never felt so embarrassed. I couldn't manage it. [...] He must have been looking for another Ferdinand, somebody much bigger than me, to help him die more easily. He was straining to figure out if there'd been any progress in the world ... Poor fellow ... Drawing up an inventory in his mind ... Wondering if people hadn't changed just a little for the better during his lifetime, if maybe he had been unfair to them without meaning to ... But there was only me, just me, me all alone, beside him, the genuine Ferdinand, who was short of everything that would make a man bigger than his own bare life, short of love for other people's lives. Of that I had none, or so little there was no use showing it. I wasn't as big as death. I was a lot smaller. (427–8)

Ferdinand himself, not that we should ever simply take him at his word, ironically undercuts Kristeva's argument that Céline's "speaking subject" has more to offer than his small self, more to say about anyone beyond himself. Of course, we have learned throughout that he is not to be trusted, and more importantly that we must distinguish between Ferdinand's utterances and Céline's "scription." Nevertheless, the narrator's derision at the self-serious fool who "distill[s] philosophical conclusions" from his "disjointed remarks" should at least signal caution to critics eager to sum up Céline's literary message.

Invoking readerly circumspection in this way, I do not mean to take away from the genuine force of Kristeva's analysis. Rather, I bring us back to the advice with which I began my discussion. I have argued from the start that, reading Kristeva on Céline, we must also read Céline. Not incidental to the latter experience, for this reader (and, in my anecdotal survey, for others), is the profoundly exasperating point, incremental and dependent on varying degrees of readerly patience, at which Céline stops engaging his reader, when he stops being funny. Describing the unremitting "horror of being," that might be as you would expect. But more significantly, he stops being interesting. The unbearability comes to seem less a writerly strategy, performatively traversing the unbearable edges of being and consciousness, and more a matter of exasperating unreadability. There are a number of points, again variously decisive, at which reading Céline can make you genuinely, physically sick. Such a readerly hazard perhaps strengthens Kristeva's argument about the "embodiment" of Célinian abjection, about his ability to inflict abjection on his readers; but it is not, for that felicitous parallel, any more pleasant to experience. If my censored account of the nauseating scene in the meat market doesn't make you feel just like Ferdinand does, for example, try reading it for yourself in its full gory glory.

More broadly speaking, such impediments to holding up Céline's entire writerly project as somehow heroic become explicitly matters of history and politics. In a crucial way, deliberately but not unproblematically sidestepped by my discussion (though not Kristeva's), Céline stops being funny when his anarchist picaresques come to be upstaged by vituperative political rantings – fascist and anti-Semitic – so extreme they eventually lead the writer to exile and prosecution. On the level of the "style" Kristeva heralds throughout *Powers of Horror*, which she gives in her last chapter the power of stemming dominant ideology and repressive symbolic discourse themselves, a reader could be forgiven for tiring of Céline's techniques. What Kristeva considers an incremental effort, in his later works, to render more stylistically explosive the experimental techniques he presents in early works can also be read as an increasingly overplayed tune. In my own case, I had had quite enough by the time I got to Céline's late efforts, in "Féerie pour une autre fois" and the exasperating (if intermittently hilarious) *Conversations with Professor Y*. The routine gets terribly old. The dashes and ellipses, the shocking declarations, the shit and the piss and the seemingly boundless stores of misanthropy eventually level out into tedium that, in my own assessment, ultimately "cancels" out Céline's initially radical power.

More than an abstract exercise in paradox or an invocation of the kinds of judgments literary critics now consider outmoded, these unresolvable questions about Céline's ultimate "message" and ultimate "value" play themselves out significantly in the course of Céline's literary and quasi-political career. By the end of his career and his life, he had become at once enormously well known and notorious, celebrated and widely published as a writer and imprisoned and discredited as an anti-Semitic *persona non grata*.

The recent special issue of *South Atlantic Quarterly* provides a larger critical canvas on which to consider Céline the artist, the political provocateur, and the savvy self-promoter. Several of its participants note that Céline zealously promoted himself and exploited his provocative reputation to the end of his life. Whereas Kristeva emphasizes his sustained radicality and beautifully declares her willingness to follow him in his project of unveiling and giving voice to the horrors of being, a number of critics offer a more sober assessment.

Bob Perelman juxtaposes to Kristeva's vision of a tireless linguistic revolutionary a personality with a keenly honed literary style to pitch:

> when you get the late Céline you have something almost like a late-night talk show guest, somebody who's got a schtick and is trying to sell books. There's that speech in *Professor Y* about the beauty of French that is funny because it's a marketing strategy by a self-destroying clown, a clown who's bitter and sharp, no denying. But it's marketing. He's trying to keep himself *amusing* and provocative. (*South Atlantic Quarterly*, p. 470)[29]

Kristeva's high-toned conclusion obscures the low-brow dimension to Céline, the shameless clown, the comic – much less the clown driven by the banal desires of market success.

And for that very reason, for the exhilarating promise and power Kristeva persists in finding in Céline, I would argue *Powers of Horror*'s critical vision *itself* has more to offer than the writer she examines so exhaustively. Like Ferdinand, Kristeva still has more to say, even at the end of the night. But unlike Ferdinand, unlike Céline himself, in her vision of the human experience there are multiple hues. Perhaps it is significant that, after Kristeva's monumental expedition through the "horror of being," she turns her critical eye to the history and vicissitudes of love.

4 Joyce's "Quashed Quotatoes"

My name is Legion: for we are many.

(Roland Barthes, "From Work to Text"[1])

"What does it matter who is speaking," someone said, "what does it matter who is speaking."

(Michel Foucault, "What is an Author?"[2])

James Joyce/Julia Kristeva

Turning from Kristeva's reading of Louis-Ferdinand Céline to her reading of James Joyce requires several adjustments, not all of them comfortable or easily approached, primarily because Joyce may be the most Kristevan writer Kristeva has never extensively written about. While her contribution to poststructural theories of intertextuality, readability, authorship, sexuality, and many others suggest potentially rich intersections with Joyce's writing (an affinity she has explicitly asserted for decades), we cannot look to her for an authoritative or well-developed reading of his texts. The association of his name with hers has not been established by the sort of extended readings she has produced on Céline, Mallarmé in *La Révolution du langage poétique*, or more recently Proust in *Time and Sense: Proust and the Experience of Literature* (1996). Despite persistent references in Kristeva's work and her featured presentation at the 1984 Frankfurt meeting of the International James Joyce Foundation – a conference including another featured reading by Derrida and panels on "Deconstructive Criticism of Joyce" and "James Joyce/Jacques Lacan" – the theoretical juxtaposition of James Joyce/Julia Kristeva is largely the story of a missed encounter, or that of an encounter yet to take place. By regularly invoking his name in her work, Kristeva gives the impression of a reading that exists without being offered, deferred, always not yet. It is as if, as she says of Céline, "[t]he enchantment will have to wait for some other time, always and forever" (*Powers of Horror*, p. 23).

Usually in the service of some broader claim, Kristeva's references to Joyce are fragmentary, oblique, parenthetical, short, casual. As analytical claims about specific textual moments in Joyce's works – critical signifiers illuminating literary signifieds – they will likely disappoint. But read another way, in a way Kristeva herself authorizes whether or not she intends, such statements suggest something else. Surveyed cumulatively, a pattern emerges that allows us to generalize about the nature of these references. Most commonly, they serve as place-holders or proper names for a larger historical moment or literary innovation Kristeva means to invoke. More subtly, they often suggest an engagement not directly with Joyce's texts themselves but with a complex critical conversation among fellow members of Tel Quel or the French intellectual establishment, which has long regarded Joyce with special indulgence. "Joyce," as a proper name signifying Joyce's texts, is repeatedly proffered as a signifier for intertextuality, for the revolutionary poetics of the avant-garde, for a writing without repression and without end, as an expression of verbal *jouissance* in the face of abjection that outpaces even Céline's. Joyce "himself" (not unproblematically) variously serves as an exemplar of the speaking subject-in-progress, the Barthesian unauthorized author, a theologically-oriented version of the Lacanian "Saint Homme," a secular and bodily transubstantialist, an artist who traverses the feminine with unique success, a prescient articulator of "the crucial issues of postmodernism: identification, representation."[3]

These lists are dense and perhaps confounding. And I mean them to be, for the moment, in order to make a point: in almost every case, Kristeva's references to Joyce are fully comprehensible only when we read them as complex signifiers within the evolution of her own theoretical project and that of her contemporaries. In a word, the word "Joyce" in Kristeva is *intertextual.*

As a literary critic of Joyce, therefore, Kristeva gives us very little. As a literary theorist engaged in a debate among critics who consider Joyce's work of paramount importance, Kristeva gives us almost too much. This situation produces a paradox for her readers: we can approach Kristeva's relationship to Joyce and find it either enormously underdeveloped or dauntingly overdetermined. In this chapter, we will navigate both possibilities – and the possibility that they are simultaneously possible. We will read Kristeva to see what she does say or could say about Joyce's texts, to see what a literary analysis extrapolated from her obliquities might look like. We will examine her reading of Joyce, augmenting it, responding to it, and critiquing it by looking to Joyce's texts themselves. Putting Kristeva's theoretical claims about Joyce's intertextuality in conversation with Joyce's own literary engagements with other texts, authorship, and the relationship between artists and their literary pasts allows us to see the largely unacknowledged way in which those same dynamics appear in her reading of Joyce. Just as she promotes, beyond the mere notion of source study, an understanding of intertextuality that regards the text as a complex interweaving of voices from a multiplicity of other discourses, so does she develop that theory – and especially, attach Joyce's name to it – by invoking a highly sedimented French tradition of Joycean criticism. Joyce's texts, in fact, offer an especially apt model of how Kristeva's own intertextuality operates. As much as Kristeva may help us read Joyce, even more so, it seems, Joyce helps us read Kristeva.

Intertextuality, intersubjectivity, and the death of the author

Kristeva's earliest references to Joyce occur in the context of her work on intertextuality, her interest in Bakhtin, and her argument about the significant linguistic break announced by key writers at the turn of the twentieth century. Kristeva grants Joyce elite membership in the group of iconoclasts who violently severed the relationship literary language traditionally had to representation. Joyce's texts – in their plurality, obscurity, sensuality, and outrageous experimentation – offer a new language, an "antilanguage" that paradoxically keeps language alive, an "unreadable" language that nevertheless engages the reader as never before.[4] Joyce's name appears in Kristeva's earliest efforts to champion a method of literary analysis skeptical about the presumed role of the "Author" and energized by an increasingly active and dynamic understanding of the "reader."

As Kristeva outlines in a 1985 interview with Margaret Waller, she first saw Mikhail Bakhtin's criticism as an exciting way to effect this change.

> I had the feeling that with his notions of dialogism and carnival we had reached an important point in moving beyond structuralism. [. . .] He was moving toward a dynamic understanding of the literary text that considered every utterance as the result of the intersection of a number of voices.[5]

While Bakhtin calls this textual condition "dialogism," Kristeva stresses that the term points to more than mere duality or literal exchange between speaking characters. Every "dialogue" is not only an interaction between a speaker (or "writing subject") and an addressee, but something more complex, where meaningful exchange and reference operate simultaneously on several registers. In one of her earliest essays on the topic, "Word, Dialogue, and Novel," Kristeva explains Bakhtin's efforts to categorize these various dialogic modes as follows: "The word's status is thus defined *horizontally* (the word in the text belongs to both writing subject and addressee) as well as *vertically* (the word in the text is oriented towards an anterior or synchronic literary corpus)" (66).[6]

Drawing on Bakhtin's formulation of the "two axes, which he calls dialogue and ambivalence," Kristeva points out the key implication of seeing the text in these terms. "[A]ny text is constructed as a mosaic of quotations," she memorably asserts, "any text is the absorption and transformation of another" (66). Practically speaking, this obligates the literary critic to hear the many voices of the text at once – to regard, say, the fictional dialogue between two characters as part of the "dialogue" among all the other voices at work in the novel, and between author and reader, and between the text and all other texts from which it draws, including the social and ideological context in which it was produced.

Kristeva has been widely credited, ironically enough, with "inventing" the theory of intertextuality.[7] She herself is usually more circumspect about laying originary claim to anything more than, perhaps, the term itself. Careful to outline "with as much intellectual honesty as possible, the source of the concept of intertextuality," Kristeva points out to Waller that the term does not appear in Bakhtin's work, but may be deduced from his work. If she does bring anything "unique" to his theory, she suggests, it stems not so much from her term as from her innovative juxtaposition of theoretical models (190). She adds a psychoanalytic component to Bakhtin's dynamic linguistics – or seen conversely, she brings his dynamic linguistics, an incipient theory of the speaking subject, to her psychoanalysis.

Kristeva first presented her reading of Bakhtin to Roland Barthes in 1966. And Bakhtin's "dynamic understanding of the literary text" indeed finds voice in the important work both critics would produce in the ensuing years. It clearly informs, for example, the distinctions Barthes draws between "monologic" and "plural" discourses in his 1971 essay "From Work to Text," as his elegant definition of intertextuality in that essay demonstrates: "The intertextual in which every text is held, it itself being the text-between of another text, is not to be confused with some origin of the text: to try to find the 'sources,' the 'influences' of a work, is to fall in with the myth of filiation; the citations which go to make up a text are anonymous, untraceable, and yet *already read*: they are quotations without inverted commas" (*Image–Music–Text*, p. 160; emphasis Barthes's). This statement reasserts the argument Barthes more notoriously presents in "The Death of the Author" (1968), where he also challenges a genealogical (and, as he sees it, implicitly theological) understanding of the literary tradition as a chain of "filiation" in which an author begets a work and in turn begets another author who does the same. Barthes argues that modern texts in particular make it difficult for critics to hold fast to the idea of the "Author-God," presiding univocally over the "message" of his work, for "[w]e know now that a text is not a line of words releasing a single 'theological' meaning [. . .] but a multi-dimensional space in which a variety of writings, none of them original, blend and clash. The text is a tissue of quotations drawn from the innumerable centres of culture" (*Image–Music–Text*, p. 146).

If we may posit any unifying principle in the face of such linguistic conditions, Barthes insists, it comes from the reader, who is "the space on which all the quotations that make up a writing are inscribed without any of them being lost; a text's unity lies not in its origin but in its destination" (*Image–Music–Text*, p. 148). As these statements suggest, however, Barthes does not simply shift the reins from an omniscient author to a reader similarly conceived. For Barthes, the reader is, like the text, analogously contingent, heterogeneous. Not "personal," and "without history, biography, psychology," Barthes's reader "is simply that *someone* who holds together in a single field all the traces by which the written text is constituted" (*Image–Music–Text*, p. 148; emphasis Barthes's). In her 1985 interview with Waller, Kristeva soberly restates Barthes's (and her own) position at the time, stripped of the provocative overtones that have misled multitudes of poststructuralism's detractors to equate his pronouncements with murder. In the plainest sense, Barthes announces a newly self-conscious and open method of literary analysis. She explains: "such an understanding of intertextuality – one that points to a dynamics involving a destruction of the creative identity and reconstitution of a new plurality – assumes at the same time that the one who reads, the reader, participates in the same dynamics" (190).

In Kristeva's work of the 1960s too, this "new plurality" exists on the level of the text, a complex intersection of "different types of texts, voices, and semantic, syntactic, and phonic systems at play," at the same time that it is at work in the reader (189). Like Barthes, Kristeva also embraces the notion of intertextuality as a way to question the traditional idea of the author as the singular, omniscient creator of a literary product by shifting attention to dynamic textuality and readerly engagement. But, more than Barthes, she *retains* a focused interest in the complicated "status of the 'creator,' the one who produces the text" in the midst of this "new plurality" (190). For her, text, reader, and author alike can be theorized within the plurality Bakhtin invites us to consider, if we bring to our analysis a similarly plural, dynamic understanding of subjectivity. Beyond Bakhtin's linguistic interest in the syntactical, phonic, and semantic manifestations of textual plurality, Kristeva wanted to explore

> the notion that the participation of different texts at different levels reveals *a particular mental activity*. And analysis should not limit itself simply to identifying texts that participate in the final texts, or to identifying their sources, but should understand that what is being dealt with is a specific *dynamic of the subject of the utterance*, who consequently, precisely because of this intertextuality, is not an individual in the etymological sense of the term, not an identity. [. . .] This *new identity* may be capable of manifesting itself as the plurality of characters the author uses; but in more recent writing, in the twentieth-century novel, it may appear as fragments of character, or fragments of ideology, or fragments of representation. (190; emphasis mine)

As the careful language of this statement suggests, Kristeva here asserts a compelling parallel between a linguistic or literary theory that understands textual production as plural, dynamic, fragmentary and a psychoanalytic theory that understands the "decentered" process of subjectivity in similar terms. The sheer population, so to speak, of characters and voices within the novel provides us with an especially rich site for exploring such dynamics; and the modern novel's explicitly experimental approach, she suggests, does so most of all.

At the same time, Kristeva's statement to Waller also asserts the theoretical position established by Barthes's "birth of the reader." She goes on to advise that noticing the complexity, indeed the doubleness, of such dynamics – simultaneously textual and "intrapsychic" – means the reader must be willing to cope with a difficulty that demands a subjective risk on the part of the reader herself. This advice echoes the call for interpretive "delirium" she advocates with regard to Céline in "Psychoanalysis and the Polis." The principled commitment to hermeneutic non-mastery she asserts in that essay presents itself here as an "aesthetic pleasure" for the "complexity of the text," a willingness, perhaps recalling Barthes, "to be reduced to zero, to the state of crisis" precipitated in the face of the "loss of meaning" (190). Only from there can we begin building diverse meanings constituted and reconstituted out of a text's intertextual free association, connotation, condensation, and polysemia.

As we have seen, then, in so many of Kristeva's efforts to lay out the principles of a literary analysis properly attuned to the precariousness of the encounter between interpreter and text, her emphasis lay on complexity and plurality, dynamic and in perpetual process. What she does not make entirely clear in her discussion here is precisely whose "subjectivity" such an approach should (or could) examine at any given moment of textual analysis – Author's or character's? Reader's or critic's? – and a certain amount of this ambiguity proves problematic in Kristeva's actual literary commentaries. Kristeva's dynamic superimposition of the concept of intersubjectivity upon the concept of intertextuality produces an exciting theory with a potential greater than the sum of its parts. By adding her specific psychoanalytic vision to the theory of intertextuality, Kristeva gains exciting new possibilities for describing literary production – as reading, writing, and the complex interaction of the two. But she engenders certain difficulties as well, which manifest themselves in her treatment of Joyce in particular. That is, between the theory of an intersubjective intertextuality and its actual, practical deployment in readings of literary texts, some puzzling issues emerge.

Kristeva's readers will be likely to experience these problems first with regard to Joyce, in trying to sort out the most basic precepts of her argument: does "Joyce" refer to the "man himself" or to a set of works whose author has that name? Does she assign authorial intention to the things his works do or say? Does she distinguish between the ideas, statements, experiences of Joyce's characters and Joyce's biographical "self"?

Given her theoretical sophistication, we would assume Kristeva's position on these matters would be clear, but in fact it is not. Often in the service of her own discursive playfulness, as we saw in her reading of Céline, Kristeva eschews sustained critical attention to intention, plot, character, and context. In this specific sense, then, "Joyce" serves as a floating signifier within Kristeva's theory, variously referencing the multiple "subjectivities" she sees operating in his multivalent texts. As we will survey, she variously refers to "Joyce" as a remarkable set of texts and as a man with a remarkable biography, or conflates a given character within those texts with the author who created them, or abstracts both the texts and the "man himself" as illustrations of an intersubjective dynamic she wishes to theorize in broad strokes. The emphatic fluidity she imposes on these conventional distinctions can make for thrilling theoretical propositions on the one hand, but also seemingly muddled literary analysis on the other. Again, as I stressed with regard to Céline, Kristeva's mode of literary analysis looks different for a reason, and its "lessons" are often oblique. But at the very least, Kristeva's complicated assertions about the intersubjective intertextuality of Joyce's work – about Joyce's "obsessions," "beliefs," his erotic, familial, national, and religious "experiences," and those of his characters, and how both make their way into the strange texts he produces – make it difficult for a careful reader to produce a rigorously "Kristevan" reading of Joyce based on her own analyses.[8]

For now, in establishing the foundations of Kristeva's theory of intertextuality, and her efforts to locate its most elaborate workings at a particular moment in literary history, it helps to return to the specific claims she makes in the Waller interview. We should note that while she says this interpretive approach "may also be applied to classical texts," modern texts absolutely *demand* it (191). Joyce's radical texts, especially his final one, urgently usher in this new kind of reading. Just after outlining the theoretical concept of intertextuality and the critical repositioning it requires, she cites the "texts of Joyce [as] a very special example of this type. It is impossible to read *Finnegan's Wake* [*sic*] without entering into the intrapsychic logic and dynamics of intertextuality" (190).[9] In this 1985 interview, originally conducted for a volume about intertextuality and contemporary American fiction, after Kristeva has written *Powers of Horror* and *Tales of Love* and while she is writing *Black Sun*, not only Joyce's name but his final work stands out as a "very special example." How or why that is the case, she does not elaborate, though important work on Joyce has been and could be done by pursuing this claim.[10] This reference turns out to be paradigmatic of the roles Joyce and Joyce's works play throughout Kristeva's theoretical career.

Kristeva's comments to Waller provide a cogent synthesis of theoretical concerns she has spent decades exploring. By outlining her debt to Bakhtin, her close work with Barthes at the time, the psychoanalytic component that makes her interest in intertextuality distinct, her emphasis on the modern novel, and her special regard for Joyce, Kristeva condenses the long evolution of a critical theory dispersed across writing from the late 1960s to the present. Some of these claims, such as her position on Joyce, have appeared consistently since her earliest work. Others, such as the foregrounding of a psychoanalytic interest in the subjective dimension of intertextuality, have developed over time.

The Menippean and a literary tradition of otherness

Including important essays such as "The Bounded Text," "Word, Dialogue, and Novel," and "Semiotics: A Critical Science and/or a Critique of Science," the 1969 publication of *Séméiotiké* demonstrates Kristeva's first efforts to conceive of the literary text "as a trans-linguistic apparatus that redistributes the order of language," as a space in which "several utterances, taken from other texts, intersect and neutralize one another."[11] It is in the course of contemplating Bakhtin's understanding of such a textual dynamic and the alternative literary history this implies that Joyce's name first appears.[12] In "Word, Dialogue, and Novel," Joyce serves as a key figure in a subversive tradition that, for its idiosyncratic historical scope and its emphatic *otherness*, curiously (no doubt unwittingly) resembles Walter Pater's "renaissance."[13] The list of names she offers here will continue to appear throughout Kristeva's career: Antoine de la Sale, Rabelais, Swift, Dostoevsky, Lautréamont, Mallarmé, Joyce, Proust, Kafka, Bataille, Artaud and certain others, with only slight variations over the decades. The list itself deserves a certain scrutiny, for it represents a literary critical intervention in its own right, first proffered by Bakhtin, but elaborated and insistently reasserted by Kristeva and the Tel Quel group with whom she worked until the late 1970s. Not arbitrarily chosen, these writers come to stand for an alternative tradition of literature – "those who have always been and still remain on the fringe of official culture" – Kristeva and her critical peers clearly privilege over the canonical figures of literary criticism ("The Bounded Text," p. 86).

Understanding this critical context, which may be traced to Bakhtin but indeed far exceeds him, proves crucial to reading the way Joyce functions as an example throughout Kristeva's work. The anti-canonical canon Kristeva everywhere invokes emphatically eschews national tradition and, in a more complicated fashion, often disdains periodization as well. It is complicated because – particularly to honor the revolutionary "break" imposed by Mallarmé, Joyce, and others – periodization becomes important to Kristeva when it needs to be. Some names are supplied by Bakhtin (Rabelais, Swift, Dostoevsky), and, as if to signify a continued debt to Bakhtin's theory, tend to turn up in Kristeva's work in just such a cluster, though she does offer a brief reading of Dostoevsky in *Powers of Horror* and devotes a long chapter to him in *Black Sun*. Others (Dante, Sade, Balzac, Artaud, Bataille) spread out in diverse directions that can leave even an initiated reader near despair, chasing half-remembered echoes from other critics (Sollers, Lacan, Barthes, and Sollers again). Kristeva's authorial citations, therefore, almost always require a certain referential decoding, where the meaning of the reference comes not from what a reader might know, specifically, about the author named but rather by recognizing in the reference an intertextual critical nod, a point of contact with a collectively constructed theory of literature of which Kristeva is only one voice.[14]

"Swift," whose name appears throughout Kristeva's work but not with nearly the regularity or privilege granted to Joyce, serves as a telling example of this dynamic. English-language readers who come to Kristeva's work, read the name "Swift" and think, "aha, the author of *Gulliver's Travels, A Tale of a Tub*, 'A Modest Proposal,' satirist of eighteenth-century British politics and Enlightenment pieties, scatologist, irreverent ironist in the tradition of Sterne, Carlyle, perhaps Wilde, and ultimately Joyce," will misconstrue her reference. For her, the name always refers to the officially unofficial "fringe," the polyphonic, "other" tradition first outlined by Bakhtin and upheld by Kristeva, Sollers, and Tel Quel more generally.[15] It never refers to the greater context of eighteenth-century literature, nor to a teemingly rich history of the novel that includes presumably non-subversive (by Kristeva's estimation) but certainly not inconsiderable writers such as Fielding, Austen, the Brontës, Thackeray, Dickens, and Hardy, to name only a few. She has not, to my knowledge, provided a substantial reading of Swift at all, much less considered him in the British political, social, and literary context in which he was writing.

With Swift, then, and occasional, idiosyncratic nods to Shakespeare (in *Tales of Love*, for example), Joyce is notably one of the very few English-language writers allowed membership in the group.[16] And the sheer quantity of references to Joyce in particular suggests a special preoccupation. For Kristeva, Joyce's radical otherness – national, traditional, stylistic, even religious – obviates any need to consider his place within English literary history. He is outside, an exception to, the British and even continental writing of his day. Irish, not British, this man who lived most of his life on the Continent becomes for Kristeva the quintessential "exile" both in his life and in his art. "James Joyce had to be [a] foreigner," she declares, sounding obliquely prescriptive, in *Strangers to Ourselves* (1991).[17]

As in so many other mentions, Kristeva here conflates the man and his work: the "foreignness" she sees in him permeates his biography and his writings. And again, the Joycean reflection occurs within a list, though here the list exhibits slight variations from her norm. Along with Joyce, she posits the foreignness of Swift – the man, his writing, his thematic concerns – Edgar Allan Poe, and Henry James, and again Rabelais. But she reserves for Joyce this final, lyrical assessment:

> And one cannot leave out James Joyce [. . .] that peculiar Irishman, himself an exile, who gave the name of Ulysses the sailor to the strangest novel of our own times, roaming through a divided culture – Greek, Jewish, Christian – in a quest of his elusive singularity. (*Strangers to Ourselves*, p. 115)

This wistfully admiring description, connecting Joyce's personal history with classical myth with Joyce's fictional characters in a romanticized genealogical blur, is typical of Kristeva's tendency to regard the man and his works alike as exceptional. Both what Joyce *does* and *is* is other. As Philippe Sollers puts it, speaking *both* of the strange "the" that ends *Finnegans Wake* and of the writer who chose to put it there, "Il fait interruption."[18]

Kristeva's understanding of the literary tradition of otherness finds its broadest elaboration in "Word, Dialogue, and Novel." Following a designation Bakhtin introduces in *Problems of Dostoevsky's Poetics* (1963), she outlines here a certain genealogy of literature that has a discernible lineage and is yet distinct from the mainstream history of literature, and is also other to normative symbolic discourse altogether. This other tradition operates polylogically, on several registers, which she catalogues with dizzying enumeration. She calls this anti-tradition, this genre that is not a genre as such, "Menippean discourse." Menippean discourse distinguishes itself for its generic hybridity, its tonal ambivalence, its satirical resistance to normative logic and "values." Its name implies an origin with historical specificity, derived from "Menippus of Gadara, a philosopher of the third century BC. His satires were lost, but we know of their existence through the writings of

Diogenes Laertius" (82). Indeed the term itself has such specificity; it was "used by the Romans to designate a genre of the first century BC (Marcus Terentius Varro's *Satirae Menippeae*)" (82). But Kristeva wants to expand the term well beyond the first century BC, both before and after.

Joyce's name appears within the multi-generic grand narrative she provides in defining the Menippean, primarily associated with the "polyphonic" novel, but exceeding it as well. Temporally speaking, by her reckoning, "the genre actually appeared much earlier" than the name Menippus itself, reappears influentially in early "Christian and Byzantine literature," and "survived through the Middle Ages, the Renaissance and the Reformation through to the present (the novels of Joyce, Kafka and Bataille)" (82). Thus it traverses history, more a spirit than a moment or mode, more an element that can appear within a text than a name to give certain works in their entirety. As if a ghostly reincarnation, the Menippean manifests itself variously, consistent only in its emphatically mocking otherness. It is against-the-grain and in-between.

Kristeva offers a description that is exhaustive and encyclopedic. The characteristics, in part, include the following:

> Menippean discourse is both comic and tragic, or rather, it is serious in the same sense as is the carnivalesque; through the status of its words, it is politically and socially disturbing. It frees speech from historical constraints, and this entails a thorough boldness in philosophical and imaginative inventiveness. [...] Phantasmagoria and an often mystical symbolism fuse with macabre naturalism. Adventures unfold in brothels, robbers' dens, taverns, fairgrounds and prisons, among erotic orgies and during sacred worship, and so forth. The word has no fear of incriminating itself. It becomes free from presupposed "values"; without distinguishing between virtue and vice. [...] Elements of the fantastic, which never appear in epic or tragic works, crop forth here. For example [...] in Lucan's *Icaromenippea*, Varro's *Endymion* and later in the works of Rabelais, Swift and Voltaire. Pathological states of the soul, such as madness, split personalities, daydreams, dreams and death, become part of the narrative (they affect the writing of Shakespeare and Calderón). (82–3)

And she goes on: the Menippean can appear "as an exploration of language and writing." It "tends towards the scandalous and eccentric in language." It is frank, "cynical," desecrating, "abrupt," at once "high and low," "made up of contrasts" and "misalliances of all kinds." It is "an all-inclusive genre, put together as a pavement of citations"; it "includes all genres (short stories, letters, speeches, mixtures of verse and prose)" (83).

It is "not cathartic," "a festival of cruelty, but also a political act." It "transmits no fixed message." It expresses " 'the eternal joy of becoming' " (a phrase given in quotation marks but not cited).[19] And perhaps most significantly for Kristeva's broader theory, it represents an historical turn in which literature "becomes conscious of itself as sign."

Parallel to such formal self-consciousness is an epistemological inwardness as well, in which man "becomes alienated from himself, discovering his 'interior' and 'reifying' this discovery in the ambivalence of Menippean writing" (84). This definitional tidal wave – and I am still editing substantially – derives its power (and perhaps its weakness) from its potential to subsume every kind of literature, or at least parts of every kind of literature. By a certain argument, we could say Kristeva has in fact defined "literariness" as such, though she herself has specifically distanced herself from that charged formalist term.[20] Whereas a number of her essays spell out the reasons for that distancing, "Word, Dialogue, and Novel" asserts them by a merely implicit methodological stance: in telling us that "Menippean writing" takes so many forms across the span of so much time, Kristeva demands a certain readerly re-alignment, a kind of perception attuned to these elements of otherness, a willingness to read against the grain.

Without getting stuck questioning the theoretical success of the "Menippean" designation, we can still notice that it says something about her understanding of Joyce. She places him within and at the contemporary *end* of a literary lineage that positions itself in "opposition" – to normative discourse, dominant literary tradition, classical logic, unified philosophy. While Kristeva's later work will largely drop the term "Menippean," its rebellious spirit lives on in other names and altered forms – "poetic language," "the semiotic," "borderline discourse," even simply "literature."

We can also take from her definition of the Menippean a specifically Kristevan claim. She points out elsewhere in "Word, Dialogue, and Novel" that placing such twentieth-century figures as Joyce within the Menippean anti-tradition, she is amending Bakhtin. "Bakhtin's examples include Rabelais, Swift, Dostoievski." But she argues we "might also add the 'modern' novel of the twentieth century – Joyce, Proust, Kafka" (71). By doing so, she extends the Menippean even further into the present. At the same time, however, she asserts a significant non-continuity. Joyce and his contemporaries keep the Menippean alive, "incorporating the carnivalesque structure" Bakhtin calls "*polyphonic*" (71; emphasis Kristeva's). Nevertheless, "Joyce, Proust, Kafka" do so on the other side of a great divide: "A break occurred at the end of the nineteenth century," separating literature that still "remains at a representative, fictitious level" in the nineteenth century from a certain literature of the twentieth. The distinction is that "our century's polyphonic novel becomes 'unreadable' (Joyce) and interior to language (Proust, Kafka). Beginning with this break – not only literary but also social, political, and philosophical in nature – the problem of intertextuality [. . .] appears as such" (71). Invoking Joyce and his "unreadable" novels, together with Proust's and Kafka's "interiorization," she asserts that rich, long-standing Menippean tradition finds its apotheosis with these writers, not only because of *what* they create, but because of the great epistemic upheaval *in which* they create.

The claim that it is at this moment that "the problem of interextuality [. . .] appears" asserts a specific literary history, but also, more subtly, describes a specific critical history as well. She follows the above claim by stating: "Bakhtin's theory itself (as well as that of Saussure's 'Anagrams') can be traced historically to this break" (71).[21] In other words, the literature of Joyce, Proust, Kafka, and the theories of Saussure and Bakhtin, are made possible by the same radical reconception of language, reference, and representation around the beginning of the twentieth century. This assertion of a break is central to Kristeva's vision of literary history, guiding her identification of the "revolution" in poetic language she will explore in the 1970s and beyond. In fact, in its ambitious effort to show intellectual convergences between literary practice and other intellectual discourses, this instance reads like the thesis of *Revolution in Poetic Language* in germinal form.

Yet, lest we get too comfortable with this distinction – that Joyce and company are inheritors of the Menippean, but with a difference that hinges on linguistic representation – Kristeva makes other claims in "Word, Dialogue, and Novel" that cloud the picture somewhat. In the midst of warning her readers about the "ambiguity one must avoid" in getting tangled in Bakhtin's own terminology, she restates this Menippean lineage a few pages on as having *always* been about representation, or more specifically about a certain counter-discourse to the dominant representational discourse. In the carnivalesque, a "tradition absorbed into Menippean discourse," "language parodies and relativizes itself, repudiating its role in representation" (79). Because "[a]ll of the most important polyphonic novels are inheritors of the Menippean, carnivalesque structure" (a long list that again includes

Joyce), its self-conscious representational mode has always been transgressive. "Its history is the history of the struggle against Christianity and its representation; this means an exploration of language (of sexuality and death), a consecration of ambivalence and of 'vice' " (80).

I think a reader would be justified in seeing these statements as somewhat contradictory, or in feeling that Kristeva so exhaustively, inclusively describes the Menippean tradition that one could, if so predisposed, identify its attributes in any text. And moreover, I can understand why it might be especially difficult in this essay to see what is so distinct about the nineteenth/twentieth-century break, when the "representational" transgressions and linguistic self-consciousness are identified throughout the tradition's long history. The issue might lead a reader to wonder whether, if the Menippean can appear in so many guises in so many periods in so many kinds of texts, it is a set of characteristics at work essentially *in* a given text, there to be found or not by discerning critics, or an attribute a critic can find if she comes to the text with certain expectations, a certain investment in reading *for* these subversive traits.[22]

Looking to other works Kristeva wrote around this time can alleviate some of this confusion, though I am not sure it ever really goes away. In "Semiotics: A Critique of Science and/or a Critical Science," also published in *Séméiotiké* in 1969, we can see that Kristeva was also concerned at this time not with treating literature as if it were an object that exhibited certain inherent features, but with looking at literature in a new way altogether. We discuss this shift in detail in Chapter 1 – the move from a static criticism of the object to a dynamic criticism involving subjectivities. And it is precisely in the context of emphasizing this shift that she references Joyce in this essay. "Word, Dialogue, and Novel" arguably runs into trouble with the dazzling definition of the Menippean by making it so historically and characteristically broad, but especially for implying therein that its characteristics inhere in certain texts and not in others.

In "Semiotics," however, Kristeva *explicitly* shifts her focus to critical methodology: the key issue becomes how we look at texts, to see what they do. With this new focus, Kristeva allows that finding writerly, subversive textuality might be a matter of methodological approach, not merely a given text's fixed qualities. In this essay, her language is more careful, if no less provocative. Here she promotes a method of analysis that regards "literature" as a "*particular semiotic practice* which has the advantage of making more accessible than others the problematics of the production of meaning" (*The Kristeva Reader*, p. 86; emphasis Kristeva's). Semiotic analysis sees "text" as "production," "practice," "productivity." In this regard, "Any 'literary' text may be envisaged as productivity," which seems to obviate the historical narrative implied, at least in part, by the "Menippean." However, she again implies that, because of the break at the end of the nineteenth century, some texts operate by means of a *more* radical productivity than others. Again, the key differences in the twentieth-century texts seem to be their self-consciousness and resistance to purely mimetic representation. Among the "modern texts which, even structurally, perceive themselves as a production that cannot be reduced to representation" are those by "Joyce, Mallarmé, Lautréamont, Roussel" (86).[23]

In "How Does One Speak to Literature?" (1971), Kristeva invokes Joyce prominently, again in order to identify the nineteenth-century "break" she notes in "Word, Dialogue, Novel" and to emphasize a newly envisioned literary theory. This essay, as we explore in Chapter 1, honors Roland Barthes for developing new critical methodologies to respond to new discourses. Language and knowledge themselves are transformed by an upheaval Kristeva deems, following Barthes, at once linguistic, philosophical, and ideological: "As capitalist society is being economically and politically choked to death, discourse is wearing thin and heading for collapse at a more rapid rate than ever before" (92). Within these dire conditions, certain discourses, she argues, are becoming ossified, retreating to an entrenched academia. Rare other discourses have remained vital: "Only one language grows more and more contemporary: the equivalent, beyond a span of thirty years, of the language of *Finnegans Wake*" (92).

As she does in the Waller interview, Kristeva here grants exemplary status to Joyce's text, prominently so, but leaves her reader to sort out the gesture's implications. In this case, the claim made by the reference lies veiled behind ambiguous syntax (identical in the original French). Is this "contemporary" language a language *like* that in *Finnegans Wake*, but not necessarily the specific language *in* Joyce's own text, a language "out in the world" that somehow *Finnegans Wake* was just uniquely able to capture? Or, more obliquely, is Kristeva suggesting that *Finnegans Wake* is as a text still "alive" in some way, a "work in progress" that still speaks, that remains unfinished? Or does she mean, more simply, that *Finnegans Wake* offers the only language that was at its inception, and continues to be, utterly "contemporary"? It remains very difficult to decide, especially because she does not reference any specific feature of the text beyond its title.

Nevertheless, a basic and incrementally familiar claim in this statement comes into view retroactively, if we examine subsequent references to Joyce in the essay. Barthes's critical theory gives new attention to "signifying systems that are trans-linguistic," "only partially linguistic," or even "anti-lingustic" (102). Such a linguistic condition "leads, in borderline experiences, to an antilanguage (Joyce), to a sacrificial language (Bataille), indicating in other respects but simultaneously a disrupted social structure" (102). Reverting, in these references, to "Joyce" rather than the name of his final revolutionary text, Kristeva makes it hard to tell just what feature of his language she envisions in this light. When she elaborates that Barthes's project identifies a kind of "writing" that "operates–constitutes the signifier but also exceeds it," we might recall her argument about Céline's stylistic excess, or we might conjure up our own images of the dizzying portmanteau language of *Finnegans Wake*.

But we largely have to do that work for ourselves. Kristeva does not elaborate. "Joyce," rather than *Finnegans Wake* specifically, seems a particularly apt locus for studying a "new 'language' [that] is […] no longer communicative" (102). Joyce stands for a kind of writing Barthes himself wants to establish as dynamic, linguistic and more, touching on the drives, on passion. For Kristeva, Barthes's insistence that writing "is always rooted in something beyond language" leads to a theory of signification beyond structuralism's. And it authorizes Kristeva's own interest in seeking signifying structures not just in language but in the psyche as well – "*the unfolding in depth of the signifying subject*" (103; emphasis Kristeva's).

A new kind of language and writing calls for a new kind of criticism. These developments are co-extensive as Barthes reads them. The utterly "contemporary language" of *Finnegans Wake* demands a new kind of criticism equipped to deal with it: "[T]he very problems we keep facing […] are called forth by this avant-garde" (114). Kristeva places Joyce at its leading edge (but then, eschewing chronology, also Rabelais), as a writer who enacts a "revolt against the language and order of a society on the wane," and produces a "new 'literature' that has us read in a new and different manner" (114). This different manner most importantly rejects the validity of viewing the text as "merely an 'object' " (114).

Transposition and the portmanteau word

In *Revolution in Poetic Language,* Joyce's name appears in the service of a similar theoretical vision, again emphasizing the contemporaneity of literature's "signifying practices" and the emergence of a theoretical apparatus prepared to account for it. "[W]ith Lautréamont, Mallarmé, Joyce, and Artaud," we see the literary articulation of a "crisis" Kristeva magisterially surveys as philosophical, political, economic, linguistic, and psychoanalytic at once (15). Their works generate meaning in a way that radically disrupts the normative representational relationship of a signifier to a signified, a "shattering of discourse" that coincides with "changes in the *status of the subject* – his relation to the body, to others and to objects" (15; emphasis Kristeva's). Throughout this text, Joyce's name appears in lists as he does here, or in parentheses, or sometimes both (85, 88, 103). Somewhat more awkwardly, if more candidly, she later proposes that "[w]e will take the names Joyce and Bataille *as emblems* of the most radical aspects of twentieth-century literature" (82; emphasis mine). This announcement, at least, prepares us for several other references to "a Joyce or a Bataille, for example," or (twice) "a Mallarmé or a Joyce" (82, 101, 218).

More theoretically significant than this collection of minor references, however, is Kristeva's effort in *Revolution in Poetic Language* to reorient the concept of intertextuality around an explicit theory of the speaking subject. The psychoanalytic component Kristeva tells Waller she initially brought to Bakhtin's textual theory emerges fully-fledged in this work. So much so, in fact, that she makes a point to give a new name to the concept itself. Having worked through a dense reading of Husserl's "thetic" in order to establish her own model of subject formation – where the inaugural "positing" of the self depends upon and comes about through enunciation – Kristeva proposes the term "transposition" as a felicitous way to describe intertextuality's at once linguistic and psychic dimensions. Because intertextuality, she explains, "has often been understood in the banal sense of 'study of sources,' we prefer the term *transposition* because it specifies that the passage from one signifying system to another demands a new articulation of the thetic – of enunciative and denotative positionality" (60; emphasis Kristeva's).

She makes a complicated argument here, and her terminology bears the weight of the meticulous Husserlian analysis that precedes it, but for our purposes we should note that, with the new term, she binds the speaking subject – that is, the *position* of the subject – inextricably to the textual processes she describes, and vice-versa. Moreover, calling transposition's "*passage from one sign system to another*" a "third 'process' " that we must add to Freud's "two fundamental 'processes' in the work of the unconscious;" clearly underscores that Kristeva sees intertextuality as not just a dynamic of texts among other texts, but as a dynamic that centrally involves speaking subjects in process (59). The gesture here recalls Kristeva's telescopic explanation to Waller that she wanted to add to Bakhtin's formulations "the notion that the participation of different texts at different levels reveals a particular mental activity."

Though we might be guilty of banal source study to say so, we can clearly see that Kristeva's insistence to Waller that intertextuality go beyond source study toward understanding "a specific dynamics of the subject of the utterance," finds its original articulation in *Revolution in Poetic Language*. Kristeva announces here, in effect, that exploring the radical textuality of Joyce and company provides a rich opportunity for exploring the strange vicissitudes of the speaking subject, in its formative beginnings, in its crises, and in its most compelling literary expressions. In this sense, "Joyce," that traveling signifier throughout this important text, reminds us that her textual theory does not derive from or come secondary to her psychoanalytic theory, thus calling on readers to "apply" her psychoanalysis of the subject to literary works. Rather, they have developed mutually, incrementally, and over time. "Literature has always been," she stresses here, "the most explicit realization of the signifying subject's condition" (82).

Kristeva's preferred new term, which she places within a Husserlian phenomenological context, also comes from classical rhetoric. While she does not explicitly acknowledge it within the theoretical "sign system" of rhetoric, "transposition" does more subtly allow Kristeva to stress that the sort of intertextuality that most interests her occurs relatively microscopically, on the level of the letter. Classically, transposition is an umbrella term for several figures of speech. One of rhetoric's four categories of change (along with addition, subtraction, and substitution), it by definition involves *rearrangement* – of letters within a word (*metathesis* or *paronomasia*), of words within a sentence (*hyperbaton*), or of the normal order of events (*hysteron proteron*). The rhetorical dimension to Kristeva's "transposition" provides an extremely suggestive tool for a textual analysis, whether Kristeva herself invokes it or not. We discussed in the previous chapter her keen interest in Céline's syntactical reordering and its rhetorical effects, which she calls neither transposition nor *hyperbaton*, but which certainly operates by such principles. Because the classical definition of transposition includes the rearrangement of letters within a word, it provides exciting potential as a model for analyzing Joyce's use of language as well, and even for seeing it within the rhetorical logic of Céline's own strategic derangements.

At one moment in her discussion of transposition, Kristeva points to "portmanteau words in Joyce" as an example of the "redistribution of the phonematic order, morphological structure, and [...] syntax" at work in the revolutionary poetics of the avant-garde (154). But her reference to Joyce's widely theorized portmanteau words, while tantalizing, remains undeveloped, and despite the reference, she cites not a single example. Clearly, Joyce's linguistically complicated, highly dynamic deployment of portmanteau words offers one of the most exciting literary specimens for Kristeva's theory of transposition one can imagine, which is why Kristeva's terseness on the matter proves especially frustrating. Joyce's technique relentlessly generates such words, punning neologisms over-stuffed with letters and meaning, as an over-packed suitcase would be stuffed with stuff.

They are what the "Shem the Penman" chapter of *Finnegans Wake* (I.7, pp. 169–95) self-reflexively derides as an inartistic, unoriginal mess of language. We can read "Shem the Penman" as a vandalized "portrait of the artist" that vengefully enumerates one "poor trait of the artless" (p. 114.32) after another, an ambiguous monologue where idealized notions of the author, artistic epiphany, and poetic language no longer hold.[24] Of course, neither do the most basic formal notions of narrator, character, or identity for that matter: it is difficult to tell just who utters this monologue, who Shem is and what role he plays in the greater "story" of the "novel," and whether it is even apt (as I am doing here) to take its assertions as broader Joycean claims about language or anything else.

Even in *A Portrait of the Artist as a Young Man*, Joyce ironizes Stephen Dedalus's naïve and self-important efforts to see the author and his creation in exalted terms. In fact, *Portrait*'s Stephen presents an aesthetic theory of the artist that sounds remarkably like the theological "Artist-God" Barthes derides in "The Death of the Author." Speaking to his unimpressed friend Lynch on a noisy Dublin street, Stephen pretentiously offers an aesthetic vision derived from Aquinas, Lessing, and Flaubert: "The artist, like the God of the creation remains within or behind or beyond or above his handiwork, invisible, refined out of existence, indifferent, paring his fingernails."[25]

Like most of Stephen's audiences, Lynch is less than convinced; by listening to him only indifferently (a type of interlocutor Joyce often opposes to his protagonist), he resists granting Stephen the serious consideration Stephen feels he deserves. With an energy, and a certain arrogance, that renders him immune to such skepticism, Stephen draws upon a history of aesthetic discourse culminating in a portrait of the artist as purely separate, lord of a creation which is itself closed and pure and wholly his: omnipotent artist, totalized artwork, in divine harmony. However, not only can Lynch not refrain from politicizing Stephen's argument ("What do you mean [...] by prating about beauty and the imagination in this miserable Godforsaken island?"), he can't help thinking about those fingernails. "Trying to refine them also out of existence," Lynch adds to the simile, offering a shade of cynicism to the portrait he puts forth, smearing Stephen's neat aesthetic borders between discrete creation and autonomous creator by bringing back into the frame of this portrait the excreta of its production.

Though denied the characters, plot, and setting of the aesthetic dialogue in *A Portrait of the Artist as a Young Man*, we can read portions of *Finnegans Wake* as an elaboration of Lynch's rhetorical questions to Stephen. Such skepticism pointedly paves the way for its "Shem the Penman" episode, a "fried-at-belief-stakes" (p. 170.33) muck-raking romp, a gleeful character-assassination that acts out the "death of the author" on the level of the letter. As "Shem" and indeed all of *Finnegans Wake* makes abundantly clear, Joyce's portmanteau words are "usylessly unreadable" (*Finnegans Wake*, p. 196.26–7) except by reading and even *hearing* them as combinations of several words in one, interwoven rearrangements of the letters of one word fused with those of another (and often another and another), referencing other names and texts and even other languages all at once.[26] When we consider that *Finnegans Wake*, not to mention *Ulysses*, gives us six hundred and twenty-eight pages of such "alphybettyformed verbage, [...] imeffible tries at speech unsyllabled, [...] once current puns, quashed quotatoes, messes of motage" created out of just such literal redistribution, the aptness of studying these dynamics under the name "transposition" is especially striking (pp. 183.13, 183.22–3).[27]

The untranslated portions of *Revolution in Poetic Language* do examine in detail linguistically complex dynamics in the works of Lautréamont and Mallarmé; these influential readings certainly contribute to the reputation Kristeva has earned as a literary theorist of intertextuality. Kristeva's interest in anagrams, after Saussure, also indicates an interest in the reordering effects of transposition on the level of the letter. She pursues some of the significatory "infinity" suggested by reading on this level in *Séméiotiké*, looking specifically at Mallarmé, but again, her terminology is different.[28]

In the context of her explicit definition of transposition, however, Kristeva's examples remain largely general and generic. She argues that the novel, for instance, engages in such transpositions in a highly dynamic way, developing its specific sense "as the result of a redistribution of several different sign systems: carnival, courtly poetry, scholastic discourse" (*Revolution in Poetic Language*, p. 59). Imagining a specific example of how such transposition would manifest itself on this generic level, we might recall the "Lemon Tree" figure in O'Brien's short story, which vigorously functions according to the formula Kristeva proposes here. As we see in that text, one says very little about the affective and semantic impact of that figure by simply tracking down its source. In O'Brien's piece, the intertextual element (from the "sign system" of sixties folk music) produces a "shattered unity" within the narrative of the story itself, which corresponds to the "shattered" psyche of the narrator and of the speaking subject who sings the song, while at the same time referring to one of the story's major themes about war's ability to "shatter" truth and death's ability, literally, to shatter human identity. Joyce belongs to the radical group of writers who most self-consciously produce texts riddled by such complex transpositional "concatenations."

New associations: music, the body, and the dissident

Kristeva's link between transposition's exchange of signifiers from one sign system to another and the actual workings of Joyce's texts thus remains fairly "emblematic" in her most explicit discussions of intertextuality, from her earliest work up to *Revolution in Poetic Language*. "Joyce" as just this sort of emblem, in fact, traverses several of Kristeva's publications in the 1970s, as her theoretical interests expand beyond this signature theoretical concept. Two essays published in her 1977 book *Polylogue*, and subsequently included in the English-language collection, *Desire* in *Language* (1980), demonstrate this usage.

In "From One Identity to Another" (1975), the name appears in an exciting early consideration of Céline, where once again Joyce belongs to a list – "Céline, Artaud, or Joyce" – of writers who irreverently, even obscenely insist upon the materiality of the letter, and who demand being read as such (*Desire in Language*, p. 142). In "The Father, Love, and Banishment" (1976), Kristeva invokes Joyce to assert a psychoanalytically inflected vision of the nineteenth-century "break," this time aligning Joyce with Freud, suggesting both were ahead of their time in representing and theorizing, respectively, a pre-symbolic femininity. She places him on the threshold of a discovery more penetrating than Freud's:

> It was not until the end of the nineteenth century and Joyce, even more than Freud, that this repression of motherhood and incest was affirmed as risky and unsettling in one's very flesh and sex. Not until then did it, by means of a language that "musicates through letters," resume within the discourse the rhythms, intonations, and echolalias of the mother–infant symbiosis – intense, pre-Oedipal, predating the father – and this in the third person. (*Desire in Language*, p. 157)

Joyce's status as example here changes according to Kristeva's evolving theoretical investments.

With its emphasis on sexuality and the negotiations of pre-Oedipal subjectivity, this particular assertion marks a subtle shift in Kristeva's focus on Joyce which corresponds to the evolution of her work more generally. The mention of Freud is also telling. Given Kristeva's prodigious contribution to the poststructural "return to Freud" (which we examine in Chapter 2), her gesture of granting Joyce "even more" insight into the shadowy workings of the unconscious than that of Freud deserves notice. Precisely what feature of (or passage from) Joyce's texts Kristeva refers to here remains ambiguous, but it comes in the course of reading Beckett's *First Love* and *Not I*, texts she does explore with readerly care.[29] Joyce's discourse serves as both contrast and close analogy to Beckett's, produced "after Joyce and in a different fashion" (157). We may surmise from the essay's earlier, equally terse references to "the overflowing Molly and Finnegan's negative awakening" that Kristeva has in mind the famously "flowing" interior monologue of the "Penelope" chapter of *Ulysses* and the supposedly "dreamy" glossolalia of *Finnegans Wake*.[30]

In "A New Type of Intellectual: the Dissident" (1977), Kristeva invokes Joyce, again, as a radical exile, writing an experimental literature that probes "the limits of identity," producing a "polyvalent, polylogic" and "playful language" that subverts the "law" of the symbolic order.[31] Overtly political, the essay is a call to action, arguing that intellectuals can either, as they typically do, slavishly uphold dominant ideology by "perceiving himself as the guardian of supposedly universal thought," or instead actively work against it (*The Kristeva Reader*, p. 293). Key tools in this revolt are the "particular kinds of speeches and *jouissance* directed against the equalizing Word," from which "another society, another community, another body start to emerge." "It is the task of the intellectual," she writes, "not just to produce" such dissident speech "but to assert its *political value*" (294; emphasis Kristeva's).

Kristeva says we may identify three specific types of intellectual dissidence, though in fact she goes on to enumerate four: the political "rebel," the psychoanalyst, the experimental writer, and women. The dissident's language, moreover, is "the language of exile," for imagining the Utopian space Kristeva identifies outside the dominant order requires "becoming a stranger to one's own country, language, sex and identity" (298). Necessarily linking dissidence with exile, Kristeva then goes on to list a number of "great generations of non-religious exiles" (298). These include the diaspora of the Jews and exiles from the Gulag. The list also includes people like Kristeva herself (who emigrated from Eastern-bloc Bulgaria to study in Paris), committed to challenging the premises of humanist rationality through a "ruthless and irreverent dismantling of the workings of discourse, thought, and existence" (299). She puts Joyce among such exiles, in another list of authors (Kafka, Joyce, and Beckett, who were in turn prefigured by Mallarmé) who created a linguistic "diaspora" of their own. They write the "languages that pluralize meaning and cross all national and linguistic barriers" (299).

While the overt political thrust of this essay may seem to distinguish it from other Joycean references we have surveyed, all the familiar associations are present here as well: Joyce as other, modern, polylogic, trans-national. Aligning the experimental writer with *jouissance* and desire, with a representation that conveys non-symbolic language through "rhythm, the conjunction of body and music," Kristeva hints at new associations as well.

In *Powers of Horror*, Kristeva again aligns Joyce with Dostoevsky, Proust, Artaud, but especially Céline. Here, the characteristic list of names appears as a series of brief textual examples, representing various writerly articulations of the abjection the book explores. The Joycean example comes from Molly's famously sensual (and unpunctuated) monologue, the last chapter of *Ulysses*, which takes on the voice of Leopold Bloom's wife. The only chapter of the book not guided by the point of view of Stephen Dedalus, Leopold Bloom, or a relatively "omniscient" narrator, it becomes for Kristeva a privileged exercise in radical writerly adventure – the "prototype of literary utterance," Kristeva calls it (on questionable, or at least unargued, grounds) (22). As we begin to see in essays such as "The Father, Love, and Banishment," Kristeva invokes Joyce's name in the context of sexuality and the body, the link between the feminine or maternal body to the dynamics of pre-Oedipal speech. The implication here that Joyce was a writer with special access to – or at least a special interest in – the "body and language" of women echoes similar claims Kristeva makes with increasing frequency throughout the 1970s and into the 1980s. Such assertions arise, for example, in "The Novel as Polylogue" (1974, 1977) and "Women's Time" (1979), if elliptically so.

In *Powers of Horror*, she regards Molly's monologue in just this way:

> *from afar*, the writer approaches the hysterical body so that it might speak, so that he might speak, using it as a springboard, of what eludes speech and turns out to be the hand to hand struggle of one woman with another, her mother of course, the absolute because primeval seat of the impossible – of the excluded, the outside-of-meaning, the abject. (22; emphasis Kristeva's)

This is heady stuff. It finds some illumination in the broader light of her theory of abjection (which we discuss in Chapters 2 and 3). But as a literary critical statement about Joyce's work, specifically his narrative technique, Kristeva's comments remain abstruse and impressionistic. If we may extract a relatively simple claim, Kristeva apparently suggests that Joyce's effort to produce an extended, interior, first-person narration in the voice of a woman – a narration moreover that mulls over issues of the body, desire, love, and sex – puts him in a special position. Kristeva makes a point, however, to stress that his innovation is not primarily "thematic." The abject "lies, beyond the themes and for Joyce generally, in the way one speaks" (23). In giving voice to "the hysterical body," he "approaches" what she here calls abjection, that place beyond normative, symbolic discourse; he does so through the language of "rhythm and music […], the ultimate sublimation of the unsignifiable" (23).

By her own accounting in *Powers of Horror*, still more important than implications of Joyce's narrative cross-gendered impersonation is the sheer linguistic audacity of his literary efforts. And again, she invokes *Finnegans Wake* as the apotheosis of a quest to create "the rhetoric of the pure signifier, of music in letters" (23). As elsewhere, Kristeva declines to elaborate on the ways in which *Finnegans Wake* specifically does this, so it is hard to speculate about just what she has in mind. In fact, perhaps appropriately, given her theory of intertextuality, the statement seems to be a reference not to Joyce's text directly, but rather to Kristeva's own description of Joyce in "The Father, Love, and Banishment." Her characterization of *Finnegans Wake* as "music in letters" recalls her assertion in that earlier essay that Joyce's language, attuned to the pre-Oedipal, "musicates in letters." (In fact, the phrases are identical in the French texts: "musique dans les lettres.") The repetition of this phrase in *Powers of Horror* acts out what Barthes calls intertextuality's "quotation without inverted commas," though, in this case, it proves difficult to tell whether we should assign the "quotation" to Joyce or to Kristeva herself, or to another source altogether.

The fact that Kristeva so often quotes without citing her sources, or quotes herself and her colleagues without even the tell-tale "inverted commas," highlights the slippery dynamics of intertextuality within critical texts as well as literary texts. Kristeva originally writes in "Father, Love, and Banishment," that Joyce radically ushers in a language "qui 'musique dans les lettres' " (*Polylogue*, p. 145). Her quotation marks suggest she is citing someone else's phrase. The fact that she has just invoked Joyce as a key purveyor of such language further implies the phrase is his own. The way that Kristeva works the supposed quotation into the syntax of her own sentence – neologizing "musique" by treating it as a verb rather than a noun – also at least mimics Joyce's strategic syntactical derangements.

The essay's English translators, in this instance, make the matter all the more confusing for readers by explicitly "Joyce-ifying" Kristeva's own wording, rendering the already strange "musics" into the even stranger "musicates." Sensing a Joycean neologism, diligent readers of Joyce concordances will search in vain for the appearance of "musicates" in his *oeuvre*, for it never appears.[32] Barthes's definition of intertextuality as "quotations without inverted commas" conjures an image of receding origins, of textual echoes whose original voice or author vanishes into a complex degree-zero of language. In "Father, Love, and Banishment," Kristeva and her translators invert such a formula, with similar results. They suggest an intertextuality of inverted commas without apparent quotation – at least not the quotation we assume we are getting.[33]

"a wildgoup's chase"[34]

The consequences of this example are in one sense banal: the uncited citation in "Father, Love, and Banishment" and its echo in *Powers of Horror* sent this reader down a brief rabbit hole of unsatisfactory source hunting, a "wildgoup's chase," from which I returned a little chastened but unscathed. The experience illustrates, for one thing, the futility of treating literary analysis as merely an exercise in source-hunting, as both Barthes's and Kristeva's theories of intertextuality assert from the beginning. On another level, however, this textual drama represents larger, more significant issues at stake in Kristeva's theory itself – her theory of intertextuality, of Joyce, and of literary criticism as such. For as I suggest much earlier, Kristeva's critical engagements with Joyce, throughout her career, say as much about an intertextual conversation with her theoretical peers (or even with her own work) as they do about Joyce's texts themselves.

One key intertextual conversation, running throughout Kristeva's Joyce commentaries and almost never acknowledged as such, takes place with her fellow critic and husband Philippe Sollers. Sollers's interest in Joyce, like Kristeva's, spans decades and manifests itself as a reflection of the complicated, shifting investments of the Tel Quel group. Unlike Kristeva, however, Sollers has grappled with Joyce on a close textual level, incorporating Joyce's style and his very words in his own novels, discussing his work in numerous critical articles and interviews, even translating (or "transforming") into French portions of *Finnegans Wake*.[35] While she has never openly acknowledged the influence of Sollers's Joycean preoccupation upon her own work, the similarities seem to run long and deep.

When Kristeva appears to quote Joyce in her 1979 "Women's Time," a ghostly, concatenating reference illustrates this critical intertextuality in a particularly dynamic light.[36] Introducing her thesis, she writes: " 'Father's time, mother's species,' as Joyce puts it; and indeed, when evoking the name and destiny of women, one thinks more of the *space* generating and forming the human species than of *time*, becoming or history" (190; emphasis Kristeva's). Joyce's statement, Kristeva suggests, aptly encapsulates the non-linear "temporal dimension" specific to female subjectivity, a dimension more properly understood in terms of "*space*" or "place" rather than time (190–1). The invocations of space and place lead Kristeva offhandedly to recall Freud's hypothesis that hysteria, the quintessential women's malady, "was linked to place"

(191). But more pointedly, it allows her to recall her own influential theory of the *chora*, which itself draws from Plato, who "designated by the aporia of the *chora*, matrix space, nourishing, unnameable, anterior to the One, to God and, consequently, defying metaphysics" (191).

This imposing, subtly free-associating list serves as the culmination of a characteristic set of moves in Kristeva's work: her own proposal about the particularity of "women's time" recalls an epigrammatically apt literary quotation, which in turn leads to an authorized observation from Freud, which in turn leads to an impressive list of all the normative structures challenged by the radicality of this "women's time," which ultimately functions in the same way as a number of other radical forces Kristeva's work has explored over the decades.

In this case, as in others, what is threatened is logocentrism, signification, metaphysics. By the end of the paragraph, Kristeva has provided an entire history of the ideas undermined by the dynamic she wishes to highlight. And retroactively, Joyce's statement at the beginning of the paragraph – which seems to *understand* something about the matriarchal space distinct from patriarchal time Kristeva theorizes – becomes a prescient articulation of this dynamic, of a force powerful enough to "defy metaphysics." Kristeva's characteristically dense synthesis (encompassing everything from literary figures to psychoanalytic observations to imposingly grand philosophical claims) is part of what makes her theory itself seem so broadly quotable and apt, indeed so profound.

Of course, critics regularly put quotations to work in this way; there is nothing remarkable about the gesture in its own right. Given her own assertions about intertextuality (and Joyce), however, the dense constellation of reference around Kristeva's initial citation of Joyce makes this particular instance worth mapping. Not only does it serve the express topic of the essay, "women's time," it also engenders a set of associations with Kristeva's larger body of work (on Freud, subject formation, signification, Plato, and the *chora*); so too does the very act of citing Joyce as someone who "puts it" particularly well call up (and reestablish) the authoritative place Joyce occupies in her literary theory.

But most remarkably, the Joycean citation does not, strictly speaking, actually cite Joyce. We might detect such a referential skewing in the fact that Joyce's supposed phrase "Father's time, mother's species" does *not* so very aptly provide the terms Kristeva ascribes to it – namely, time and space. She draws "space" ("one thinks more of the *space* generating") from "species," while simultaneously retaining "species" ("and forming the human species"). According to the accepted code for reading Joyce's portmanteau words, deriving a double meaning by means of a slight translation is not unjustifiable. But Kristeva nevertheless treats the translation, from "species" to "space," as a given.[37] It turns out, in this case, that Kristeva likely has other reasons for reading the word in this way, beyond the usual allowances for Joyce's multiply referential portmanteaus.

That is to say, Kristeva indeed has a clear reason for associating Joyce's supposed statement with "space." But what chiefly authorizes Kristeva's reading is a set of associations all but invisible on the pages of the essay itself. For if one goes looking for "Father's time, mother's species" in Joyce's *oeuvre*, it is not to be found. The phrase, in that specific form, does appear, but in another language, in another form. Philippe Sollers's highly Joycean novel *Lois* (1972) mulls over and chews up bits of *Finnegans Wake* throughout. The beginning of his second chapter contains, in the midst of a dizzying wordplay about fathers and mothers, what Geert Lernout supposes is a "mangled version" of a Joycean phrase: "pépé-durée de mèrespacée" (Lernout, *The French Joyce*, p. 166; *Lois*, p. 41).[38] Sollers's "mèrespacée" indicates what Kristeva's "mother's species" does not: a linguistic connection to the notion of "space." And that connection leads back to what is indeed Joyce's original phrase in *Finnegans Wake*, which is different from what Kristeva purports to take from Joyce: "Father Times and Mother Spacies" (*Finnegans Wake*, 600.2–3). This statement occurs in Book IV of *Finnegans Wake*, the final chapter of the book, that which Sollers translated in 1973 for the pages of *Tel Quel*. Book IV begins with the words "Sandyhas! Sandyhas! Sandyhas!" (593.1). Sollers's *Lois* includes those same three words in that same form on the first page of chapter 2, a few sentences from his "mangled" quotation of Joyce's "Father Times and Mother Spacies."

Given this textual web and Kristeva's domestic proximity to it (as Sollers' wife), her supposed citation of Joyce in "Women's Time" is far more likely, or more precisely, a translated citation of Sollers's translated citation of Joyce. Ironically, while the phrase appears nowhere in Joyce in the form Kristeva gives, it does reappear as such in the autobiography of Maria-Antonietta Macciocchi, a student of Sollers who writes in detail about the French intellectual culture of the 1970s and the 1980s and about Sollers's central role within it.[39] As Lernout points out, Macchiocchi revives this phrase (in English) in her conclusion, as she reflects on "the role that time and space have played in her life" (Lernout, *The French Joyce*, p. 166). She writes: "the key to all that may be in what Joyce said: '*Father's time, mother's species*' " (587).

Probably unwittingly, Macciocchi helpfully completes an intertextual circle. Claiming to cite Joyce while reflecting on her experience in the French intellectual scene, she more precisely quotes Kristeva's purported citation of Joyce. Yet it is likely that both are, in fact, citing (and re-translating) a version of Sollers's translated citation of Joyce. Macchiocchi demonstrates, by means of her own weirdly refracted citation, the diffusely solar influence that Sollers's Joyce seems to have had in French intellectual culture – which in turn sheds light on Kristeva's own interest in Joyce.

Identification, transubstantiation, and love

Because it represents the most sustained commentary on Joyce Kristeva has ever given, "Joyce the 'Gracehoper,' or Orpheus' Return," a featured lecture at the 1984 International James Joyce Symposium in Frankfurt (subsequently included in her *New Maladies of the Soul*, 1995) plays out these dynamics on an exponentially more complex scale than any of the isolated references we have surveyed so far. Most prominently, it represents another stage in the shifting emblematic function of "Joyce" throughout Kristeva's career. We can still see basic elements of her previous claims – that Joyce's language works by means of shifting signifiers and multiple referentiality; that his writing exists in an "other" tradition of literature; that he writes from the position of exile and (religious) dissident; that he "embodies" feminine sexuality through Molly, and so on.

But distinctively new preoccupations come to the fore as well; and so does her deep, if unacknowledged, conversation with Sollers's similarly evolving reading of Joyce. Finally, the very occasion of Kristeva's lecture draws up associations: she and Jacques Derrida were both featured speakers at the event, and both delivered their essays in French (Derrida's "Deux mots pour Joyce" lasted two hours) to the largely English- and German-speaking audiences. Clearly, echoes of the 1975 Paris conference – where Lacan, Sollers, and others staged a noisy intervention into Joyce studies – were stirred by Kristeva's and Derrida's presence; indeed, Bernard Benstock explicitly thematizes the return of the "French Joyce" in his introduction to the published proceedings of the conference.[40]

Kristeva's elliptical references to the notion of Joyce as a "Saint Homme" (which she goes on to reject) and his writing as "symptom" (which she more subtly endorses) indicate that she too acknowledged the occasional significance of her remarks, and some of the associations they were likely to bring up. For both concepts had been featured in Lacan's keynote address, entitled "Joyce the Symbol," at the 1975 Symposium the impact of which Jean-Michel Rabaté vividly recounts in *Jacques Lacan: Psychoanalysis and the Subject of Literature* (2001):

> I was present when Lacan gave his memorable speech at the Sorbonne, and could not help feeling some unease in the face of Lacan's mixture of brilliant insights and trite biographical explanations. It took me years to disentangle the remarkably original readings from a groping and fumbling approach […]. One can say on the whole that Lacan decided early on to play the role of the uninitiated reader, distinguishing his approach as that of a psychoanalyst from that of all the specialists who thrive on Joyce in the universities. (159)

In a number of ways, Rabaté's characterizations of Lacan's address are apt for Kristeva's as well. The most apparent of these is the "uncomfortable" mixture of provocative theory with what Rabaté regretfully calls "trite biographical explanations." Throughout the essay, Kristeva not only makes fairly absolute links between Joyce's personal life and his texts, but also asserts that the appearance of certain themes in his texts reflects clear "aware[ness]," even "obsession[s]" – claims that often seem like blatant, if not naïve, deployments of the intentional fallacy (*New Maladies of the Soul*, pp. 175, 174). We will address these, and their implications, below; they warrant criticism, especially given Kristeva's repeated invocation of Joyce's texts as exemplary models of a radical intertextuality in which such biographical links to an author are rendered suspect, the relics of an outmoded criticism Kristeva claims to move beyond.

More subtly, Kristeva situates herself among the Joyceans she addresses, and proceeds in a manner that bears rhetorical and methodological similarities to Lacan's address a decade earlier. She too begins by announcing a certain inadequacy to the task at hand: "We all know that any attempt to speak about Joyce proves to be difficult, absurd, disappointing" (172). But she, unlike Lacan, does not admit to being a novice or an outsider to Joyce criticism; or rather she does so only for the sake of distancing herself from a literary criticism ("or what is left of it") "reluctant" to read literature as a site for the psychoanalytic dynamics she wishes to privilege (172). That is to say, like Lacan, Kristeva very much presents herself as a psychoanalyst reading a literary text (*Ulysses*) and the presumed motivations of an author (Joyce) in light of the complex workings of unconscious functions: "intrapsychic identification" (174), "the return of the repressed" (174), the maintenance of "psychic space" through literary expression (175), "the secret of femininity" (176), the two "amorous" logics of "eros and agape" (173, 177), "verbal [and] trans- or preverbal" representation (177), and others as well.

The critical focus *feels* different here. Kristeva does not present her argument as an analysis of literary language, as her long history of references to Joyce might lead us to expect. Obviously, her claim that literary expression is a privileged way of coping with and articulating the struggles of being invokes a long-standing and fundamental feature of her theory of literature, as do her references to the "trans- or preverbal" elements of Joyce's language. But Kristeva largely subordinates these to concepts *not* specific to a theory of how to read literature, how literary language functions, or what role literature plays as a discourse among others in the culture at large.

My assessment requires explanation, for it would be easy to counter that indeed this is the most detailed literary analysis of Joyce Kristeva has ever offered, with a lengthy discussion of the "Scylla and Charybdis" episode in *Ulysses,* in which Stephen Dedalus presents his own literary analysis of Shakespeare's *Hamlet.* One could also counter that Kristeva – by looking at Joyce's religious thematics – highlights exciting new connections between metaphor and the psychic workings of transference, and furthermore that this theory of metaphor, in *Time and Sense,* plays an especially central role in Kristeva's most sustained literary analysis to date. What I mean to suggest is that "Joyce the 'Gracehoper,' " like so many of Kristeva's comments about Joyce's texts, says at least as much, if not more, about a certain moment in her own theoretical trajectory as it does about Joyce.

More than a reading of *Ulysses,* the essay provides a re-articulation of *Tales of Love,* Kristeva's magisterial meditation on Freudian transference, identification, metaphor, and the history of "*love* as a discourse" (specifically, *Eros* and *Agape*) throughout Western discourse (*Tales of Love,* p. 31). It also foregrounds "the Catholic element" in Joyce, as it plays itself out in the thematics of the trinity, the Eucharist, and transubstantiation – an element that Kristeva, like Sollers, had come to deem "the heart of the question" when it comes to reading Joyce.[41]

Tales of Love is widely regarded as the second installment in the trilogy of major works Kristeva produced in the 1980s, highly psychoanalytic explorations of the "borderline discourses" of abjection, love, and melancholia – which underpin not only the human subject, but also the cultural institutions subjects have created. Like *Powers of Horror* and *Black Sun*, the works that come before and after it, *Tales of Love* draws heavily from Freud's pioneering speculations on each topic; in this instance, Freud's attention to the role of *transference* in the analytic situation provides a paradigmatic structure for Kristeva's study, which ranges from Plato, Aristotle, and Aquinas to an experience of subjective desire she finds uniquely at work in the contemporary struggles of the subject (her own patients, specifically). As do abjection and melancholia, love occasions a subjective crisis in which a discernible, stable object evanesces, and in which, thus, an unstable relationship between subject and object comes into play.

Closely recalling the compelling descriptions of abjection in the opening chapter of *Powers of Horror*, both in style and substance, the first chapter of *Tales of Love* describes another condition that paradoxically mingles pleasure and pain and pushes the subject to its limits: "I am, in love, at the zenith of my subjectivity" (6). In Chapter 2, we noted that Freud makes a similar observation about the strange identificatory experience of love in *Civilization and Its Discontents*, calling it one of the moments in subjective life where the clear borders between self and other break down. Curiously, Kristeva's own description of the psychic impact of such a phenomenon does not acknowledge Freud's account. Instead, she seems to draw her models from aesthetic discourse, though not avowedly so. In its violent conjunction of opposite affects, Kristeva links the experience of love to the sublime, a connection that has indeed been asserted for millennia.

In probably *the* founding text on sublimity, Longinus (*not* a figure who appears in Kristeva's study, while less likely ancients do), cites as his first example of sublime discourse the poetry of Sappho, in particular a poem in which she describes passionate love as a kind of bodily dissolution, an exquisite pain that exposes the lover to an extreme barely distinguishable from near-death. Similarly, in Kristeva's rendering, love brings us to a "fragile crest where death and regeneration vie for dominance" (6). Her poetic descriptions of such love echo, almost image for image, the Sappho poem Longinus rapturously admires. Enviously praising the man who holds the affections of the woman Sappho's speaker loves, she says: "When I see you only for a moment, I cannot speak; / my tongue is broken, a subtle fire runs under my skin; my eyes cannot see, my ears hum; / cold sweat pours off me."[42]

Similarly, Kristeva speaks of

> A body swept away, present in all its limbs through a delightful absence – shaky voice, dry throat, starry eyes, flushed or clammy skin, throbbing heart ... Would the symptoms of love be the symptoms of fear? Both a fear and a need of no longer being limited, held back, but going beyond. Dread of transgressing not only proprieties or taboos, but also, and above all, fear of crossing and desire to cross the boundaries of the self. (7)

Longinus praises Sappho's description of near-death bodily dissolution as a triumph of poetic organic unity; while Kristeva eschews the notion of such unity, whether poetic or psychic, Kristeva too sees powerful *linguistic* or *discursive* potential in amatory experience of this kind.

For her, Freud most profoundly realized this potential in the psychoanalytic relationship between analyst and patient. "First among the moderns," she writes, "Sigmund Freud [...] thought of turning love into a cure" (8). Furthermore, he recognized "the disorder that love reveals (rather than induces) in the speaking being" (8). The "talking cure" of psychoanalysis exploits this condition of the speaking being by precisely acknowledging the ways in which therapy (the speaking interactions between analyst and analysand) are indeed predicated on establishing a relationship that is not unlike "love," so defined.

Freud calls this phenomenon *transference*. A situation in which the analysand imagines a relationship with the analyst that bears the markers of love, or "amatory identification," transference depends in fact upon a complex logic of associations and displacements. It is a dynamic that the analyst must recognize ("and if he forgets it he dooms himself not to perform an analysis"), but *not* because it is an unavoidably unwelcome side-effect of the intense affections analytic trust and compassion are likely to elicit (13). Rather, it signals a more fundamental process of meaning-making within the unconscious, related to the "displacement of meaning and intensity" Freud outlines in *The Interpretation of Dreams* (343). Just as, in dreams, elements appear in a way that "displaces" their true meaning or significance for the dreaming subject – a dream about buying salmon may not be about salmon at all, to crudely summarize one of Freud's brilliant dream interpretations – so too, in analysis, does the analysand "displace" all kinds of feelings on to the person of the analyst himself. Kristeva calls this latter form "[a]nalysis love."[43]

Kristeva gives detailed attention to Freud's concept of transference, noting its earliest associations with dream logic and its evolution into a theory of the identificatory relationships that develop in the analytic situation. She notes that the two transferences, in Freud's theoretical trajectory, are not identical: "one [in the dreamwork] is a matter of *logic,* there is a play between the meanings of words; the other [in analysis love] is *economic,* it displaces love upon a stranger who is only a stand-in" (13; emphasis Kristeva's).

By beginning her outline of transference with Freud's earliest understanding of the term (tied to the logic of the dreamwork), she underscores an aspect of Freud's dream analysis that subsequent theorists – Lacan and Kristeva chief among them – have considered central: namely, that condensation, displacement, representability, puns, and censorship essentially operate figuratively, like a language. Following Freud, Kristeva points out that transference or distortion depends upon a logic of substitution, where a signifier is wrested from its "normal" referential relationship to a signified and made to point elsewhere. Put simply, *transference acts like metaphor.*

While she distinguishes Freud's "logical" description of transference from the "economic" one that he applies to the workings of transference love, she also emphatically keeps in circulation the constellation of similarities between them. In the two versions of transference, a similar significatory structure nevertheless organizes both. In both cases, meaning *travels,* signifiers *shift,* and an indirect series of substitutive *identifications* come to define the people and ideas involved. In *analysis* love, the dynamic involves

> three people: the *subject* (the analysand), his imaginary or real *object* of love (the other with whom what is being played out is the whole interusbjective drama of neurosis or, in more severe cases, of the disintegration of identity leading to psychosis), and the *Third Party,* the stand-in for potential Ideal, possible Power. The analyst occupies that place of the *Other.* (13)

Befitting Lacan's and Kristeva's long-standing assumption that the unconscious can be read as a language, the linguistic implications of this argument are undeniable: transference, in both cases, acts out a drama of meaning, fundamentally discursive. And in this sense, this drama of meaning is also, at the same time and inextricably, a drama of subjective crisis as such. Transference "suggests that the Province of Meaning is no longer held within a strictly referential univocity" – a lesson of so many poststructural studies of language, literature, philosophy, and the self (14). Kristeva's capital letters – "the Province of Meaning" – signal that the stakes here are high and the implications far-reaching.

The borders of any such "Province" – or rather the presumption that such a "place" exists – come under threat with Kristeva's critique, but primarily because she announces that transference itself threatens the borders of "referential univocity." We have seen these gestures, and explored similar dynamics, throughout Kristeva's work. *Powers of Horror* and her other works have prepared us for the broader set of associations she will bring to the study of transference love so defined: "it ushers in that passion of signs exemplified by free association, displacement, condensation, and so forth, [...] as disturbing and intense as the cathartic effects of great art" (14). The "passion of signs" played out in love, in the complex psychic work love represents, is part of the motor force that generates art. Like the complementary (if opposite) phenonemenon of abjection, "amorous and/or transference discourse [amounts] to a permanent stabilization–destabilization between the *symbolic* [and] the *semiotic*" (16).

Without too much oversimplification, we could say that we have once again, with love, a powerful borderline discourse that has spanned history and finds expression in the furthest reaches of religion, philosophy, literature, but also in the fundamental "*experience of the speaking being*" (17; emphasis Kristeva's). From the very earliest, pre-Oedipal associations of self with other, these dynamics begin to play themselves out. Again, this "experience" is fundamentally fraught, incomplete, founded on an "emptiness, which is at the root of the human psyche" (23).[44] As she has asserted from *Revolution in Poetic Language* to *Powers of Horror*, literature remains one of the privileged signifiers, or rather privileged domains, for articulating that emptiness in a way that is cathartic, productive. It is not, she argues, "a matter of filling [the subject's] 'crisis' – his emptiness – with meaning" (380). Rather, art, like analysis, allows articulations of one's supposed "own proper self" that are provisional, contingent, so-to-speak, "floating, empty at times, inauthentic, obviously lying" (380).

At the end of *Tales of Love*, she writes provocatively of its almost Utopian power, recalling the last pages of *Powers of Horror* in both tone and vision:

> I speak in favor of imagination as an antidote for the crisis. Not in favor of "power to the imagination," which is the rallying cry of perverts longing for the law. But in favor of saturating powers and counterpowers with imaginary constructions – phantasmatic, daring, violent, critical,

> demanding, shy ... Let them speak [...] Imagination succeeds where the narcissist becomes hollowed out and the paranoid fails. (381)

Kristeva's style and meaning here might be confounding if we were not already so familiar with the foundations on which she makes such claims. The notion of literature (among other marginal discourses) as an expression of continual "work in progress," of the *sujet-en-procès,* as we have seen, persists as a dominant theme throughout Kristeva's career.

The argument and focus of *Tales of Love* pervades Kristeva's Frankfurt address on Joyce. Without at least this cursory understanding of her interest in transference as a psychoanalytic concept with linguistic and literary implications, without the specific definition of "love" understood precisely within that theoretical context, the argument of "Joyce the 'Gracehoper' " remains quite opaque. When she opens by considering the "symptom" she accuses other literary critics of ignoring in Joyce, we can – in light of *Tales of Love* – read that to mean the symptom of the subject's "emptiness" within the "uncanny adventure of human meaning" ("Gracehoper," p. 173). The symptom also refers to the psychoanalytic decentered subject more generally, the one who – recalling Lacan's mirror stage – is fundamentally incomplete, defined by a series of identifications (between self and other) that are always unstable, illusory, grounded in discrepancy and lack. Here, she glosses this psychoanalytic context telescopically: "my entire psychic experience consists of failed identifications" (177).

The special privilege she grants Joyce throughout her address derives specifically from the unique ability he apparently had to analyze "the *symptom* of writing within its intrapsychic dimension, which is contingent upon the speaking being's capacity to *identify* with an aspect or feature of another subject or object" (173; emphasis Kristeva's). Joyce seems to know this condition and act it out in his texts' themes and characterizations: "Joyce is the author who possesses the daunting advantage of having mirrored, experienced, and revealed the inner workings of identification, which governs the evolution of the imaginary, that is fiction" (173).

Putting aside the somewhat startling intentionality she grants to Joyce here (as in "Father, Love, and Banishment," he manages to become somehow more Freudian than Freud), we can see that she means to posit Joyce as an exemplar of the specific psychic dynamics that dominate her work at the time. This statement also sets the tone, and implies the method, of the literary analysis to follow. In giving dominant focus to the psychoanalytic dynamic she sees Joyce playing out, Kristeva abandons the close, rhetorical focus she insisted upon with regard to Céline – that is, to style and meaning acted out jointly in "the rhythm of the sentence," as Nietzsche puts it (*Powers of Horror*, p. 133). Her analysis of Joyce's interest in "transubstantiation" and how that interest manifests itself in Stephen's theory of *Hamlet* (dramatized in the "Scylla and Charybdis" chapter of *Ulysses*) is largely thematic.[45]

It is also, at moments, expressly biographical and, in a way quite distinct from Kristeva's earlier preoccupations with Joyce, emphatically concerned with religion. Without overly asserting a crude "source-study" or biographical referent to explain this focus, I would point out that Philippe Sollers's 1980 interview "La Trinité de Joyce" must have been second only to *Tales of Love* as a motivation for Kristeva's comments in "Gracehoper." Lernout chronicles Sollers's own flamboyant turn to Catholicism around this same time, and the "Trinité" interview clearly shows that Sollers extended that interest to his reading of Joyce. Nearly every one of Kristeva's examples (including those I study below) occur in the Sollers text as well. After her initial claim about the pertinence of Joyce's works to the study of identification, Kristeva draws attention to "Joyce's Catholicism, which consisted of his profound experience with Trinitarian religion as well as his mockery of it" (173). Of course, regardless of Sollers's interests, or their influence on Kristeva's, Joyce's own "Catholicism" is a fairly uncontroversial fact. Somewhat more self-serving is the importance Kristeva attaches to it, as in her subsequent claim that it "impelled him to contemplate" the Eucharist.

Indeed, there are a number of well-studied invocations of this ritual in Joyce – most notably, Buck Mulligan's mocking first words in *Ulysses*. But for Kristeva, Joyce's references mean that he thought through the Eucharist, and by extension transubstantiation, in precisely the terms her existing theoretical models have set up: "the ritual par excellence of identification with God's body and a springboard for all other identifications, including that of artistic profusion" (173–4). That Joyce's texts do not merely provide a felicitous site for exploring these concepts, particularly the links between the religious logic of the ritual and the psychodynamics of identification, but, more strangely, *do* Kristeva's theoretical work *before* her, comes across in the biographical speculation that follows:

> It is likely that the cultural context of Catholicism – which Joyce had completely assimilated – was challenged by a biographical event that

> endangered his identity and enabled him to focus his writing on the identificatory substratum of psychic functioning, which he so masterfully laid out against the backdrop of the grandest religion. (174)

In a similarly biographical vein, Kristeva proceeds to explore Joyce's "obsession" with the Eucharist theme, for which she gives a handful of loose textual examples.

She cites, for instance, a single word (which Sollers also cites) – "contransmagnificandjewbangtantiality" – that arises in the "Proteus" chapter of *Ulysses*, while Stephen walks on Sandymount Strand, contemplating abstract philosophies, his own role as an artist, as well as more mundane concerns. In its narrative context, Stephen is thinking about his own dead mother, while he also wonders, skeptically, about "the divine substance wherein Father and Son are consubstantial?" (3.49–50). Surely, the ideas of fathers and sons, Stephen as son, Stephen as literary son to the tradition he also contemplates in these very pages, the libidinal and the cerebral self, and so many more, circulate around this passage. And Kristeva is right to draw associations with the Trinity and transubstantiation from "Joyce's umbrella word," but to call it an "obsession" of Joyce's (a term she uses more than once) pointedly takes the claim beyond a reading of the text itself, and in fact ignores much of the narrative context – indeed the deeply overdetermined irony – in which so many of Stephen's meditations take place.

Kristeva links this word to another, more narratively developed, exploration of the idea of transubstantiation: "the consubstantiality between father and son in Shakespeare's *Hamlet* and between Shakespeare, his father, [and] his son Hamnet" (174). This set of associations refers us to a famous episode in *Ulysses* in which Stephen Dedalus gives a highly idiosyncratic – and dubiously biographical – analysis of *Hamlet*, one it is not absolutely clear he entirely believes. Joyce sets up his readers to be skeptical of this "interpretation" from the beginning of the novel, where Stephen's irreverent roommate, Buck Mulligan, summarizes the argument as follows: "He proves by algebra that Hamlet's grandson is Shakespeare's grandfather and that he himself is the ghost of his own father" (1.555–7).

But Kristeva treats the argument quite gravely, perhaps because it does give such fertile ground to the intersecting ideas of literary production (wherein an author "identifies" with a character in complex ways) and familial love (Hamlet's and Shakespeare's own). She prefaces one long passage from Stephen's theorizing, by telling us that "*Joyce patiently traces* the equivalence between the dead father, Shakespeare the author, and his artistic transmutation that leads from being a 'spectre' to being his own son – the text" (182; emphasis mine). Kristeva then extensively quotes Stephen's somewhat pretentious rhetorical questions and energetic over-associations, which read like mad metaphorizings, too many equivalents and substitutions:

> To a son he speaks, the son of his soul, the prince, young Hamlet and to the son of his body, Hamnet Shakespear, who has died in Stratford that his namesake may live forever.
>
> – Is it possible that that player Shakespeare, a ghost by absence, and in the vesture of buried Denmark, a ghost by death, speaking his own words to his own son's name (had Hamnet Shakespeare lived he would have been prince Hamlet's twin) is it possible, I want to know, or probable that he did not draw or foresee the son: I am the murdered father: your mother is the guilty queen. Ann Shakespeare, born Hathaway. (Joyce, quoted by Kristeva, pp. 182–3)

Yet Kristeva does not follow up this densely baffling "algebra" with an explanation, much less a textual analysis. Rather, she follows with a theoretical assertion about the passage that, seemingly unwittingly, matches Stephen's own abstruseness, concatenating an intricate weave of her own concerns that bear little ostensible connection to the passage from Joyce:

> The father dies so that the son might live; the son dies so that the father might be embodied in his work and transformed into his own son. In this "Dedalan" maze, we must search for the woman. The Christian agape of transubstantiation was in opposition with Greek eros. (183)

Kristeva continues for another paragraph and a half in this vein, drawing together an entire history by way of references to Plato, psychoanalytic development narratives, narcissism, imagination, sacrifice, and even "transposition" (which we can recall as another term for intertextuality). Yet these associations are left floating, without synthesis, without an indication of how they collectively comment on the Joycean text she has just quoted.

Almost mockingly, she concludes: "To sum up, identification, understood as a heterogeneous transference (body and meaning, metaphor and mystic metamorphosis) onto the realm of the father, begins by placing me in improbability and uncertainty – that is, in meaning" (183–4). It is not at all clear what Kristeva has indeed summed up, but somehow we return to the terms from *Tales of Love* with which we began – transference and metaphor, uncertain subjectivity and the struggle for meaning. Her own loosely associative prose puts us, as readers (or, originally, as listeners) in that precarious "uncertainty" ourselves. Unfortunately, whereas I read such performative effects as highly strategic and meticulous in much of Kristeva's work – in *Powers of Horror*, for instance – here they seem merely sloppy.

We begin this chapter by looking at Kristeva's recent interview with Margaret Waller, where she asserts the necessity of reading Joyce intertextually, observing that his texts demand such reading. Yet she seems to forget much of the practical thrust behind that imperative in this reading of Joyce. What she does retain is the notion of textuality as a complex "dialogue" of subjectivities, intersubjectivities, where the "subject" of the author is disseminated across the pages of his texts in the myriad subjectivities his fictions create. Certainly, this loosely understood dialogism underwrites Kristeva's links between the "person" of Joyce and his characters (as she has done in a number of works where she refers to Joyce's remarkable "incarnation" of Molly in the final chapter of *Ulysses*). But I don't believe she ever clearly works out the implications of such a claim, and in practice they can appear simplistically biographical and thematic. She quotes long passages from Stephen's Shakespeare theory, which is more than Kristeva usually gives us from Joyce. But even the way she introduces and frames the passages suggests a disappointing lack of attention to context, to the simple matter of *who's speaking*.

A number of complicating factors make Kristeva's reading of "Scylla and Charybdis" quite problematic, if interestingly so. Ironically, her argument relies to a large extent on a presumed biographical continuum between the man and his works, between Joyce "himself," that is, and the "life" and words of his characters – ironically, because this presumption drives Stephen's own argument about Shakespeare. The notion that Joyce merely endorses Stephen's theory is undermined in a number of fairly obvious ways throughout "Scylla and Charybdis" and beyond, a fact Kristeva would have to concede had she given any substantive consideration to the context of Stephen's utterances. To use her own terminology, Stephen's statements are at once dialogic and intertextual, in both simple and complex ways. Narratively speaking, Stephen's argument occurs within an intellectual conversation involving several people, most of whom regard his argument with skepticism if not outright derision; and it takes place within the walls of a library alive with the ghosts of the literary past. That is to say, the conversation alludes to Shakespeare, but also to Mallarmé and Swinburne, as well as to the literary scene of contemporary Dublin – which, not incidentally, conspicuously excludes Stephen.

In its entirety, the fictionally framed Shakespearean theory perhaps most urgently references Oscar Wilde's equally slippery "Portrait of Mr. W. H." In fact, one of Stephen's interlocutors explicitly cites Wilde's strange piece (a fairly bad literary "analysis" framed by a story about bad critics) as a dazzling example of willful, self-identifying Shakespeare criticism. "Has no-one made him out to be an Irishman?" John Englinton asks dubiously as Stephen begins his argument (9.519–20). Joyce implies an ironic frame for the discussion that will take place, and draws attention to its context within the "story" of *Ulysses* itself, when Mr. Best says: "The most brilliant of all is that story of Wilde's [...] That *Portrait of Mr. W. H.* where he proves that the sonnets were written by a Willie Hughes, a man of all hues" (9.522–4). Both texts, Wilde's and Joyce's, offer their protagonists' analysis as both superficially plausible and fundamentally insupportable. In Stephen's case, even he doesn't quite believe what he says.

In the case of Wilde's fictional critic, the cost of an overly self-interested theory lacking evidence is death: the inventor of the Shakespeare theory forges a picture as "evidence," then kills himself. The consequences of Kristeva's argument, offered as a featured presentation at an international conference populated by participants likely to be both supportive of fellow readers and cognizant of Kristeva's authoritative theoretical status, would hardly be so dire. Yet it is remarkable that Kristeva's and Stephen's arguments rely on a set of similar critical moves. Given the long history of Kristeva's participation in a theory of textuality that so incisively critiques our unexamined assumptions about authors, textual utterances, their sources and echoes of other texts, and our own implication in the great intertextual dialogue they engender, her most "complete" reading of Joyce to date strikes a strange chord.

Ultimately, I believe it leaves us with usefully cautionary questions about the juxtaposition posed by this book from the start: what is the relationship between Julia Kristeva and literary theory? Does she offer one? If so, how can we produce one in kind? What I hope to convey, even in the final confusing light of the "Gracehoper" essay, is that those questions need constantly to be asked, their answers never taken for granted. While Kristeva herself has for decades profoundly asked those questions, where she does not, we must ask them for her.

What does it matter who's speaking?

In "The Death of the Author," Roland Barthes bases his provocative vision of a new type of reading on the very practical fact that, in the Balzac passage he quotes at the essay's outset, *we cannot tell* who is speaking. As we have explored, this "death of the author" ushers "the birth of the reader," who must navigate texts in the midst of this uncertainty, vigilantly attentive to it. Michel Foucault directly responds to Barthes's essay with a provocative essay of his own, "What is an Author?" He argues that Barthes's declarations do not settle the matter, particularly when it comes to the actual practice – personal and institutional – of reading texts. To say the author is dead, Foucault argues, does not obviate us from knowing what we mean when we talk about the author, or the reader for that matter, or even what we're doing with the texts that have affixed to them an author's name.

To make this point, he cites an intriguing, characteristically cryptic, statement from Samuel Beckett – which I myself cite in the epigraph to this chapter: " 'What does it matter who is speaking,' someone said, 'what does it matter who is speaking.' " The status of the citation in Foucault's argument remains somewhat ambiguous; there are indications that he cites it as an emblematic pose, rendering the question outmoded, as if it *does not* matter. In his conclusion, he suggests another connotation to the question as well. He can envision an era of the future, where different terms hold sway. Foucault acknowledges that, "In saying this, I seem to call for a form of culture in which fiction would not be limited by the figure of the author" (119). Under some new system, not accidentally resembling Foucault's own theoretical vision:

> We would no longer hear the questions that have been rehashed for so long: Who really spoke? Is it really he and not someone else? With what authenticity or originality? And what part of his deepest self did he express in his discourse? Instead, there would be other questions, like these: What are the modes of existence of this discourse? Where has it been used, how can it circulate, and who can appropriate it for himself? What are the places in it where there is room for possible subjects? Who can assume these various subject functions? (119–20)

In its messianic tone, Foucault's statement here resembles many of Kristeva's own visionary conceptions of an infinite intertextuality, imbricated by an equally infinite set of intersubjectivities. Her "Gracehoper" essay, while at best an incomplete project of exploring such concepts with regard to Joyce, demonstrates the continued potential for new readings guided by the provocative set of questions her own theory poses. But Foucault cleverly draws himself up short at the end of "What is an Author?" Following this set of questions for a future theory of reading, a nagging voice remains: "And behind all these questions, we would hear hardly anything but the stirring of an indifference: What difference does it make who is speaking?" (120).

Beckett's question returns, if it is in fact Beckett's question: Foucault doesn't tell us where it comes from, who speaks those words in what play, though the double quotation suggests that it is the statement of a character. With the question lingering the way it does at the end of his essay, Foucault's answer, how he would have us read the answer, remains unspoken. We could take it two ways, I believe, and the two ways make a difference. "What difference does it make who is speaking?" in the first sense has too often been (mis)taken as the slogan of a blithe, relativistic poststructuralist theory that doesn't give a damn what the difference is. In Kristeva's most difficult, most sweeping readings, she arguably asserts as much herself: Stephen and Joyce, Ferdinand and Céline, what difference does it make? But Foucault leaves room for another reading as well: *it makes all the difference*, precisely when (and because) it is so hard to tell.

Practically speaking, we can translate this to mean it *matters* how carefully we read, how assiduously we assign context or agency to the utterance of a character, and author, or a critic. The complex condition of intertextuality that puts all such determinations in infinite regress does not absolve the reader from knowing (or trying to know) the difference – between author and character, between an original assertion and a quotation of another, and so on. Rather, it raises the stakes of those determinations, ideally putting the careful reader in a state of constant attentiveness, even if impossibly so.

It makes a difference, for instance, to notice that not only Foucault's urgent questions about the future of reading in the face of an infinitely complex textuality, but Barthes's and Kristeva's own questions as well, find a curious voice in a prior text, written by a quietly devastating theorist none of them cite. Before "The Death of the Author," "What is an Author?" and any of Kristeva's numerous meditations, Maurice Blanchot wrote an essay on Samuel Beckett, "Where Now? Who Now?" (1959), that anticipates every one of these theorists' fundamental claims about the nature of textuality and the conditions of reading. In the essay (collected in a book suggestively titled *Le Livre à venir*),

Blanchot begins by asking what now seems like a very familiar question: "Who speaks in Samuel Beckett's books?"[46] He ends with a long quotation from Beckett's *The Unnameable*, reading in it an indication of what makes the "artistic" exploration of "origins," the persistent questions of who speaks and from where, "such a risky undertaking – both for the artist and for art" (198). The persistent questions of who speaks and from where in Beckett's books take us to the "point where language ceases to speak but is, where nothing begins, nothing is said, but where language is always reborn and always starts afresh" (197). But for Blanchot, the linguistic conditions that make "artistic creation" risky are also precisely what make it important. As Kristeva's own explorations so powerfully suggest, even when they fall short, the same risks and rewards attend the work of the critic.

5 Wordsworth's Tales of Love

Poststructuralism's "other Wordsworth"

William Wordsworth is a poet about whom Julia Kristeva never has written, and probably never would. He is English, Romantic, an avowedly plain-spoken "man writing to men," writing a poetry that aspires to the prosaic, that devotes itself to representing the extraordinary within the commonplace – the contemplative profundity the "meanest flower" can evoke, the lessons learned by a poignant encounter with a leech gatherer or a little girl, the mundane marvels of a rural tourist's trip to teeming London. Wordsworth offers the very opposite, we might say, of Céline, whose explosive prose utters in "poetic" cadences the horror of extreme experience, of madness, brutality, and war; or, for that matter, of Joyce, who rendered even an everyman's banal errand or a trip to the pub in the most unmistakably challenging language and style English literature had ever seen. Wordsworth's piety and earnestness decidedly disqualify him from inclusion in the irreverently ironic Menippean tradition, which, we might gather from Kristeva's and Bakhtin's accounts, apparently skips his generation. Wordsworth, in other words, is precisely not avant-garde. *His* "revolution" in poetic language sought to overthrow a much different literary and social regime (the elite, mannered wit of the eighteenth century) than the one against which Kristeva's literary heroes battled. Indeed, Wordsworth's brand of idealized liberal humanism serves as the central target of the radical campaign Kristeva's theory studies but also wages.

Or so it would seem. For of course, to characterize Wordsworth this way means subscribing to a version of his work and his poetic project he may himself underwrite – most famously in the "Preface" to *Lyrical Ballads* – but nevertheless remarkably *contradicts* in poetry subtly veiled by linguistic, stylistic, and even thematic unremarkability. From within the supposedly reassuring domesticity of Wordsworth's poetry and in spite of domesticating critical assessments of the quiet, stately Lake poet, another picture emerges. In "Wordsworth and the Victorians," Paul de Man notably adumbrates this *other* Wordsworth, a poet who explores the "ever-threatening undoing" of consciousness in a language, and through an epistemology, far more radical than it looks.[1] De Man wryly concedes that he understands why Wordsworth has been associated with stoical matter-of-factness and pious reassurance, and why he has attracted noteworthy parodists, for Wordsworth has indeed "produced some of the flattest lines of which the English language is capable" (87). Nevertheless, he finds a "daring" and "risk" to Wordsworth's verse in spite of such risible flatness, a "danger[ous]" poetic engagement that makes his work urgently germane to the central questions of linguistic signification, reference, and constructions of subjectivity in contemporary theory.[2]

We can see this other Wordsworth clearly in "passages that are so radically unpredictable, so audacious in the sparseness of their means" that they resist literary historical classification or even precedent (87). What is harder to see, and thus what de Man would have us see, is that this other, stranger Wordsworth dwells uncannily within that familiar, domestic and domesticated, Victorian Wordsworth: "All remains implicit, inward, sheltered within the unsuspected nuances of common speech" (87).

In conversation and sometimes at odds with Paul de Man, Geoffrey Hartman offers a similar critical re-evaluation in *The Unremarkable Wordsworth*, whose main conceit I have just borrowed, by arguing that the "curious vigor of Wordsworth's clichés (or unremarkable phrases) remains to be explored" (211). Hartman's own understatement in that call glosses an energetic mobilization in critical theory to do just that. In fact, it was an exploration that was well underway, with no little help from Hartman himself, by the time he published the book. Nearly every chapter of *The Unremarkable Wordsworth* had appeared previously, before and after the 1984 publication of de Man's *Rhetoric of Romanticism* and even in direct collaboration with de Man. Chapter 7, "Words, Wish, Worth," appeared in the conspicuous 1979 publication of *Deconstruction and Criticism*, jointly edited by Harold Bloom, Paul de Man, Jacques Derrida, Geoffrey Hartman, and J. Hillis Miller.

While the preface to that book, written by Hartman, denies that it stands as a "manifesto" for anything, it was nevertheless taken by many as a provocative instantiation of "The Yale School," a term that names a certain kind of American deconstruction inextricably tied to re-reading Wordsworthian language, and to the project of re-situating romanticism within literary history more generally. In his preface, Hartman deliberately distinguishes his own work (and Bloom's) from what he calls the "merciless and consequent" readings of the real "boa-deconstructors": Derrida, Miller, and de Man.[3] Judging whether that assessment is fair or right, or more importantly, addressing what a huge critical conversation it telescopes, falls well beyond the purview of this discussion – though it is tempting to pursue some obvious intersections (in the signature, "Derrida," for instance) with the French theoretical scene and the poststructuralist preoccupations we have considered in other portions of this book.

What I mean to emphasize here is the emergence of a new reading of Wordsworth, equally if differently invested in the poststructuralist reflections on language and subjectivity that so deeply inform Kristeva's critical theory. In his "Foreword" to Hartman's *Unremarkable Wordsworth,* Donald G. Marshall concludes that, despite Hartman's meticulous efforts to uncover the uncannily "precarious subjectivity of the poet," Wordsworth nevertheless

> certainly has his limits. He knows little or nothing of a darker side [of human existence, religion, and culture] that runs from Coleridge through Poe and Baudelaire and whose manifestations in modern literature, full of troubling political implications, are brought out in Julia Kristeva's analysis of the "abject" and of Céline in *Powers of Horror*. (xx, xxii)

Other critics involved in this rereading of Wordsworth – what we might call a second generation of "Yale School" romanticists – have pointedly disagreed with this assessment. That is, they have argued that Kristeva's theory does indeed have something to offer literary analyses of Wordsworth. These arguments appear in close chronological proximity to Marshall's Wordsworth/Kristeva link (or rather, non-link). While they have never, in my opinion, been adequately developed, they nevertheless prove intriguing, subtle, and worth examining.

In their very underdevelopment, their tentativeness, they remind us that theoretical "applications" need to proceed with caution, if not quite so much caution as Marshall's near-juxtaposition expresses. They demonstrate that, in drawing Kristeva's theory into unfamiliar terrain – for, as we will examine, deconstruction just as much as Wordsworth's poetry often works from contexts seemingly antithetical to Kristeva's precepts – it is crucial to acknowledge the *differences* between the literary author they examine and the heterogeneous theoretical frameworks they invoke to do so. These readings also serve as an apt conclusion to our own study, for they suggest just how promising and still largely uncharted the rich intersection between "Julia Kristeva" and "literary theory" continues to be.

The poet at the "end of the line"

In *The End of the Line: Essays on Psychoanalysis and the Sublime*, Neil Hertz turns to Kristeva in his final chapter, a long "Afterword" that mulls the implications of the various readings he has conducted of Longinus, Kant, Wordsworth, George Eliot, Freud, Courbet, and others. He credits her essay "L'Abjet d'amour," an essay written after *Powers of Horror* that appears in revised form in *Tales of Love*, with providing "an account" of subject formation and its threats "that seems particularly appropriate to the texts and paintings we have been considering" (231). In a phrase borrowed from Kenneth Burke, Hertz argues that we might understand sublimity as an "end of the line" crisis in which "differentiation," between subjects and objects, but also in the perceptual or representational ability to distinguish objects, breaks down or is momentarily "blocked."

Wordsworth, Hertz observes, depends on this logic of sublime blockage throughout *The Prelude*. Wordsworth dramatically narrates moments where the senses, perception, meaning, and indeed the borders of the self are radically threatened, only to be recuperated all the more triumphantly by the superior power of the poet.[4] Such moments are so prevalent in Wordsworth's poetry that the task of exhaustively identifying them seems itself sublime, but Hertz points suggestively to the famous "Blind Beggar" episode in Book VII of *The Prelude* as a paradigmatic instance, the culmination of disturbing horrors the poet faces during a trip to London. But in an important sense, Hertz is more interested in those preceding moments of horror, for "it is in response to them that the Blind Beggar is brought into the poem" (59). The Blind Beggar allows Wordsworth a revelatory recognition of "the utmost that we know, / Both of ourselves and of the universe" (VII, lines 617–18; 1805) that, in turn, leads to a reassuring assertion of the poetic faculties, of "such structures as the mind / Builds for itself" (VII, lines 626–7; 1805).

A series of earlier encounters, however, "tell of a moment, a recurrent moment, of thoroughgoing self-loss – not the recuperable baffled self associated with scenarios of blockage, but a more radical flux and dispersion of the subject" (59). Wordsworth represents London's assaulting chaos and din, generically speaking, as the epic's requisite descent into the underworld. Its lurid figures (limbless "cripple[s]," tacky pantomimes, crowds of strangers, noisy signs and advertisements, and so on) cumulatively impose upon the poet a crisis of meaning that is simultaneously a crisis of self. Wordsworth sums up the significance London's horrors at the end of Book VII, from the relatively comfortable position of having survived them:

> Oh, blank confusion! true epitome
> Of what the mighty City is herself
> To thousands upon thousands of her sons,
> Living amid the same perpetual whirl
> Of trivial objects, melted and reduced
> To one identity, by differences
> That have no law, no meaning, and no end –
> Oppression, under which even highest minds
> Must labour, whence the strongest are not free.
> (lines 722–30)[5]

Hertz draws us to this passage to indicate a broader logic demonstrated in a number of episodes throughout Book VII, but also among critics of the sublime: sublime overload, which baffles and thwarts man's thinking faculties, is specifically dramatized as a problem of reading. Or rather, the problem of consciousness, of "man thinking," finds increasing representation in instances of "man reading": "the self cannot simply think but must read the confirmation of its own integrity, which is only legible in a specular structure" (54–5).

Hertz's "end of the line" formulation allows us to see a number of Wordsworth's encounters with London's "blank confusion" as instances where difference (between subject and object, between object and object) is rendered so opaque that the "specular structure" itself collapses. Wordsworth's account of Bartholomew Fair further underscores just the readerly "[o]ppression" facing the mind confronted with an "undistinguishable world" by more explicitly rendering its horror as a representational overload, where the details of the scene become a strangely symbolic, indeed book-like, procession:

> Shop after shop, with symbols, blazoned names,
> And all the tradesman's honours overhead:
> Here, fronts of houses, like a title-page,

> With letters huge inscribed from top to toe,
> Stationed above the door, like guardian saints;
> There, allegoric shapes, female or male,
> Or physiognomies of real men.
>
> (Book VII, lines 158–64)

Hertz points out that, in its overload of signification, even the narrative control of Wordsworth's account devolves into mere listing, "until everything comes to seem like reading matter" not easily read (57). Wordsworth elevates unreadability to the level of human condition when he laments that, among the London throng, "the face of every one / That passes by me is a mystery" (VII, lines 596–7).

In the final lines of this reflection, just two lines before the seemingly prophetic encounter with the Blind Beggar makes his mind "turn round," Wordsworth describes the subjective impact of these readerly breakdowns in especially devastating terms:

> And all the ballast of familiar life,
> The present, and the past; hope, fear; all stays,
> All laws of acting, thinking, speaking man
> Went from me, neither knowing me, nor known.
>
> (Book VII, lines 603–6)

Hertz does not point out that Wordsworth says expressly that he was immersed in this unsettled frame of mind when " 'twas my chance / Abruptly" to come across the frightening but ultimately felicitous figure of the beggar. But he does argue, as I say above, that the logic of this sequence of horrors requires his appearance, for it "keeps the poet-impressario from tumbling into his text" (60). In other words, it *re-establishes* a structure of difference (between the poet and London's crush of indecipherable, undifferentiated objects, "melted and reduced / To one identity") and thereby also reasserts the very borders of the threatened self (losing the "ballast" of "[a]ll laws of acting, thinking, speaking man") who struggled to perceive them. After the Blind Beggar and the requisite summary of what the trip to London has led him to understand, Wordsworth concludes Book VII with restored "Composure and ennobling harmony," as if ultimately conquering chaos (VII, line 741).[6]

Kristeva and the pre-Oedipal Wordsworth

By now, the resonances with Kristeva's own theoretical frameworks are probably obvious: London's series of horrors and the impact they have on the poet–subject who encounters them, while mild compared with Kristeva's own examples and too neatly resolved for her critical vision, easily call up Kristeva's vivid accounts of abjection. But Hertz's own links between Wordsworth and abjection are only lightly sketched, and the questions he draws out when he does invoke Kristeva serve Hertz in a broader series of speculations about sublimity, representation, subjectivity, and gender. With his emphasis on these episodes as scenes of reading, as crises of readability, Hertz situates himself within a key conversation in deconstructive romanticism, and he fluently converses in its idiom. In the "boa-deconstructive" rhetorical readings of Paul de Man, psychoanalysis has no place (or so de Man says), but Hertz's critical method is more catholic. The book includes essays "on psychoanalysis": two chapters dealing exclusively with Freud, and another on the figure of the Medusa, which draws centrally on Freud's own Medusa essay. Just as significantly, however, it invokes psychoanalytic theory as a provocative tool in his essays "on the sublime." Throughout his book, Hertz makes significant inroads into contemporary theories of the sublime (it is now regularly cited as a key poststructuralist text on sublimity) by means of the careful way in which he mediates between deconstructive rhetorical reading and psychoanalysis.

One thesis of the book is that existing efforts at that mediation – most specifically, Thomas Weiskel's equally seminal book, *The Romantic Sublime: Studies in the Structure and Psychology of Transcendence* – had depended on a too strictly Oedipal model for talking about subjective crisis in sublimity. Hertz "give[s] Weiskel credit for dwelling as long as he did on the puzzles and anxieties of the pre-Oedipal," but he also notes Weiskel's symptomatic "relief he seemed to have experienced as an interpreter in at last bringing it all home to the Father" (230). Weiskel's book was published in 1976, as Hertz points out.[7] And since then,

> developments within psychoanalytic practice have converged with the work of feminist and post-structuralist theorists in providing counterirritants to those [critical] anxieties and encouraging more, and more varied, exploration of the earliest stages of infancy. (230–1)

For this reason, Hertz finds Kristeva important, especially the account of primary narcissism that arises from her theory of abjection. Because Kristeva's exploration of narcissism dwells so insistently in the murky, troubled waters of the subject's struggles with not-yet-objects and non-objects, Hertz sees suggestive parallels to his own "end of the line" model for describing sublime crisis. But he specifically singles out Kristeva for offering a potential antitode to the patriarchal or Oedipal bias of critics and artists of sublimity who tend to bring it "all home to the Father."

Hertz sees Kristeva's work as part of a larger poststructuralist effort to re-read Freud by way of Saussurian linguistics (as we explore in Chapter 2). In fact, he notes, she describes the infant's "primal separation" in terms that imply "more than a resemblance" to the bar that separates Saussure's signifier and signified (231).[8] Lacan does the same thing, but in Kristeva, Hertz argues, this separation is not yet gendered, not yet "Lacan's Symbolic Father" (231). This bar, *vide*, "blankness" – surely Hertz wants us to recall Wordsworth's "blank confusion" – represents, in his words, "a placeholder whose role is to maintain the separation between infant and mother that is the guarantee of the infant's acquisition of an identity and of language, for this is also the gap between signifier and signified, the gap that makes language possible" (231–2).

Hertz also emphasizes the strongly charged "equivocation" and ambivalence of Kristeva's account of narcissism, the fact that it serves both "to mask, but also to protect" (232). Subject formation depends upon abjecting "that which could have been a chaos," expelling what is not me and what threatens me, even if that separation is never as complete as Wordsworth's final lines of Book VII suggests it is (Hertz, 232, quoting Kristeva). Hertz's reading of the interrelated passages that lead up to the harmonious conclusion of Book VII – particularly his contention that Wordsworth needs the Blind Beggar in order to abject, as it were, the chaos and confusion and subjective dissolution described leading up to it – makes his turn to Kristeva at the end of his own book even more intriguing.[9]

By his own admission, he makes the final turn to Kristeva "a little too rapidly" (231). But it makes a gesture that is standard practice for a good conclusion: it signals where one could go from there, what work remains to be done beyond the borders of his own text. "For our purposes," Kristeva's "emphasis on the rudimentary nature of both 'subject' and 'object' in narcissistic configurations" suggests a promising route for further interrogating the subjective and linguistic dimensions of sublime experience (232). Hertz has followed his own implicit call in two subsequent articles analyzing not only

Wordsworth's poetic language but also Paul de Man's critical language about Wordsworth.

In "Lurid Figures" (1989) and "More Lurid Figures" (1990), he probes the curious rhetorical logic at work in de Man's analyses of poetic figuration.[10] In particular, he wonders about de Man's "characteristic – and characteristically unsettling [...] way of combining analysis and pathos," of describing the seemingly "affectless" workings of rhetoric in a critical language, and by means of literary examples, in which the "recurrent figures are strongly marked and whose themes are emotively charged, not to say melodramatic" ("Lurid Figures," p. 82). He argues that rhetorical pattern derives its force by evoking the "pathos of uncertain agency." De Man repeatedly describes linguistic undecidability and the inherent "indifference" of language through strangely personified, even melodramatic tropes. In identifying the strangeness of the "other Wordsworth" in "Wordsworth and the Victorians," for example, de Man points to moments of daring in which Wordsworth's language threatens to break down clear lines of epistemological demarcation (in this case between philosophy and poetry) as if it were a scene of seduction. He describes it, in other words, as if it were a subjective drama, when he purports to be talking about "the integrity of modes of discourse" (85). This blending of psychoanalytic models with rhetorical analysis would not be remarkable if it were not de Man he was talking about. But de Man's discourse, Hertz stresses, "is committed to questioning" psychoanalytic subjectivity's "privilege as an interpretive category" (85).

Hertz's answer as to how and why de Man's "lurid figures" operate the way they do is painstaking and complex, and its stakes lie far beyond the question of how Kristeva and Wordsworth might meet in the arena of contemporary literary theory. In these essays, Hertz joins them by pointing out that Kristeva helps us to notice that de Man's subtle dramas of subjectivity are gendered, emphatically unstable, and often tinged with violence in ways that recall her dynamic theory of narcissism. In "Wordsworth and the Victorians," de Man's account of the threatening breakdown between different modes of discourse in Wordsworth's poetry sounds like Kristeva's own accounts of subjective crisis. "[T]he danger that prompts the urge to reestablish clear demarcating lines" in de Man's lurid linguistic drama "would seem to be the threatened collapse of [the Oedipal] triangle into a more archaic structure, at once cognitively unsettling and menacing to the integrity of the preoedipal subject" (85).

Reading love in the "Blessed Babe"

Even more compellingly, de Man's privileged example in "Wordsworth and the Victorians" is the psychoanalytically ripe "Blessed Babe" episode from Book II of *The Prelude*:

> Blessed the infant Babe,
> (For with my best conjecture I would trace
> The progress of our being) blest the Babe,
> Nurs'd in his Mother's arms, the Babe who sleeps
> Upon his Mother's breast, who, when his soul
> Claims manifest kindred with an earthly soul,
> Doth gather passion from his Mother's eye!
> Like an awakening breeze, and hence his mind
> Even in the first trial of its powers
> Is prompt and watchful, eager to combine
> In one appearance, all the elements
> And parts of the same object, else detach'd
> And loth to coalesce.
>
> (Book II, lines 237–50)

Again, more concerned with reading de Man's reading of the passage than with commenting on Wordsworth's lines themselves, Hertz only incidentally notes the aptness of the passage for "partisans of the mirror stage" (97). Instead, he maps the way de Man redirects readerly focus away from the obvious figures in the scene of infantile/maternal love, from the burgeoning differentiation of a new subject "in the first trial of its powers," toward another story involving less apparent agents: "The characters in de Man's story of origins are named 'eye' and 'face' and 'language' " (98). Hertz wonders what it means for de Man, in effect, to erase the mother from the scene and regard it instead as an allegory of reading.

In this sense, Hertz suggests, Kristeva might once more offer insight into the motivations for the "abjection" of the maternal figure – that is, where a strongly gendered scene is at once exploited for its emotive force, yet drained of the question of sexual difference. Hertz once more invokes Kristeva's name obliquely, in the service of a project yet to come: "it has been left to [de Man's] readers to begin the work of articulating his implicit positions with those of other discourses, Derrida's, for example, or Lacan's or Kristeva's" (100).

De Man reads the "Blessed Babe" as a dynamic and formative "face-to-face" encounter. But when the child "Doth gather passion from his

Mother's eye," de Man suggests he is indeed looking at "language" as much as at his mother. Or that is a crude synopsis, for it implies a simple subject/object relation, whereas de Man means to emphasize the way Wordsworth indeed describes the "Blessed Babe's" perception of the mother's powerful "discipline of love" (II, line 251) as a formative, inaugural act, a positing, "a moment of abrupt performance" (96). For de Man, Hertz says, " 'language' is not an object; 'language' is already there in the looking" (96).

Hertz wonders whether de Man's critical decision to privilege this scene as an act of reading at the exclusion of seeing it as an instance of a (linguistically grounded) coalescence of subjectivity commits, on a critical level, a kind of maternal abjection. On the other hand, he points out that Wordsworth's poetry itself asserts a kind of matricidal gesture by strangely announcing the death, or at least the disappearance, of the mother several lines after the "Blessed Babe" episode: "The props of my affection were removed" (II, line 294). Wordsworth goes on to stress that the formative "infant sensibility" those initial experiences of the profound infant/mother intercourse (which not only gave him a crucial, dynamic paradigm for love, but also lay the framework for "the filial bond / Of Nature that connect him with the world") are but a step along a path toward higher consciousness and a more autonomously sustained selfhood.

Through "mute dialogues with my mother's heart," the poet establishes "the infant sensibility / Great birthright of our being"; that formative love, from the beginning, "was in me / Augmented and sustained (II, lines 283, 285–7). Yet in a typical Wordsworthian turn, that loving comfort of a connection (to a loved one, to nature, to a reading or an understanding) is thrown into doubt, only to be rescued by an awareness of a self-generated power or a willed faith that, as he says in "Tintern Abbey," "Nature never did betray / The heart that loved her" (lines 122–3).

The simple fact that so many Wordsworthian episodes derive their force from experiences that powerfully, if not entirely, threaten the prayerful faith of that maxim makes Wordsworth's poetry a profoundly rich, and indeed radically unstable, site for psychoanalytically informed readings of early subject formation as an evolving literary construct. Because Wordsworth makes prodigious efforts to describe the "growth of the poet's mind" by so often narrating its inaugural moments in densely conflictual terms, and by, moreover, perpetually testing the integrity of that poetic mind through radically unsettling "borderline" experiences, critics invested in the deconstructive rereading of Wordsworth and romanticism have marshaled psychoanalytic models of interpretation as powerful tools in the effort to understand the "other Wordsworth."

In the work of Neil Hertz – but also, notably, in that of Cynthia Chase, who also ambitiously inserts Kristeva into the rhetorical criticism of Wordsworthian figuration – psychoanalytic theory is apt precisely because it is *itself* also a rhetorical theory. Especially in the hands of Julia Kristeva, accounting for the earliest struggles to establish self in relation to other means *necessarily* talking about the fundamental structures of signification. As a "speaking subject," the effort *to become* is inextricable from the effort *to read* and *to mean*. In "Primary Narcissism and the Giving of Figure," an essay that represents the most sustained effort to date to probe the potential links between de Man's rhetorical theory and Kristeva's theory of the speaking subject by way of Wordsworth's poetry, Chase argues that what links all three discourses is that each describes an inaugural act of reading – a performative decision – that asserts a differentiation in the face of undifferentiability.[11] Put more simply, de Man, Kristeva, and Wordsworth (particularly in the "Blessed Babe" episode) all find "at the origin of signification" a constitutive decision, a sorting that "repudiate[es] [...] the uncertainty about those marks that may or may not be significative" (127). Kristeva calls this process abjection. De Man, as Hertz points out, seems similarly interested in such moments where readerly undecidability becomes most charged. For Wordsworth, these "borderline crises" allow for more triumphant assertions of the self-generated powers of the poet.

Because she considers Kristeva's theory of maternal, narcissistic love as principally "an account of reading," Chase argues that Kristeva actually offers a way to clarify just what is at stake in those puzzling "dramas of uncertain agency" Hertz sees throughout de Man. Seeing de Man, Kristeva, and Wordsworth together allows "the articulation of an enigma. How are the signifying and the sign held together, and held apart?" (125).[12] Wordsworth startlingly describes the Blessed Babe's lovingly enclosed effort to perceive the objects of his affection as a unifying whole as one menaced by the threat of non-differentiation:

> eager to combine
> In one appearance, all the elements
> And parts of the same object, else detach'd
> And loth to coalesce.
>
> (Book II, lines 247–50)

Chase locates this threat not only in the dispersion of objects "loth to coalesce," but also in what she calls, quoting Kristeva, "a *coagulation* of the mother and her desire" (128; emphasis Kristeva's).

Part of what rescues the infant from the potentially consuming "passion" of his "mother's eye," Wordsworth tells us, is the "gravitation[al]" power of another love: "the filial bond / Of Nature that connect[s] him with the world" (II, lines 263–4). In Wordsworth's account, as in Kristevan primary narcissism, the profound dynamics of the infant's "first affections" – a phrase I draw from *Tales of Love*, by the way, though it sounds remarkably Wordsworthian – produce the poetic mind and the speaking subject. These struggles represent "the first trial of its powers" (Kristeva, p. 27; Wordsworth, Book II, line 246). In both the literary as well as the theoretical accounts, "what blurs [...] is the distinction from what is read and what is read from or not read," Chase tells us (128). If Wordsworth produces such moments where that distinction becomes dramatically indistinct to serve as "blockages" that will ultimately be sublimely overcome, as Hertz contends, Kristeva gives us a way to account for what is at stake in such crises. Chase argues: "Kristeva's work on 'abjection' and melancholia I take to be an exploration of the consequences of the failure of this distinction, of the fact that the differentiation of the sign and the other fails to take place" (128).

New Narcissi and a criticism to come

Throughout this discussion, I repeatedly emphasize the sublime turn Wordsworth triumphantly insists upon at every moment when he confronts this crisis of reading, which Chase, like Kristeva, considers a *general condition* of reading but also of existence. As Chase puts it, with jarring lucidity, "To read [...] is precisely not to know" (127). Nevertheless, the critical efforts of de Man, Hertz, Chase, and so many others to re-read Wordsworthian romanticism convincingly suggest that the "other Wordsworth" might indeed be the Wordsworth whose legacy endures. These post-romantic critiques, indeed, might themselves come to constitute Kristeva's heralded "revolution in poetic language." The Wordsworth of lurid figures and figurations, of linguistic daring and devastating accounts of subjective dissolution, engages in a far more fraught struggle for "ennobling" poetic authority through humanistic love of self, the human family, and nature than his own homiletic assurances of Nature's love and the poet's power so memorably assert. In our conventional, canonical assessment, a certain Wordsworth holds a kingly seat in literary and intellectual history; as he himself avows, he is a poet more "philosophic" for having endured his trials and more triumphant for establishing a final composed, ennobling place above "the press / Of self-destroying, transitory things" ("Immortality Ode," line 186; *Prelude*, Book VII, lines 739–40).

But another Wordsworth continues to haunt, as well, revived by contemporary critical efforts to see an ironically greater, or *more* profound, poetic force in Wordsworth's brushes with poetic "failure" than in his announcements of poetic "success." Kristeva's silence on the high romantic poets, her privileging of other eras, seems to suggest that Wordsworth would be, for her, one of those writers dispiritingly in the thrall of the symbolic order as they "continue their long march toward idols and truths of all kinds," repressing the "nurturing horror that they attend to pushing aside by purifying, systematizing [...] the horror they seize on in order to build themselves up and function" (*Powers of Horror*, p. 210). Hertz's account of the logic of blockage in Wordsworth's poetry supports that assessment, in which the horrors of London are "seized" in the effort to build and valorize the poetic mind that survives them. Yet Hertz's turn to Kristeva precisely to describe the considerable force and complexity of Wordsworth's negotiation of "horror" suggests that we might see Wordsworth working not *only* out of a "righteous," repressive faith in the stability of the symbolic order. Hertz and Chase draw Wordsworth closer to Kristeva by pointing out how much the critical language and critical vision of the de Manian Wordsworth – a poet strongest when he dwells most precariously in the borderline regions of linguistic dissolution – resonates with the intense dramas of subjectivity at work in Kristeva's understanding of narcissism.

Viewed in this light, Wordsworth might not be the Romanticist protector of "the old psychic space," but something closer to the "post-Romanticist" Narcissus Kristeva envisions in *Tales of Love* (379, 381). Her final call in that work for a criticism that properly attends to the radical "instability of the *narcissistic subject*" identifies psychoanalysis as a discipline well-suited to survey the terrain of such a subject without recourse to falsely consoling theoretical explanations (374, 379; emphasis Kristeva's). Hers will not be a psychoanalysis "concerned with rebuilding their own proper space, a 'home,' for contemporary Narcissi: repair the father, soothe the mother, allow them to build a solid, introspective inside, master of its losses and wanderings, assuming that such a goal is attainable." Instead, she means to "follow, impel, favor breakaways, driftings," for psychoanalysis is rather "the instrument of a departure from that enclosure, not [...] its warden" (379).

Under the unsettling scrutiny of the "merciless and consequent" critical eye of de Man and others, the domestic, Victorian Wordsworth is shown to be precisely the opposite. Not homey, but uncanny. The supposed "shelter" of his common speech, they demonstrate, conceals "the break that has always been hidden within it" (de Man, "Victorians," p. 85). Hertz and Chase show that one promising critical avenue for the "departure" Kristeva envisions could include a re-evaluation of Wordsworth's poetic language, tracking by what means he purports to "build a solid, introspective inside" and at what great cost he declares himself "master of its losses and wanderings." They suggest, by way of Kristeva's powerful formulations, that Wordsworth claims his hard-fought, supposed composure and harmony by the reflection of Narcissus' turbulent pool.

Glossary

This glossary does not provide a comprehensive list of Kristeva's key theoretical terms, but rather highlights those with the most direct relevance to her discussions of – or theory of – literature as I have explored them in this book. It also looks at psychoanalytic terminology that most crucially informs her literary theory, as well as neologisms whose meanings are not otherwise self-evident (such as *signifiance* and *semanalysis*). I give brief "definitions" of terms Kristeva has spent entire monographs defining (most notably, *abjection*), and which my earlier chapters discuss with much greater attention to context and nuance. In the case of these especially rich and multifaceted terms, definitions here often overlap with discussions provided in the earlier chapters of this book – text, intertextuality, the subject, the semiotic, and so on. As such, the entries provided in the glossary should serve only for quick reference and should not replace those discussions; nor, most importantly, should they obviate the reader from reading Kristeva's own explanations of her terms or from attending to the arguments in which she deploys them. In keeping with this broad ethic of reading – that summaries and abstracted explanations cannot replace the work of actually reading Kristeva – I fashion most of these definitions with close reference to texts in which Kristeva formatively uses the terms themselves.

Readers seeking further terminological guidance should consult the pithy and lucid glossary provided in *The Kristeva Critical Reader*, ed. John Lechte and Mary Zournazi (Edinburgh: Edinburgh University Press, 2003). John Lechte's *Julia Kristeva* (New York: Routledge, 1990) also addresses all of Kristeva's major terms. Kelly Oliver, in *Reading Kristeva: Unraveling the Double-bind* (Indiana: Indiana University Press, 1993), gives excellent expositions of Kristeva's psychoanalytic lexicon, particularly as it relates to Kristeva's accounts of motherhood, pre-Oedipal subject formation, and the symbolic system. Toril Moi's editorial introductions in *The Kristeva Reader* (New York: Columbia University Press, 1986) clearly highlight the key terms at work in each selection. And Michael Payne's *Reading Theory: An Introduction to Lacan, Derrida, and Kristeva* (Oxford: Blackwell, 1993) provides the indispensable service of navigating the reader through the dense and allusive theoretical vocabulary of *Revolution in Poetic Language* (it also includes a brief glossary as an appendix).

Abjection

Kristeva's major treatise on abjection is, of course, *Powers of Horror*, and the best way to understand her definition of the concept is carefully to read (and re-read) chapter 1 of that text, "Approaching Abjection," where her difficult and fascinating prose not only describes the idea of the abject, but also acts out its strange force. For Kristeva's own efforts to name and categorize abjection demonstrates perhaps its most crucial feature: its resistance to definition, its objectless negativity. "The abject has only one quality of the object – that of being opposed to *I*" (*Powers of Horror*, p. 1). Abjection looms and threatens, jettisons the subject to a borderland of horror, and at once beseeches and repulses the subject, radically defying categorization: "Not me. Not that. But not nothing, either. A 'something' that I do not recognize as a thing. A weight of meaninglessness about which there is nothing insignificant, and which crushes me" (2). A term initially borrowed from Georges Bataille (who regarded abjection as the squalid, hypocritical, corrupt), Kristeva's abjection refers to an extreme state of subjectivity – a crisis in which the borders of self and other radically break down. But it is also, more importantly, a precondition of subjectivity itself, one of the key dynamics by which those borders of the self get established in the first place.

Through Kristeva's account – and in her examinations of food loathing, maternal rejection, criminality, defilement rites, the Freudian theory of phobia, the Oedipus myth, and, most compellingly, the literary works of Louis-Ferdinand Céline – we come to understand abjection as much more than a mere developmental account of infantile separation. That is, abjection refers at once (1) to an infantile, originary moment in the subject's individual history, (2) to something the subject might experience throughout its existence at moments of extreme crisis, and (3) to a collective condition of our humanity. It manifests itself in the most exceptional instances of human horror, both personal and collective, but also in the deepest structures of cultural taboo, and even in what we hold to be our highest cultural achievements.

Agape/Eros

Kristeva says that she undertook her study of love because it provided her, following *Powers of Horror,* with another rich "elaboration of a history of subjectivity" (*Tales of Love,* p. 16). While largely psychoanalytic in its focus, *Tales of Love* also gives newly concentrated attention to philosophically and theologically grounded "*images of love* in the West" (16; emphasis Kristeva's). Thus she looks to "Greek *Eros,* Jewish *Ahav,* Christian *Agape,* and the various dynamics affecting the amorous protagonists who emerge out of them: Narcissus, Don Juan, Romeo and Juliet, or the Mother with her child of which the Virgin Mary is our prototype" (16). We see in earlier works such as "Stabat Mater" how Kristeva's theoretical investment in the Virgin Mary allows her to expand and revise Lacan's theory of feminine *jouissance* (see *jouissance* entry below); but here, the Virgin Mary is but one of many amorous paradigms that demonstrate an intricately open system that "manifest[s] the semiotic flow within symbolicity" (16).

Through these explorations, Kristeva introduces the *Eros/Agape* opposition in order to illustrate the different logics of subject/object relations in erotic and religious love, respectively. In *Eros,* Kristeva argues, the subject must rise in order to unify: the separation from the mother allows the subject to produce an ego, and this production expresses itself in terms of an ego-ideal, which makes it possible for the subject to love. The consequence of the ego-ideal, however, is a certain failure of ideality, from which the subject experiences a rupture between its object and its desire. A feeling of loss accompanies the formation of the ego, and the relationship between the subject and object becomes critically complex. *Agape,* on the other hand, which Kristeva traces to Paul's discussion of God, describes a relationship between subject and object as one that subordinates the subject to its object in order to fuse the two as a single expression of subjectivity. At heart is a basic recognition of the other as oneself; and as such, the subject descends into the ideal rather than rising to it. Kristeva regards Joyce as an author who, while capable of highly erotic representations of love (particularly in the "Penelope" chapter of *Ulysses* and in his notoriously racy correspondence with Nora Barnacle), nevertheless explored

Agape in a uniquely probing manner. She made this argument in her address to the 1984 Joyce Symposium in Frankfurt. Kristeva provides an in-depth analysis of the *Eros*/*Agape* distinction in *Tales of Love*, pages 145–80.

Carnival/Carnivalesque

Indebted to Bakhtin's discussion of carnival in *Rabelais and His World* and in his analysis of Dostoevsky's novels, Kristeva uses the terms "carnival" and "carnivalesque" to mean a general process of transgressing literary, political, or social norms. Bakhtin saw significance in the cultural phenomenon of the carnival, an occasion in which the normal order and hierarchies of society are, for a time and in a given place, temporarily suspended. The carnivalesque tradition in literature not only depicts instances of this phenomenon, but acts out its dynamics on the level of representation and discourse. Swift's grotesques and Joyce's portmanteau language both belong to this tradition. As a specifically literary discourse, the carnivalesque is "essentially dialogical," and indeed the "[f]igures germane to carnivalesque language, including repetition [. . .] produce a more flagrant dialogism than any other discourse" ("Word, Dialogue, and Novel," in *The Kristeva Reader*, p. 48).

Epic and carnival are the "two currents" of the European narrative tradition (50). Whereas epic tends toward the theological and upholds normative "belief," carnival "challenges God, authority and social law" (49). Kristeva seeks to distance "carnival" from its commonplace associations with burlesque and parody; those understandings are pejorative and overly ambiguous, ignoring carnival's more subversive, "transformative" dimensions. It may produce laughter, but of the most serious kind, a laughter that is comic and tragic at once. For according to both Bakhtin and Kristeva, carnival has a more radical relation to the law than mere parody. It does not simply reverse states of affairs; it does not reflect or mirror. Instead, carnival enacts a complex set of identities, in which the boundary between what is normal and what is abnormal subsumes the very concept of the boundary within a larger dynamic of transgression. In other words, carnival is not an 'other side' to boundary; it is, rather, the incorporation of that other into the identity of the one who transgresses; it is the doubling of structure in terms of the other.

Part of the broader trajectory of Menippean discourse, the carnivalesque tradition finds modern voice in the "polyphonic novel[s]" of

"Rabelais, Cervantes, Swift, Sade, Lautréamont, Dostoevsky, Joyce and Kafka" (50). In *Powers of Horror*, by way of introducing his works, Kristeva argues that Céline's deliriously abject narratives may superficially be called "carnivalesque," but that the term proves inadequate to account for his true radicality. "Céline's effect is quite other" (*Powers of Horror*, p. 134).

Chora

A notoriously difficult term to define, *chora* has long suffered the distinction as one of the most opaque concepts in Kristeva's *oeuvre*. She introduces the term early in *Revolution in Poetic Language*, as she endeavors to lay out the relationship between the semiotic and the symbolic in early subject formation, and in the subject's initial situating and positing in the modalities of the signifying process. Kristeva takes the term, if somewhat abstrusely, from Plato's *Timaeus*, where it means "receptacle" (and is called "nourishing and maternal") and refers to a space or potentiality more than a representable entity (*Revolution in Poetic Language*, pp. 25, 26). For Kristeva, the Platonic borrowing allows her "to denote an essentially mobile and extremely provisional articulation constituted by movements and their ephemeral stases" (25).

Intimately tied to Kristeva's notion of the body as a language-driven and language-driving process, the chora is primarily a drive-determined and determining locus of what is itself unrepresentable to and by language. "Chora" expresses a distinct "motility"; in contrast to the symbolic order of the ego, it cannot be represented spatially or geometrically. Instead, the chora is associated with the semiotic, although it is itself not of the semiotic. Rather, the chora is that which makes possible or serves to structure the signifying processes of the semiotic; it is a force or dynamic, not a place. As such, the chora is wholly process. The signifying drives of language find their home in the chora, which enables and determines language as a bodily process, not a mechanical system. In fact, Kristeva, drawing heavily on Freud, characterizes the chora as maternal, emphasizing the pre-symbolic. Although Kristeva discusses the chora throughout her work, she most extensively analyzes the concept in *Revolution in Poetic Language*; most useful may be pages 25–35 in the English translation and 450–60 in the French. Toril Moi also anthologizes this chapter, "The Semiotic Chora Ordering the Drives," in *The Kristeva Reader*, pp. 93–8.

Dialogic/dialogism

As initially theorized by Mikhail Bakhtin with respect to the works of Dostoevsky, the concept of "dialogism" conceives of language as an intersection or interaction of unique properties, voices, or horizons of social and political expression. Dialogism is the "double-voicing" of language; in all discourse there is a fundamental tension between the impulse to centralize and the necessity to decentralize, a tension that renders discourse abundant with tones and meanings in excess of any single intention or expression. In this regard, the text is a process of tonalities, all of which exist simultaneously within textuality itself. To support this notion, Bakhtin argues that all levels of the text are similarly dialogic: the single word, the phrase, and the structure of the novel all equally possess dialogic properties. The concept of the dialogic or dialogism, becomes increasingly important to Kristeva's view of poetic language, particularly in her discussions of Mallarmé and Lautréamont in *Revolution in Poetic Language.*

Intertextuality

Although predominantly attributed to Kristeva, the notion of intertextuality finds articulation in the works of Barthes, Jakobson, and especially Bakhtin. In "From Work to Text," for example, Barthes memorably defines intertextuality as "quotations without inverted commas" (*Image–Music–Text,* p. 160). But he means more than just citations and their sources, for intertextuality instead names a dynamic in which all texts participate; no text exists in self-sufficient isolation from other texts. In "Word, Dialogue, and Novel" and "The Bounded Text," Kristeva abstracts this notion in order to reconceive language itself as a general process of intertextuality, much in the manner of Bakhtin. She credits Bakhtin, in fact, with being the first literary theorist to contend with the idea that "any text is the absorption and transformation of another" ("Word, Dialogue, and Novel," in *The Kristeva Reader*, p. 37). In *Revolution in Poetic Language,* she expresses concern that Bakhtin's "transformational" emphasis has been overlooked by readers of her own work, so she re-introduces intertextuality under the name "transposition" to stress the "passage from one sign system to another" that takes place as one text creates itself out of the thematic and generic materials of another text

(*Revolution in Poetic Language*, p. 59; emphasis Kristeva's). Readings of Mallarmé and Lautréamont in *Revolution in Poetic Language* are guided by this insight. Most abstractly, she shows that the interpenetration and interdependence of all language acts foreground the very capacity for meaning to exist.

Not simply a network of allusions or quotations, Kristeva's intertextuality exists as a semiotic superstructure, a kind of requisite for language systems to function. In this sense, intertextuality is not something that happens at a particular moment in literary history; it is something that simply happens in language as such. In another sense, however, Kristeva does associate this linguistic phenomenon with the specific seismic shifts engendered by the modern era – Nerval's or Mallarmé's "great condensation and great polysemia," for example, or Joyce's *Finnegans Wake*, which is "impossible" to read "without entering into the intrapsychic logic and dynamics of intertextuality" (*Julia Kristeva Interviews*, p. 191). Kristeva's literary theoretical claims, in this regard, draw closely from Bakhtin's ideas of *dialogism* and *polyphony*, but the psychoanalytic implications of intertextuality also play an important part, as her comment on Joyce suggests.

The kaleidoscopic multiplicity Bakhtin and Barthes see in textuality so conceived, Kristeva sees in the workings of the speaking subject as well. Simply put, the subject is itself "intertextual." Accordingly, Kristeva sees in the polyphonic twentieth-century novel, for example, "fragments of character, or fragments of ideology, or fragments of representation" (190). But she also believes this new order of representation implies important changes in the formation of identities as well; her "understanding of intertextuality [. . .] points to a dynamics involving a destruction of the creative identity and reconstitution of a new plurality" (190).

Jouissance

In his Seminar XX (1972–3), "God and the *Jouissance* of Woman: A Love Letter," Jacques Lacan proposes that feminine *jouissance* indicates something "beyond" – beyond the phallus, beyond the notion of Woman purely within a paternal symbolic system, perhaps beyond language. He cites the mystics as those who may have sensed "that there must be a *jouissance* which goes beyond" (*Feminine Sexuality*, p. 147). Lest anyone overlook the strong sexual connotation to the term *jouissance*, Lacan refers us to the ecstatic expression of

Saint Theresa captured in Bernini's marble: "you only have to go and look at Bernini's statue in Rome to understand immediately that she's coming, there is no doubt about it" (147).

Outrageousness aside, Lacan's proposals here are notoriously complex, and their implications contested. But we could say at the very least that Kristeva invokes the term with the Lacanian context in mind. She herself will first consider feminine *jouissance* in the context of Christian martyrs (*About Chinese Women*, pp. 25–33), but quickly sets her sights on the Virgin Mary rather than Saint Theresa. Kristeva pointedly argues that Christianity prefers its heroines to be virgins, as a way of managing its understanding of motherhood and cordoning off any feminine *jouissance* not in the service of the paternal, the Symbolic, and the Word. The shift indicates that Kristeva is interested in the *jouissance* of the mother, of motherhood, as a "beyond" that patriarchal culture – and indeed even Lacan – are not prepared to acknowledge, much less assimilate. Kristeva argues that the cult of the Virgin Mary (indeed, the very insistence on Christ's birth as a virgin birth) indicates the "cleverly balanced architecture" of the "Western symbolic economy" ("Stabat Mater," in *The Kristeva Reader*, pp. 182, 174). A bold-typed parallel text crowds the pages on which Kristeva makes this argument, a vivid, visceral first-person narrative that articulates the *jouissance* her critical text aims to theorize. "Stabat Mater" was reprinted in Kristeva's *Tales of Love*, where she considers *jouissance* in the broader context of Western history's many discourses on love – those of the mystics, philosophers, poets, and patients.

Jouissance always, of course, describes a certain relation to language, an extreme state in which language and subjectivity mutually break down. In "The True-Real," hallucinatory experiences, close to psychosis, leave "a hole in the subject's discourse" and conjure up "an unutterable *jouissance* that endangers the symbolic resources of the speaking being" ("The True-Real," in *The Kristeva Reader*, p. 228). Thus in *Tales of Love*, as in *Powers of Horror* and elsewhere, Kristeva gives *jouissance* an emphatically literary valence as well: it is linked to art, imagination, the "work in progress" of those who aim to articulate the dissolving power of subjective crisis (love, horror) rather than repress it. In this sense, *jouissance* is related to sublimation (what Freud called the efforts of artists and others to redirect the drives towards culturally productive ends) and the sublime.

Kristeva even extends *jouissance* to the work of the critic or the analyst, for instance in "Psychoanalysis and the Polis." Here, *jouissance* is the vertigo or "delirium" one experiences in confronting a text or a patient who resists interpretive mastery. As this essay title suggests, Kristeva's methodology is proudly psychoanalytic, but the term harkens to her literary critical mentors as well. In *The Pleasure of the Text*, Roland Barthes identifies *jouissance* as that which "imposes a state of loss" or "discomfort" on the processes of interpretation, reading, and decoding; it startles into awareness (9). *Jouissance* is a kind of bliss or euphoria associated with the breakdown of conventional practices, especially literary and hermeneutic ones. This breakdown, which still retains the sexual connotations of the more psychoanalytic usage, forces the reader to confront language itself, stimulating a liberation from mere pleasure (*plaisir*) by initiating the reader into a higher, more ecstatic anxiety, the *jouissance* of subversion, ambiguity, play. Barthes asserts that *jouissance* characterizes the "writerly" text and opens up the text for *signifiance*, an unconstrained interplay of semiological drives.

Menippean

Menippean discourse, a kind of tradition of subversion, acts to undermine the centripetal force of discourse by embracing tonal indeterminacy, hybrid structures, and a capacity for transgression. Menippean discourse derives, as Kristeva notes, from Menippus of Gadara; however, the term does not factually have an origin, in that Menippean discourse existed before and exists after Menippus. The Menippean tradition is one of satire, mockery, complexity, and above all, dialogism. Kristeva, in "Word, Dialogue, and Novel," identifies the Menippean with open texts, *signifiance*, and *jouissance* in general.

Novel

In a 1988 interview Kristeva conducted for French radio, she offers an interesting account of how the tumultuous, experimental culture of Paris in the mid-sixties ("good times for intellectuals") first led her to consider the birth of the novel. She came to Paris intent on writing a thesis on the *nouveau roman*, but quickly changed her course: "Rather than investigate the way the *nouveau roman* decomposed the form of the novel, I wanted to pose a different question: how did the novel establish itself as a genre? So I shifted my focus from the end to the beginning" (*Julia Kristeva Interviews*, pp. 5, 6).

In her eventual thesis, *Le Texte du roman: approche sémiologique d'une structure discursive transformationnelle* (1970), Kristeva studies the work of fifteenth-century prose writer Antoine de la Sale, arguing that his work demonstrates a crucial historical change in the way the sign was understood, and that it is with this new understanding that the genre of the novel comes into being. One of the few portions of the text available in English translation, "From Symbol to Sign" (*The Kristeva Reader*, pp. 62–73) provides a cogent overview of this ambitious argument. "We shall use the term novel to describe the kind of narrative that starts to emerge clearly at the end of the Middle Ages and the beginning of the Renaissance" (63). The kind of narrative that interests her marks a literary historical "transition" from the "epic system" (see the discussion of "carnival," above, for an indication of how Kristeva understands "epic") to "another way of thinking"; but also, more pertinently, it marks another way of *representing*, "a passage from the *symbol* to the *sign*" (63). With its roots in the theater and in the carnivalesque, and its Menippean spirit, de la Sale's little-known novella *Jehan de Saintré* provides a "perfect example of such a narrative" (63).

Kristeva meticulously draws the symbol/sign distinction by way of C. S. Peirce and Saussure, but generally speaking, the symbol and the sign *mean* by different logics. The symbol *refers* to a transcendental idea, rigidly and (supposedly) non-arbitrarily, but the novel's semiotic practices began to call into question the "transcendental unity supporting the symbol – its other-worldly wrapping" (65). In the wake of the "capsize[d]" symbol came the *sign*, a "new signifying relation between two elements, both located in the 'real,' concrete world" (65). With the sign, not only did signifying become "more and more 'material,' " it also became unstable, ambivalent, opaque, self-referential.

Kristeva sees de la Sale's image of the Sybil as a key example of the shift from symbol to sign, a "hybrid, double, ambiguous" figure we have seen from time to time in antiquity and the end of the Middle Ages, which has proliferated "all over Europe" by the end of the fifteenth century (67). But Kristeva views the relative instability of the sign over the symbol not as a weakness, but as a liberating potentiality. She sees in the figure of the Sybil a figure of the monumental shift from symbol to sign itself. The sign allows for a new "infinitization of discourse," and in the figure of the Sybil we might imagine this new plurality, "the word as it were liberated from its dependence on the symbol and enjoying the 'arbitrariness' of the sign" (68). In its infinity, in the "unlimited possibilities" its mode of representation opens up at the end of the Middle

Ages, the novel cannot properly be dissociated from the *dialogic*, as Kristeva theorizes elsewhere, since each depends heavily on the dynamic between time, or context, and utterance, or location.

Drawing mainly on an essay by Bakhtin collected in *The Dialogic Imagination*, Kristeva in "Word, Dialogue, and Novel" argues that the novel is necessarily open-ended in that it constructs a plot through the infusion of distinct systems or methods of signification, integrated into a generalized, but specific, sequence of linguistic events. This renders the "meaning" of the text, as traditionally understood, indistinct from the "form," and so changes the process of reading from one of decoding to one of experiencing; the reader does not analyze a text so much as be *affected* by it, intellectually as well as psychologically and emotionally. Her analysis of Céline's novels in *Powers of Horror* – a literary criticism that is inextricably an analysis of the "strange state" Céline's narratives impose on their readers (including herself) – demonstrates this point with virtuosity. "Read for yourself," she tells her readers, in effect.

Poetic language

The phrase "poetic language" was popularized by Russian formalism in the early decades of the twentieth century. Ossip Brik's establishment of the "Society for the Study of Poetic Language" in 1917, for instance, announced a new distinction as well as a new theoretical enterprise. As Boris Eichenbaum also outlines in "The Theory of the 'Formal' Method," formalists were interested in distinguishing "practical language" (which exists largely to communicate fact or information) from "poetic language" (which has an *other* purpose, if a "purpose," as such, at all).

While Kristeva revives the phrase with clear awareness of its formalist legacy, she also seeks to distance herself from that legacy. For Kristeva, the formalist opposition proves too rigid, and is unequipped to account for the permeability of these different forms. In other words, elements of "poetic language" can and do exist everywhere. Thus, as Léon Roudiez explains in the "Introduction" to *Revolution in Poetic Language*, in Kristeva's theory, the phrase "stands for the infinite possibilities of all language, and all other language acts are merely partial realizations of the possibilities inherent in 'poetic language'" (*Revolution in Poetic Language*, p. 2). That is, Kristeva's use of "poetic language" vastly exceeds what one normally understands "poetic" to mean; for Kristeva, the poetic is a feature of all language, not just those instances of linguistic versification traditionally identified as poetry. Instead, the novels of Joyce and Sollers, the prose visions of Lautréamont, and the opaque sign systems of music all qualify as poetic language.

Semanalysis

Sème, from the Greek *séméîon*, means "sign," but also trace, mark, distinctive feature, imprint, figuration (*Revolution in Poetic Language*, p. 25). In Kristeva's work, the term underscores the basic materiality of language and recalls the organizational logic of language – of the signifier and the signified – theorized by Ferdinand de Saussure in the *Course in General Linguistics*. While Saussure and the structural linguists working in his wake made great strides in *semiology* – the study of the sign and signification – Kristeva seeks a theoretical system that addresses and moves beyond semiology's methodological limitations.

In "The System and the Speaking Subject," Kristeva outlines these distinctions by introducing her term, *semanalysis*. *Semanalysis* (or semiotics), as she envisions it, might replace the formal, static science of the sign practiced by Saussure and others. While it necessarily "carries on the semiotic discovery" of their work, semanalysis also sharply distinguishes itself in its approach and in its basic understanding of the thing it studies ("The System and the Speaking Subject," in *The Kristeva Reader*, p. 32). *Semanalysis* would acknowledge language as a dynamic (a "signifying process") rather than a static system (a "sign-system"); and most importantly, it would recognize the central role of a "speaking, historical" subject in the formation of language systems (28). Kristeva's term underscores the theoretical shift she effects, from a semiological "science of linguistics that has no way of apprehending anything in language which belongs not with the social contract but with play, pleasure or desire" towards something new. *Semanalysis* is the name she gives to a new critical discourse that could apprehend such marginal "signifying practices" – that could, for instance, theorize elements of signification falling outside of the normative signifying structure of the "social contract," such as "ellipses, non-recoverable deletions, indefinite embeddings" (28). Most emphatically, *semanalysis* focuses on the irregular, drive-motivated symbolic processes (the "primary processes" such as displacement and condensation) of the unconscious, as they find their way into the "signifying code and the fragmented body of the speaking subject" (29).

The gesture of creating a new term signals, Kristeva hopes, a theoretical project to come. It highlights what she calls in an important early essay, "The Ethics of Linguistics" – namely, a linguistics that would work from different premises by different means. As opposed to structural linguistics' presumably scientific "semiology of systems," *semanalysis* would be a self-conscious discourse, poised for self-critique. As a discourse about discourse, it would not presume itself scientifically or objectively outside its object of study.

Semiotic/symbolic

A crucial part of Kristeva's thought depends upon the distinction between two distinct linguistic forces – "*two modalities* [...] within the same *signifying process* that constitutes language" – the semiotic and the symbolic (*Revolution in Poetic Language*, pp. 23–4; emphasis Kristeva's). Although the semiotic seems to receive privileged attention in Kristeva (and among her commentators) as the more radical, unknowable, artistically productive modality, in fact neither language nor subjectivity can ever be "purely" semiotic or symbolic. While the fascinating "nonverbal signifying systems" Kristeva examines (such as primary narcissism or abjection, or even music) are "constructed exclusively on the basis of the semiotic," she insists that "this exclusivity is relative." Because "the subject is *both* semiotic *and* symbolic, no signifying system he produces can be either 'exclusively' semiotic or 'exclusively' symbolic, and is instead necessarily marked by an indebtedness to both" (24; emphasis Kristeva's).

The semiotic and the symbolic function "*synchronically within the signifying process of the subject himself.*" In a narrowly archaeological sense, nevertheless, we could say that the semiotic comes first. Psychoanalytically, it is associated with the "primary processes," the drives, the unconscious logic of condensation and displacement, as well as the workings of the body, rhythms, and sound (25). The symbolic, by contrast, is the "social" domain of signification: science, logic, the law "established through the objective constraints of biological (including sexual) differences and concrete, historical family structures"

(29). Closely related to both *jouissance* and the chora, it cannot be represented in terms of the symbolic.

Arguably, feminist theory's primary interest in Kristeva stemmed from the gendered parental dynamics she has associated with the semiotic/symbolic relationship. The semiotic, a kind of language before language, is closely related to the mother. Opposed to the maternal semiotic, the symbolic finds its origin in the father, or more accurately, the phallus; the symbolic introduces a rift in the subject that separates subject from mother, thus making possible the formation of the ego. Lacan, identifying the unconscious with just this process of separation and ego-formation, revolutionizes the unconscious by calling it symbolic. The ego, narcissism, and language are all symbolic operations. It is in conflict with the symbolic that phenomena such as repression, abjection, and fear often arise. While critics are often divided about Kristeva's supposed privileging of one domain or the other (some accuse her of essentializing or overly valorizing a stereotypically "feminine" semiotic; others accuse her of working too heavily in the thrall of the symbolic), Kristeva has insisted upon their dynamic interdependence throughout her career; each realizes itself through the other, much in the way that the ego achieves self-awareness through narcissism in Kristeva's analysis of love in *Tales of Love*. Kristeva shrewdly analyzes the semiotic in the early pages of *Polylogue* (pp. 14–50), as well as in *Revolution in Poetic Language* (pp. 19–90).

Signifiance

Signifiance is not a mere synonym for significance, though your computer's spell-checker might suggest otherwise. In the provocative "Prolegomenon" to *Revolution in Poetic Language*, Kristeva invokes, or coins, the term *signifiance* to describe the heterogeneous signifying practices that attest to a "crisis" in representation and in the structure of the human subject. These are, in fact, joint phenomena for Kristeva, and when she speaks of "crisis," she refers to a rather specific moment in literary history (the emergence of Lautréamont, Mallarmé, Joyce, and others) in which "linguistic changes" actually "constitute changes in the *status of the subject*" (*Revolution in Poetic Language*, p. 15; emphasis Kristeva's). Kristeva argues that, at the margins and on the other side of normative discourses, there exist signifying practices that are emphatically bodily and material. These significations articulate "the sum of the unconscious, subjective, and social relations in gestures of confrontation and appropriation, destruction and construction – productive violence, in short" (16). We have historically discounted such discourses as madness, magic, poetry, but Kristeva seeks to give them theoretical coherence – and revolutionary force – under the imprimatur of her new term.

Signifiance, thus, serves as a building block in Kristeva's effort to define "literature," the "text," and "poetic language" within her broad understanding of the dialectic between the subject and society, between "biological urges" and their cultural incorporation "into the code of linguistic and social communication" (17). *Signifiance* dwells closer to the "destructuring and a-signifying" processes of the unconscious than it does to the kind of signification structural linguistics was able to describe, though it permeates the latter as well (17). In the final paragraph of the "Prolegomenon," Kristeva at once elegantly defines her term and underscores its importance for her effort to trace revolution in poetic language:

> What we call *signifiance*, then, is precisely this unlimited and unbounded generating process, this unceasing operation of the drives toward, in, and through language; toward, in, and through the exchange system and its protagonists – the subject and his institutions. This heterogeneous process [...] is a structuring and destructuring *practice*, a passage to the outer *boundaries* of the subject and society. Then – and only then – can it be jouissance and revolution." (17; emphasis Kristeva's)

Subject

Perhaps *the* central concept in Kristeva's theory from the 1960s to the present, the "subject" and "subjectivity," of course, resist simple definition. As I outline in Chapter 2, the subject is for Kristeva, as it is for psychoanalysis and poststructuralist theory more generally, a "decentered subject." In other words, Kristeva emphatically distinguishes her understanding of the subject from that of rationalist or idealist philosophy. Whereas the Cartesian *cogito* (the subject who can say "I think, therefore I am") implies a subjectivity founded on cognition, logic, and most importantly *presence*, the Kristevan subject is other, elsewhere, unconscious, drive-motivated.

Freud and Lacan did much of the crucial groundwork in theorizing this decentered subject, but Kristeva's account differs from theirs in key ways. Kristeva stresses, for one, that the subject is a "speaking body." That is, the subject is constituted in and through language, but is also a material being, who becomes a meaningful self before and outside symbolic language through the "language" of cries and touch, tears and blood and milk, the flesh and that which the flesh expels. The bodily emphasis she gives to subject formation allows her to offer acute analyses of cultural prohibitions, taboos, and defilement rites; it also has led her to find a way to theorize aspects of signification that fall outside "normative" systems of meaning. For while the negotiations of body and language seem most fraught in the earliest stages of subject formation (in the relations between an infant and his mother, or in the infant's understanding of his own body), in fact these struggles persist throughout the life of the subject and indeed pervade all cultural organization.

It is for this reason that Kristeva insists on calling the subject a "*sujet-en-procès*" – that is, a subject-in-process and a subject-on-trial. This dynamic, process-oriented understanding of subjectivity, constantly negotiating between the semiotic and the symbolic aspects of signification, is arguably Kristeva's most singular contribution to the "subject" in contemporary theory, particularly psychoanalytic theory.

Symbol/sign

See "Novel"

Text

See "Intertextuality"

Thetic

The "thetic" refers to the act of "positing" or "positioning" that is a necessary precondition to any enunciation, and thus to any establishment of the speaking subject. I would argue that understanding the place and meaning of the "thetic" in Kristeva's theoretical system is one of the most difficult tasks facing serious readers of her work. Her use of the term – along with her effort to situate it in an explicitly psychoanalytic framework – signals a complex conversation with other difficult theoreticians such as Hjelmslev, Frege, Husserl, and Lacan. Part I of *Revolution in Poetic Language*, particularly chapters 3 through 8, explore the concept of the thetic and place it within her larger model of semiotic and symbolic signification, the chora, enunciation, and the formation of the subject; Michael Payne's *Reading Theory* (171–8) offers the most lucid explication of these chapters I have seen.

The term comes from Edmund Husserl, the phenomenologist who, in aiming to describe the founding structures of consciousness, asserts that a "first philosophy" (in the manner of Descartes's *Meditations*) leaves him with "The General Thesis of the Natural Standpoint" (*Ideas*, p. 20; quoted in Payne, *Reading Theory*, p. 171). This "thesis" means that, doubting everything, he still must allow or *posit* that the world exists, is out there, as a fact. Posing this thesis is a significant *act* in itself, thus the term *thetic*, which connotes the activeness of the act, its inaugural, situating, constitutive dimension – qualities Kristeva's theory almost always highlights in her dynamic, process-driven understanding of signification and subjectivity. According to Kristeva, the thetic, or the projected exteriority of the object in terms of its subject, creates a stable opposition in which ego exists clearly in reference to what is outside of the subject.

In Chapters 3 through 6 of *Revolution in Poetic Language* (32–50), Kristeva argues that Husserl's phenomenological method provides an indispensable, but ultimately limited account of the thetic aspect of language. For the transcendental ego to function properly, a rigorous distinction must be maintained between signifier and signified, a limitation that restricts the process of language to a series of oppositions. However, as Kristeva clearly illustrates, the thetic, since it can be traced to the ego's development during the mirror stage, underlies *all* meaningful communication.

Notes

1 The Objects, Objectives, and Objectivity of Textual Analysis

1. Léon Roudiez, "Introduction" to Julia Kristeva's *Revolution in Poetic Language*. trans. Margaret Waller (New York: Columbia University Press, 1984). *La Révolution du langage poétique* was originally published in French in 1974 (Paris: Seuil), in full. The English edition translates only the first third of the French text. See Annotated Bibliography.
2. Jonathan Culler, *Literary Theory: A Very Short Introduction* (Oxford: Oxford University Press, 1997), p. 1, emphasis Culler's.
3. In his introduction to another translated volume of Julia Kristeva's texts, *Desire in Language: A Semiotic Approach to Literature and Art* (New York: Columbia University Press, 1980), Roudiez pointedly distinguishes Kristeva's own critical procedure from mere application; she is "[n]ot 'applying' a theory, but allowing practice to test theory, letting the two enter into a dialectical relationship" (1).
4. See Paul de Man's *The Resistance to Theory* (Minneapolis: University of Minnesota Press, 1986), which argues that "the approaches to literature that developed during the sixties and that now, under a variety of designations, make up the ill-defined and somewhat chaotic field of literary theory" have little indisputably in common with each other besides an approach newly focused on the "linguistic," in which the "object of discussion is no longer the meaning or value" of the work "but the modalities of [its] production" (7). I am suggesting that applying Kristeva's concepts in the service of conventional literary analysis, privileging thematic analysis over rhetorical, content over form, enacts the kind of "resistance" de Man outlines: "The resistance to theory is a resistance to the use of language about language. It is therefore a resistance to language itself or to the possibility that language contains factors or functions that cannot be reduced to intuition. But we seem to assume all too readily that, when we refer to something called 'language,' we know what it is we are talking about, although there is probably no word to be found in the language that is as overdetermined, self-evasive, disfigured and disfiguring as 'language' " (12–13).
5. A recent *New York Times* article (Alan Riding, July 14, 2001) characterizes this reception (somewhat simplistically) as an instance of typical Franco-American misunderstanding and overzealous "political correctness." Kristeva's own statement on the matter supports these fairly tired journalistic tropes for discussing theory: "She feels she has been misunderstood in the United States by the very circles that have embraced her as an icon of feminism and multiculturalism. 'Many of our American colleagues have taken what we proposed and simplified it, caricatured it and made it politically correct,' she said. 'I no longer recognize myself.' "

6. Philip Lewis, "Revolutionary Semiotics," *Diacritics*, 4(3) (1974): 28–32. Lewis memorably argues in this review essay that "interdisciplinary is an inadequate epithet" not only for her mode of inquiry, but also for its aim and effects. "The crucial issues," for Kristeva, "are 'superdisciplinary' – conceptual and epistemological." That is, like so many of her contemporaries (Foucault, Lacan, Derrida, for instance), Kristeva's work persistently pursues "the most fundamental philosophical questions of intelligibility" in any number of significatory phenomena (28).
7. Julia Kristeva, Jean-Claude Milner, and Nicolas Ruwet (eds), *Langue, discours, société* (Paris: Seuil, 1975), p. 230, quoted by Roudiez, *Revolution in Poetic Language*, p. 5.
8. "The System and the Speaking Subject," *The Kristeva Reader*, ed. Toril Moi (New York: Columbia University Press, 1986), p. 27.
9. Kristeva calls these philosophies "embodiments of the Idea," which obviously glosses a long history of philosophy and indicates that the scope of her critique exceeds the field of linguistics. In fact, this phrase, together with the remarkable rhetorical posturing in this passage, suggestively recall *The German Ideology* of Karl Marx, which also boldly takes aim at a purportedly wrong-headed intellectual tradition (philosophical idealism), for ignoring man's "real, active existence," his material conditions and their means of production. Given Kristeva's engagement with Marx, this resemblance or echo is likely not to be accidental.
10. In his introduction to *Desire in Language: A Semiotic Approach to Literature and Art*, ed. Léon S. Roudiez, trans. Thomas Gora, Alice Jardine, and Léon S. Roudiez (New York: Columbia University Press, 1980), Roudiez reflects on Kristeva's eccentric engagement with these intellectual models: "She is nearly always, if ever so slightly, off-centered in relation to all established doctrines (Marxian, Freudian, Saussurian, Chomskian, for instance). To put it another way, while she may borrow terminology from several disciplines and theoretical writers, her discourse is not the orthodox discourse of any one of them: the vocabulary is theirs but the syntax is her own" (12–13).
11. See Michael Payne's *Reading Theory: An Introduction to Lacan, Derrida, Kristeva* (Oxford: Blackwell, 1993), which suggests that Kristeva herself discourages treating literature, or "the text," as a "unified, aestheticized object or a well-wrought urn" (165).
12. Kristeva identifies "the various formalisms, either linguistic or not, Russian or New Critical" as the focus of her critique in at least one important essay that I will discuss below ("How Does One Speak to Literature?" *Desire in Language*, p. 95). In the Anglo-American context, the institutional force of New Criticism has been particularly strong and is arguably still felt in the structure and curricula of many departments of English. It is worth recognizing, however, that the objective and scientific claims of formalism and New Criticism deserve a more nuanced examination than they are often given. Boris Eichenbaum, for instance, begins his influential survey of Russian formalism with an epigraph from the Swiss botanist Alphonse de Candolle: "The worst, in my opinion, are those who describe science as if it were settled." He goes on to insist that the methodological dogmatism associated with Russian formalism is a misrepresentation and that in their own efforts, "We posit specific principles and adhere to them insofar as the material justifies them. [...] There is no ready-made science" ("The Theory of the 'Formal Method,' " *Russian Formalist Criticism*, trans. Lee T. Lemon and Marion J. Reis [Lincoln: University of Nebraska Press, 1965], p. 102). He does everywhere, however, assume that objectivity is both ideal and achievable. Similarly, John Crowe Ransom, in

"Criticism, Inc." (*The World's Body* [Baton Rouge: Louisiana State University Press, 1968], p. 329), asserts that the literary analysis he calls for "shall be objective" and "[s]cientific," but also allows that it "will never be a very exact science, or even a nearly exact one."

13. Roudiez, in the Introduction to *Revolution in Poetic Language*, in specifically advises that the latter phrase – "textual analysis" – more accurately describes Kristeva's approach to literature (5).
14. "Semiotics: a Critical Science and/or a Critique of Science" *The Kristeva Reader*, p. 87. Originally published in *Séméiotiké. Recherches pour une sémanalyse* (Paris: Seuil, 1969). Earlier in this same essay, she states her position in starker terms: "literature does not exist for semiotics. It does not exist as an utterance [*parole*] like others and even less as an aesthetic object. It is a *particular semiotic practice* which has the advantage of making more accessible than others the problematics of the production of meaning posed by a new semiotics, and consequently it is of interest only to the extent that it ('literature') is envisaged as irreducible to the level of an object for normative linguistics" (86; emphasis Kristeva's). "Literature" and the "literary," "poetry" and especially "poetic language," of course, remain dominant (and arguably "valorized") terms in Kristeva's discourse, if in this highly specialized sense. See also Roudiez, *Revolution in Poetic Language* (5–7, 9), on Kristeva's position on the "literary."
15. Leo Jakubinsky, "On the Sounds of Poetic Language," cited in Boris Eichenbaum, "The Theory of the 'Formal Method,' " *Russian Formalist Criticism*, trans. Lee T. Lemon and Marion J. Reis (Lincoln: University of Nebraska Press, 1965), p. 108.
16. Julia Kristeva, "From One Identity to Another," *Desire in Language*, pp. 124–5. Originally "*D'une identité à l'autre*," *Tel Quel*, 62 (1975); reprinted in *Polylogue* (Paris: Seuil, 1977), pp. 149–72.
17. "How Does One Speak to Literature?" *Desire in Language: A Semiotic Approach to Literature and Art*, ed. Léon Roudiez (New York: Columbia University Press, 1980), p. 93.
18. W. K. Wimsatt, Jr. and Monroe C. Beardsley, "The Intentional Fallacy," *The Verbal Icon: Studies in the Meaning of Poetry* (Lexington, KT: University of Kentucky Press, 1954), p. 4; emphasis theirs.
19. Kristeva, "How Does One Speak to Literature?" p. 114.
20. Of course, so do many poststructuralists critical of the assumptions of formalism and New Criticism. Perhaps most memorable, if also most misunderstood, is Derrida's claim that "il n'y a pas d'hors-texte" (*Of Grammatology*, trans. Gayatri Chakravorty Spivak (Baltimore: Johns Hopkins University Press, 1974), 158). The editor's introduction to *The Norton Anthology of Theory and Criticism*, ed. Vincent B. Leitch (New York: Norton, 2001) gives a succinct overview of the inside/outside distinction asserted in "The Intentional Fallacy" and the critiques it has solicited by Kenneth Burke, Harold Bloom, Stanley Fish and others (1371–4).
21. This interdisciplinarity is not the "simple confrontation of specialist branches of knowledge" (155). It, is, rather the sort of "superdisciplinarity" Phillip Lewis attributes to Kristeva's *Revolution in Poetic Language*. In a spirit comparable to Kristeva's "Prolegomenon," Barthes specifies: "What is new and which affects the idea of the work comes not necessarily from the internal recasting of each of these disciplines, but rather from their encounter in relation to an object which traditionally is the province of none of them" (155).

22. Barthes's most famous essay on the "relativization" of writer, reader, and critic and its bearing on the text is "The Death of the Author," also included in *Image–Music–Text*. Originally published as "*La mort de l'auteur*," *Mantéia*, V (1968).
23. On the issue of privileged examples, Barthes continues: "In particular, the tendency must be avoided to say that the work is classic, the text avant-garde; it is not a question of drawing up a crude honours list in the name of modernity" (156). Looking at the broad spectrum of Kristeva's textual analyses, we could say that she, too, aims to avoid that tendency. Yet "modernity" and the "avant-garde" do clearly enjoy a privileged status in Kristeva's theory as well. For an excellent critique of Kristeva's evolving and overdetermined investments in these concepts, see Leslie Hill, "Julia Kristeva: Theorizing the Avant-Garde?" in *Abjection, Melancholia, and Love: The Works of Julia Kristeva*, ed. John Fletcher and Andrew Benjamin (London: Routledge, 1991), pp. 137–56.
24. The presentation was subsequently published as "Bakhtine, le mot, le dialogue et le roman," *Critique*, XXIII (1967), included, as "Le mot, le dialogue et le roman," in the 1969 edition of her book *Séméiotiké*.
25. Kristeva, "From One Identity to Another," *Desire in Language*, p. 128.
26. Jacques Lacan, "The Agency of the Letter in the Unconscious; or Reason Since Freud," *Écrits*, trans. Alan Sheridan (New York: Norton, 1977), 153. Originally "L'instance de la lettre dans l'inconscient; ou la raison depuis Freud," *La Psychanalyse*, 3 (1957): 47–81, and published in the French *Écrits* (Paris: Seuil, 1966). Lacan argues, "it is easy to see that only the correlations between signifier and signifier provide the standard for all research into signification" (p. 153). Like Barthes, Kristeva, and Derrida, Lacan is at once indebted to, and critical of, Saussure's formulation of meaning and reference: "The linearity that Saussure holds to be constitutive of the chain of discourse [...] is not sufficient. [... O]ne has only to listen to poetry, which Saussure was no doubt in the habit of doing, for a polyphony to be heard, for it to become clear that all discourse is aligned along the several staves of a score" (154).
27. Richard Howard, "Preface" to Barthes's *S/Z*, trans. Richard Miller (New York: Noonday, 1974), p. x; emphasis Howard's. Originally published in Paris, by Seuil, 1970.
28. In Jonathan Culler, *Structuralist Poetics* (Ithaca: Cornell University Press, 1975), a book instrumental in bringing Barthes's and Kristeva's work to an Anglo-American audience, Culler places a similar emphasis on this new "objective." He argues that "we might do well to look to the work of the French structuralists" in answering the questions crucial to literary study as a whole, namely, "What is literary criticism for? What is its task and what is its value?" (vii). Citing Barthes among the "chief" (3) figures of French structuralism, Culler proposes that the "type of literary study which structuralism helps one to envisage would not be primarily interpretive; it would not offer a method which, when applied to literary works, produced new and hitherto unexpected meanings. Rather than a criticism which discovers or assigns meanings, it would be a poetics which strives to define the conditions of meaning. Granting new attention to the activity of reading, it would attempt to specify how we go about making sense of texts, what are the interpretive operations on which literature itself, as an institution, is based" (viii).
29. Shoshana Felman, "Introduction," *Literature and Psychoanalysis: The Question of Reading: Otherwise*, ed. Shoshana Felman (Baltimore, MD: Johns Hopkins University

Press, 1982), pp. 8–9. Originally published as a double issue of *Yale French Studies*, 55/56 (1977).

2 The Subject, the Abject, and Psychoanalysis

1. Jacques Lacan, "The Freudian Thing, or the Meaning of the Return to Freud in Psychoanalysis," *Écrits*, trans. Alan Sheridan (New York: W.W. Norton, 1977), p. 118.
2. See Lacan, "The Freudian Thing": "What such a return involves for me is not a return of the repressed, but rather taking the antithesis constituted by the phase in the history of the psychoanalytic movement since the death of Freud, showing what psychoanalysis is not, and seeking with you the means of revitalizing that which has continued to sustain it … . The meaning of a return to Freud is a return to the meaning of Freud" (116–17).
3. Jacques Lacan, "The Agency of the Letter in the Unconscious," *Écrits*, trans. Alan Sheridan (New York: W. W. Norton, 1977), p. 163.
4. "Psychoanalysis and the Polis," *The Kristeva Reader*, ed. Toril Moi (New York: Columbia University Press, 1986), pp. 306, 303. Originally published in *Critical Inquiry*, 9(1) (1982), and reprinted in *The Politics of Interpretation*, ed. W. J. T. Mitchell (Chicago: University of Chicago Press, 1983).
5. Freud expresses this sentiment in particularly devastating terms in *Beyond the Pleasure Principle*, trans. James Strachey (New York: W.W. Norton, 1961): "It may be difficult, too, for us to abandon the belief that there is an instinct towards perfection at work in human beings, which has brought them to their present high level of intellectual achievement and ethical sublimation and which may be expected to watch over their development as supermen. I have no faith, however, in the existence of any such internal instinct and I cannot see how this benevolent illusion is to be preserved" (36). Freud focuses here on the contradictory impulses of the drives (*Eros* and *Thanatos*), an idea that deeply informs Kristeva's turbulent vision of subjectivity.
6. Jacques Lacan, "The Mirror Stage as Formative of the Function of the I as Revealed in Psychoanalytic Experience," *Écrits*, trans. Alan Sheridan (New York: W.W. Norton, 1977), p. 1. Other important poststructuralist projects, of course, are devoted to this critique as well. Jacques Derrida's life's work has been to deconstruct Western philosophy's "determination of being as *presence* in all senses of this word" (Derrida, quoted by Spivak, "Introduction," *Of Grammatology*, trans. Gayatri Chakravorty Spivak [Baltimore: Johns Hopkins University Press, 1974], p xxi). Michel Foucault's role is also central; in *The Archaeology of Knowledge and the Discourse on Language*, trans. A. M. Sheridan Smith (New York: Pantheon, 1972), he begins by considering humanism's tenacious effort to preserve "a privileged shelter for the sovereignty of consciousness" in the face of the "decentering operated by Marx [and] Nietzsche" and "more recently, […] the researches of psychoanalysis, linguistics, and ethnology" (12–13).
7. For a good explanation of the place of the psychoanalytic "unconscious" in the history of the subject from Rousseau to current literary theory, see Françoise Meltzer, "Unconscious," *Critical Terms for Literary Study*, ed. Frank Lentricchia and Thomas McLaughlin (Chicago: University of Chicago Press, 1995), pp. 147–62. See also Jonathan Culler, *Literary Theory: A Very Short Introduction* (Oxford: Oxford University

Press, 2000), chapter 8, "Identity, Identification, and the Subject" (104–15). For Kristeva's place in this history, see Toril Moi, *Sexual/Textual Politics: Feminist Literary Theory* (London: Routledge, 1985), pp. 150–72. Moi makes clear that Kristeva's theory of the speaking subject (as a speaking *body*) can only be understood "if one avoids defining [it] as any kind of transcendental or Cartesian ego. The speaking subject must instead be constructed in the field of thought developed after Marx, Freud, and Nietzsche. Without the divided, decentred, overdetermined and differential notion of the subject proposed by these thinkers, Kristevan semiotics is unthinkable" (152). See also John Lechte, *Julia Kristeva* (London: Routledge, 1990), pp. 16–17.

8. Lacan stresses, as do Kristeva and others, that his critique of the *cogito*, or the "transcendental subject," is necessary for a vigilant critique of modern forms of thought that have either forgotten or failed to learn Freud's lesson. (Among those forms, Lacan includes Sartrean existentialism and American ego-psychology.) "It is nonetheless true that the philosophical *cogito* is at the center of the mirage that renders modern man so sure of being himself even in his uncertainties about himself, and even in the mistrust he has learned to practice against the traps of self-love" (165).
9. Nietzsche's role in this decentering is similarly instrumental, as Foucault, Derrida, and numerous others have emphasized (e.g., Gilles Deleuze, Paul de Man, Sarah Kofman). See, for example, Nietzsche's essay "On Truth and Lies in a Non-Moral Sense," on the folly of man's presumed place in the world: "the intellect is human, and only its own possessor and progenitor regards it with such pathos, as if it housed the axis around which the entire world revolved [...] and just as every bearer of burdens wants to be admired, so the proudest man of all, the philosopher, wants to see, on all sides, the eyes of the universe trained, as through telescopes, on his thoughts and deeds" (*The Birth of Tragedy and Other Writings*, ed. Raymond Guess and Ronald Spiers, trans. Ronald Spiers [Cambridge: Cambridge University Press, 1999], p. 141).
10. Ferdinand de Saussure, *Course in General Linguistics*, trans. Wade Baskin (New York: McGraw-Hill, 1959), pp. 111, 120; emphasis Saussure's. On this juxtaposition of Freud and Saussure in Lacan's thought, see Samuel Weber, *The Return to Freud: Jacques Lacan's Dislocation of Psychoanalysis*, trans. Michael Levine (Cambridge: Cambridge University Press, 1991). For lucid summaries of Saussure's semiology and its impact, see Culler, *Literary Theory: A Very Short Introduction*, pp. 54–7; Jonathan Culler, *Structuralist Poetics: Structuralism, Linguistics and the Study of Poetry* (Ithaca: Cornell University Press, 1975); Jonathan Culler, *Ferdinand de Saussure* (Ithaca: Cornell Univeristy Press, 1985); David Holdcroft, *Saussure: Signs, Systems, and Arbitrariness* (Cambridge: Cambridge University Press, 1991).
11. For a discussion of subjectivity as a "taking place," see Weber, *Return to Freud*, chapter 6 (76–98).
12. Kristeva repeatedly insists that her narratives of the subject in process should not be taken as literal accounts of anyone's or everyone's actual "experience," though she is often accused of doing just that. Derrida aptly describes the poststructuralist's necessarily awkward approach to "experience" in *Of Grammatology*: "As for the concept of experience, it is most unwieldy here. Like all the notions I am using, it belongs to the history of metaphysics and we can only use it under erasure. 'Experience' has always designated a relationship with a presence, whether that relationship had the form of consciousness or not. Yet we must, by means of the sort of contortion and contention that discourse is obliged to undergo, exhaust the resources of the

concept of experience before attaining and in order to attain, by deconstruction, its ultimate foundation. It is the only way to escape the 'empiricism' and the 'naïve' critiques of experience at the same time" (60).

13. Sigmund Freud, *Civilization and Its Discontents*, trans. and ed. James Strachey (New York: W. W. Norton, 1961), p. 11.
14. Notably, the only specific example Freud gives of such a crisis is not a "pathological" state at all. "There is only one state – admittedly an unusual state, but not one that can be stigmatized as pathological," in which the ego cannot maintain its "clear and sharp lines of demarcation." It is the state of "being in love" (13). Freud's passing observation will become the commanding locus of Kristeva's *Tales of Love*.
15. "I is an other" [*Je est un autre*], as Lacan puts it – quoting Rimbaud – in "Aggressivity in Psychoanalysis" [*Écrits*, trans. Alan Sheridan (New York: W.W. Norton, 1977), p. 23].
16. Julia Kristeva, *Powers of Horror: An Essay on Abjection*, trans. Léon Roudiez (New York: Columbia University Press, 1982), p. 10. On the temporal dynamics of this moment in Lacan, see Weber's discussion of the "future anterior" in *Return to Freud* (7–10).
17. Over the course of Lacan's career, the "real" becomes an increasingly significant element of his theory, a "third term, linked to the imaginary and the symbolic," as translator Alan Sheridan explains: "it stands for what is neither symbolic nor imaginary, and remains foreclosed from the analytic experience" (*Écrits*, p. ix).
18. Julia Kristeva, "Place Names," *Desire in Language: A Semiotic Approach to Literature and Art*, ed. Léon Roudiez, trans. Thomas Gora, Alice Jardine, and Léon Roudiez (New York: Columbia University Press, 1980), p. 283. Originally published as "Noms de Lieu," *Tel Quel*, 68 (1976), and revised in *Polylogue* (Paris: Seuil, 1977), pp. 467–91.
19. Again, it is important to stress the dialectical relationship between the semiotic and the symbolic, and a strictly developmental account of Kristeva's theory can oversimplify the temporality at work. The semiotic does not simply precede the symbolic. Using similar language, Kristeva asserts that *Revolution in Poetic Language* (indeed the very section quoted above) "posit[s] the *logical and chronological priority of the symbolic* in any organization of the semiotic" (Julia Kristeva, "Within the Microcosm of the 'Talking Cure,' " W. Kerriya and J. Smith (eds), trans. T. Gora and M. Waller, *Psychiatry and the Humanities*, vol. 6 [New Haven: Yale, University Press, 1983], p. 34; emphasis mine). Nor can a description of the semiotic pinpoint a moment of origin for the subject: "this semiotic mode has no primacy, no point of origin" (37).
20. "Within the Microcosm of the 'Talking Cure,' " p. 33.
21. For a more detailed examination of Kristeva's critique of Lacan and her objection that he "does not allow for nonmeaning or what is heterogeneous to meaning within the realm of signification," see Kelly Oliver, *Reading Kristeva: Unraveling the Double-bind* (Bloomington: Indiana University Press, 1993), pp. 18–47.
22. "Cultural Strangeness and the Subject in Crisis," interview with Suzanne Clark and Kathleen Hulley, in *Julia Kristeva Interviews*, ed. Ross Guberman (New York: Columbia University Press, 1996), p. 37.
23. Céline's work and Kristeva's reading of it are the topic of Chapter 3.
24. On the book's initial reception, see Léon Roudiez, "Translator's Note," in Kristeva, *Powers of Horror*, pp. vii–viii.
25. Samuel Weber, *The Legend of Freud* (Minneapolis, MN: University of Minnesota Press, 1982; reissued Stanford, CA: Stanford University Press, 2000).

3 Céline's Pharmacy

1. In Jaques Derrida, *Dissemination*, trans. Barbara Johnson (Chicago: University of Chicago Press, 1981), p. 169. Originally published in *Tel Quel*, 32 and 33 (1968).
2. See Chapter 1, note 4, on the distinction between rhetorical and thematic reading (according to Paul de Man's terminology), or Chapter 1, note 28, which describes the same method as a distinction between poetics and hermeneutics (according to Jonathan Culler).
3. I am using the terms "constative" and "performative" in accordance with speech act theory. Constative utterances report facts, refer to an existing state of affairs, are either true or false. By contrast, performative utterances perform or indeed create the action to which they refer. The performativity of language, as Kristeva's work richly demonstrates, has been an important preoccupation for a wide spectrum of poststructuralist theories.
4. "Céline: Neither Actor Nor Martyr" is the title to chapter 6, of *Powers of Horror.*
5. As not only Graves' 1949 statement suggests, it would be inaccurate to deem this critical gesture new, or to suppose that Céline's style uniquely demands it (though again, Kristeva's provocative tone suggests it is and it does).
6. From "Louis-Ferdinand Céline vous parle," *Romans*, vol. II (Paris: Gallimard, 1974), p. 934. Léon Roudiez's translation of the last phrase differs from Margaret Waller's in "Psychoanalysis and the Polis." She translates: "This involves taking sentences, I was telling you, and unhinging them" (*The Kristeva Reader*, pp. 314–15).
7. This summary statement is not meant to be blithe, for, as a voluminous body of scholarship attests, the issue of anti-Semitism is anything but peripheral to a consideration of Céline's life and writings. The same is true for the importance of feminine abjection and the role of the mother in Kristeva's own theoretical project. Rather, my selectivity reflects an effort to focus on the elements of Kristeva's literary analysis that tend to be eclipsed by the incendiary glow of those topics, and that have been given relatively little attention in critical commentary of Kristeva on Céline.
8. Along with Alcide, Ferdinand's exceptional companion in the seething jungles of Africa, Bébert is arguably the only character – certainly the only patient – Ferdinand regards with apparently unironic warmth. Some of that warmth extends to Bébert's aunt, who stays in Ferdinand's thoughts even after he leaves Rancy.
9. "The filthy thing" does not fully convey the multivalent obscenity of the term. In Manheim's translation of *Journey*, he variously translates "la vache" (which literally means "cow") as "slut," "bastard." In "Psychoanalysis and the Polis," Kristeva quotes the same statement from *Journey*; essay translator Margaret Waller renders "la vache" as "bitch."
10. Gérard Gerette, *Narrative Discourse: An Essay in Method*, trans. Jane E. Lewin (Ithaca: Cornell University Press, 1980).
11. Roudiez cites Ralph Manheim's translation of *Rigadoon* (New York: Dell, 1974), pp.125–6. The ellipses and italicized words vary slightly in the French. Of course, the onomatopoeia does as well.
12. Longinus, "On Sublimity," trans. D. A. Russell, *Ancient Literary Criticism: Principal Texts and New Translations*, ed. D. A. Russell and M. Winterbottom (Oxford: Oxford University Press, 1972), in *The Norton Anthology of Theory and Criticism*, ed. Vincent Leitch (New York: W.W. Norton, 2001), p. 147.

13. This claim is problematic for a number of reasons, which I will explore further in the next chapter.
14. Roudiez's translation of Céline is different from the Manheim translation I quote. It reads: "One can be a virgin with respect to Horror as one is virgin towards Voluptuousness" (140). The French reads: "On est puceau de l'Horreur comme on est puceau de la Volupté."
15. A number of key works of World War I literature, arguably grounding a new genre in itself, in fact pre-date Céline's 1932 publication of *Journey to the End of the Night*: the poetry of Siegfried Sassoon, Wilfred Owen, and Isaac Rosenberg; Edmund Blunden's *Undertones of War* (1928), Robert Graves' *Goodbye to All That* (1929).
16. I am borrowing this chiasmus – the distinction between the "rhetoric of violence" and the "violence of rhetoric" – from Teresa de Lauretis, *Technologies of Gender: Essays on Theory, Film, and Fiction* (Bloomington: Indiana University Press, 1987), p. 32.
17. *The Aeneid*, Book II, 722–9, trans. Robert Fitzgerald (New York: Vintage, 1990).
18. Tim O'Brien, "How to Tell a True War Story," in *The Things They Carried* (New York: Broadway Books, 1990), p. 78.
19. The coincidence of the food motif with death in these passages seems to effect what Kristeva observes in Samuel Beckett's *How It Is* [*Comment c'est*]: "a trans-substantiation in reverse; no longer from food to body, but from body to refuse" ["The True-Real," trans. Seán Hand, *The Kristeva Reader*, ed. Toril Moi (New York: Columbia University Press, 1986), p. 233].
20. Signund Freud, *The Interpretation of Dreams*, trans. and ed. James Strachey (New York: Avon, 1965), pp. 143, 564. Kristeva cites Freud's concept of the "umbilical" in "Psychoanalysis and the Polis" as a suggestive trope for the "*unnameable*" within analysis, "that which is necessarily enclosed in every questionable, interpretable, enigmatic object" (310; emphasis Kristeva's).
21. Jacques Lacan, "Tuché and Automaton," in *Four Fundamental Concepts of Psychoanalysis*, ed. Jacques-Allain Miller, trans. Alan Sheridan (New York: W.W. Norton, 1978), pp. 53–64.
22. Sigmund Freud, *Beyond the Pleasure Principle*, trans. James Strachey (New York: W.W. Norton, 1961), pp. 10–17.
23. O'Brien never explicitly cites the song, nor does he indicate what lyrics Bowker sings. But we can infer that the reference is to Will Holt's "Lemon Tree" (Boulder Music Corporation, BMI), popularized by Peter, Paul, and Mary (*Peter, Paul, and Mary*. Warner Brothers Records, 1962).
24. Angus Fletcher, *Allegory: The Theory of a Symbolic Mode* (Ithaca: Cornell University Press, 1964), p. 241n., in part citing Quintilian's *Institutio Oratoria*, VIII, vi, 37–9.
25. "Metalepsis," *Silva Rhetoricae*, ed. Gideon O. Burton. Brigham Young University, July 3, 2003. <http://www.rhetoric.byu.edu>.
26. Sigmund Freud, "Medusa's Head" (1922), in *Sexuality and the Psychology of Love*, ed. Philip Rieff, trans. James Strachey (New York: Collier, 1963), pp. 212–13.
27. *The Princeton Encyclopedia of Poetry and Poetics*, ed. Alex Preminger and T. V. F. Brogan (Princeton NJ: Princeton University Press, 1993), p. 759.
28. Will Holt, "Lemon Tree" (Boulder Music Corporation – BMI).
29. Bob Perelman (and conference participants), "Commentary and Discussion," *Céline, USA, South Atlantic Quarterly*, 93(2), ed. Alice Yaeger Kaplan and Philippe Roussin, 1994.

4 Joyce's "Quashed Quotatoes"

1. Roland Barthes, quoting the New Testament, Mark, 5: 9. He offers the statement, "the words of the man possessed by demons" in Mark's telling, as an apt "motto" for textuality as he sees it: "The plural of demoniacal texture which opposes text to work can bring with it fundamental changes in reading, and precisely in the areas where monologism appears to be the Law" ("From Work to Text," *Image–Music–Text*, p. 160).
2. Michel Foucault, quoting Samuel Beckett, "What is an Author?" trans. Josué V. Harari, in *The Foucault Reader*, ed. Paul Rabinow (New York: Pantheon Books, 1984), p. 101.
3. Julia Kristeva, "Joyce 'The Gracehoper' or Orpheus' Return," *New Maladies of the Soul*, trans. and ed. Ross Guberman (New York: Columbia University Press, 1995), p. 187. All subsequent references are from this edition. The essay first appears in the published proceedings of the Frankfurt conference, translated by Jacques Aubert and Shari Benstock (Kristeva and Derrida both delivered their lectures in French). See *James Joyce: The Augmented Ninth*, ed. Bernard Benstock (Syracuse, NY: Syracuse University Press, 1988), pp. 167–80.
4. These statements occur in Julia Kristeva, "How Does One Speak to Literature?" (1971) (an essay dedicated to the work of Roland Barthes, which I discuss in Chapter 1) and Julia Kristeva, "Word, Dialogue, and Novel," from *Séméiotiké: Recherches pour une Sémanalyse* (Paris: Seuil, 1969), respectively.
5. Julia Kristeva, "Intertextuality and Literary Interpretation," in *Julia Kristeva Interviews*, ed. Ross Guberman (New York: Columbia University Press, 1996), p. 189.
6. All citations are taken from Julia Kristeva, *Desire in Language: A Semiotic Approach to Literature and Art*, trans. Thomas Gora, Alice Jardine, and Léon S. Roudiez, ed. Léon S. Roudiez (New York: Columbia University Press, 1980). The essay also appears in *The Kristeva Reader*, trans. Sean Hand and L. S. Roudiez, ed. Toril Moi (New York: Columbia University Press, 1986).
7. See Léon Roudiez's introduction to Julia Kristeva, *Revolution in Poetic Language*, trans. Margaret Waller (New York: Columbia University Press, 1984), for example, or M. H. Abrams' *Glossary of Literary Terms* (Fort Worth, TX: Harcourt, 1993). For more detailed discussion of the concept, which situates Kristeva's work in a larger theoretical debate, see Graham Allen's *Intertextuality* (London: Routledge, 2000). A good anthology of essays, a number of which discuss Kristeva (granting her varying degrees of original authorship of the term), is in Jay Clayton and Eric Rothstein (eds), *Influence and Intertextuality in Literary History* (Madison, WI: University of Wisconsin Press, 1991). *Intertextuality and Contemporary American Fiction*, ed. Patrick O'Connell and Robert Con Davis, includes the original publication of Kristeva's Waller interview, as well as an excellent overview essay on the history of the concept by Thaïs Morgan.
8. These claims arise specifically in her "Gracehoper" presentation to the International James Joyce Symposium in 1984, which we will discuss in a later section of the chapter.
9. The egregious apostrophe in the title of Joyce's final work – a felony offense to a Joycean – does not appear in the original publication of this interview (O'Connell and Davis (eds), *Intertextuality and Contemporary American Fiction*, 1989). And because it was an interview, of course, we cannot attribute the crime to Kristeva herself; one cannot *say* "Finnegans" with an apostrophe, or without one for that matter. While a quibble about punctuation seems trivial in one regard, in another it speaks directly to the very issues Kristeva addresses: Who speaks when the text speaks? Whose error is this, and by what process of intertextuality does it appear?

10. The range of work on Joyce influenced by poststructuralists' special preoccupation with Joyce's works (as a kind of limit-case of a boundless textuality) is too voluminous to outline adequately here. Derek Attridge and Daniel Ferrer's collection, *The Post-structuralist Joyce* (Cambridge: Cambridge University Press, 1984) does so, including essays such as Stephen Heath's "Ambioviolences," which first appeared in *Tel Quel* at the "commission" of Philippe Sollers; it is heavily indebted to Kristeva's theory of intertextuality and quotes her liberally. Geert Lernout offers the most comprehensive (if often unforgiving) survey of French Joyce studies and Anglo-American work influenced by it in *The French Joyce* (Ann Arbor: University of Michigan Press, 1990). See the Annotated Bibliography on both texts.
11. Julia Kristeva, "The Bounded Text," *Desire in Language*. First published in *Séméiotiké* (Paris: Seuil, 1969), pp. 113–42.
12. See Kristeva, *Séméiotiké*, chapter 1, note 24. The chapter was first published in essay form in April of 1967, as "Bakhtine, le mot, le dialogue et le roman," *Critique*, XXIII, 239 (1967): 438–65. It was her second publication.
13. At the time, especially enraging art historians who held to a much narrower use of this term, Pater traces this "renaissance" from the thirteenth century to the eighteenth, with echoes both before and after. Bakhtin's provocative use of the term "novel," wrenched from a strict literary historical or generic designation, makes a similar gesture.
14. While I will examine certain curious moments of this critical polyvalence with regard to Joyce, its vast and very complicated scope prevents summary here. The best resource for navigating the French and more broadly poststructural engagement with Joyce, from which Kristeva's reading thoroughly derives, is Lernout *The French Joyce*. For a good historical overview, focused particularly on the Tel Quel group, see Patrick ffrench, *The Time of Theory: A History of Tel Quel (1960–1983)* (Oxford: Clarendon; New York: Oxford University Press, 1995); *The Tel Quel Reader*, ed. Patrick ffrench and Roland-François Lack (London and New York: Routledge, 1998), provides a similar introduction, and includes key texts from the group (see the Annotated Bibliography). Elisabeth Roudinesco's voluminous *Jacques Lacan & Co.: A History of Psychoanalysis in France, 1925–1985*, trans. Jeffrey Mehlman (Chicago: University of Chicago Press, 1990), differently focused as the title suggests, serves as another helpful resource. Jonathan Culler's *Structuralist Poetics* offers an incisive critique of Tel Quel's literary theory. Finally, Kristeva herself has written a fairly revealing, fairly autobiographical novel, *The Samurai*, trans. Barbara Bray (New York: Columbia University Press, 1990), detailing her involvement with French intellectual culture and its key figures; Philippe Sollers's *Women*, trans. Barbara Bray (New York: Columbia University Press, 1990) is a similar *roman à clef*.
15. References in "Word, Dialogue, and Novel," "How Does One Speak to Literature?" and "The Novel as Polylogue" demonstrate this referential code clearly. See Kristeva, *Desire in Language*, pp. 71, 79, 83, 86, 109, 181.
16. See Julia Kristeva, "Romeo and Juliet: Love–Hatred in the Couple," *Tales of Love*, trans. Léon S. Roudiez (New York: Columbia University Press, 1985), pp. 209–33.
17. Kristeva, *Strangers to Ourselves*, trans. Léon Roudiez (New York: Columbia University Press, 1991), p. 21.
18. Jean-Louis Houdebine and Philippe Sollers, "La Trinité de Joyce II," *Tel Quel* 83 (1980): 85. Houdebine and Sollers, discussing the meaning of *Finnegans Wake*'s final word, disdain the dominant and "très banal" critical interpretation, which typically

reads the "the" as a sign of the text's recirculation, referring us back to its first word, "riverrrun." Instead, Houdebine argues that a more potent reading, apparently authorized by Joyce's own comments, sees the "the" in an altogether other sense, as a blank or silence or lack. It is "la marque anaphorique, la plus 'silencieuse' qui soit, dit-il, de quelque chose qui manqué ...". Sollers agrees and includes Joyce in general to the radical effect of that final word. Both the word and the man himself "interrupt" sense, tradition, and so on. For a detailed catalogue and analysis of Joyce's "heroic" status as Other in French Joycean criticism, see Lernout, *The French Joyce*, especially pp. 153–6 and 224–6.

19. V. N. Volosinov's *Marxism and the Philosophy of Language*, trans. Latislav Matejka and I. R. Titunik (Cambridge: Harvard University Press, 1986), a work conventionally attributed to Bakhtin, may contain the phrase Kristeva cites. Tracking it back from the English translation of Kristeva's French to Volosinov's original Russian, however, makes such a connection at best only speculative – and perhaps misguided, given Kristeva's own arguments about source-hunting in the face of intertextuality. In *Marxism*, Volosinov suggests that an "objective" view of language as a synchronic system (a view he ultimately rejects) presents language as "a ceaseless flow of becoming," which is close to Kristeva's phrase but not decisively so (66).
20. At the end of "The Bounded Text," Kristeva reasserts that her concept of intertexuality and "writing" calls for a "re-evaluation of 'literature,' and that, in her assessment, simple recourse to the idea of the "author" or the "book" belongs to a now outmoded formalism. Speaking of the "misled" Russian Formalists and their terms, she concludes: "It is evident that the concepts of 'arbitrariness' or 'literariness' can only be accepted within an ideology of valorization of the oeuvre [...] to the detriment of writing (textual productivity); in other words, only within a bounded (cultural) text" (58–9).
21. The reference here to Saussure's controversial theory of "Anagrams" is also a reference to Kristeva's own work. "Towards a Semiology of Paragrams" offers her reading of Saussure, but also notably positions itself as a sort of manifesto on the "infinity" of poetic language and the critical imperative to examine it as such. The essay first appeared in *Tel Quel*, 29 (1967) and was subsequently published, in altered form, in *Séméiotiké*. The first version of the essay has recently been translated into English by Roland-François Lack and included in ffrench and Lack (eds), *The Tel Quel Reader*, pp. 25–49. See the Annotated Bibliography for an overview of the essay's argument.
22. Jonathan Culler provides an incisive critique of this ambiguity in recent theories of intertextuality, including Kristeva's, in "Presupposition and Intertextuality," in *The Pursuit of Signs: Semiotics, Literature, Deconstruction* (Ithaca: Cornell University Press, 1981).
23. I have altered the syntax to avoid an awkward quotation. In the full sentence, the list of authors appears in parentheses directly after the phrase ending with "representation." Aside from demonstrating a noticeable tic in Kristeva's writing (a penchant for supplying exemplary authors by name, in parentheses, and without explanation), the full syntax of the sentence suggests that the list "Joyce, Mallarmé, Lautréamont, Roussel" names texts rather than authors. I would argue that slipperiness, which runs through Kristeva's works, is problematic, especially when it lends itself to claims that sound merely biographical. I will explore this issue below.
24. Puns on the name of Joyce's first novel appear in variously discernible forms throughout *Finnegans Wake*. The one I quote here does not appear in "Shem," but

rather two chapters earlier (Book I, chapter 5) in what is conventionally called "The Letter Chapter." The original context of the phrase also suggestively invokes issues of intertextual complexity. Here, questions of testimony, reliability, hearsay, signature, and letters circulate around a supposed story about ALP and HCE, the shadowy "main characters" of *Finnegans Wake*. On the subject of whether a seemingly anonymous letter provides verifiable testimony of an original event concerning these characters, the narration hedges: "whether it be thumbprint, mademark or just a poor trait of the artless, its importance in establishing the identities in the writer complexus [...] will be best appreciated by never forgetting that both before and after the battle of the Boyne it was a habit not to sign letters always. Tip. And it is surely a lesser ignorance to write a word with every consonant too few than to add all too many. The end? Say it with missiles then and thus arabesque the page. [...] So why, pray, sign anything as long as every word, letter, penstroke, paperspace is a perfect signature of its own?" (pp. 114.31–115.8).

25. James Joyce, *A Portrait of the Artist as a Young Man*, the Viking Critical Library, ed. Chester G. Anderson (New York: Penguin, 1968), p. 215. Notes to the Viking edition offer the following background: "Joyce found this metaphor in Flaubert's Letter to Mlle. Leroyer de Chantepie, March 18, 1857 [...] '*Madame Bovary* n'a rien de vrai. C'est une histoire totalement inventée. [...] L'illusion [...] vient au contraire de l'impersonalité de l'oeuvre. C'est un de mes principes: qu'il ne faut pas s'écrire. L'artiste doit être dans son oeuvre comme Dieu dans la Création, invisible et tout-puissant, qu'on le sente partout, mais qu'on ne le voie pas.' (Quoted in *Critical Writings*, p. 141n.)."
26. James Joyce, *Finnegans Wake* (New York: Penguin Books, 1967).
27. Maud Ellmann, one of the critics best able to bring psychoanalytic theory to considerations of literature, cites Joyce's "quashed quotatoes" in an essay on Kristeva and T. S. Eliot, contrasting the spirits in which Joyce and Eliot linguistically scavenge "among the relics of the literary past" (180). See "Eliot's Abjection," in *Abjection, Melancholia, and Love: The Work of Julia Kristeva*, ed. John Fletcher and Andrew Benjamin (London: Routledge, 1990), pp. 178–200. See the Annotated Bibliography.
28. See Jonathan Culler, *Structuralist Poetics* (Ithaca: Cornell University Press, 1975), pp. 246–7, for a discussion of Kristeva's reading of the anagrammatic (or "metathetic") possibilities in Mallarmé's "Un Coup de dés."
29. For an informative and patient exposition of Kristeva's reading of Beckett in this essay, see Jennifer Birkett, "French Feminists and Anglo-Irish Modernists: Cixous, Kristeva, Beckett and Joyce," *Miscelánea: A Journal of English and American Studies*, 18 (1997): 1–19.
30. For superb discussions of the way both these truisms – that Molly "flows" and Finnegan "dreams" – have been established primarily by Joyce criticism, rather than by the authority of Joycean textual evidence, see Derek Attridge, "Molly's Flow," in *Joyce Effects: On Language, History and Theory* (New York: Cambridge University Press, 2000), and "Deconstructing Digression: the Backbone of *Finnegans Wake* and the Margins of Culture" in *Peculiar Language: Literature as Difference from the Renaissance to James Joyce* (Ithaca, NY: Cornell University Press, 1988).
31. *The Kristeva Reader*, p. 295. Originally published as an editorial in *Tel Quel*, 74 (1977): 3–8.
32. I appreciate Margot Norris's help in tracking down the supposed origin of the word "musicates" in Joyce's work (that is, in verifying that it isn't to be found).

33. It remains quite possible that the phrase in quotation marks does indeed cite a source of which I am unaware. Kristeva's husband, Philippe Sollers, had for years been producing novels (particularly *Lois*, 1972) deeply informed by Joycean language and showcasing critical examinations of Joyce in *Tel Quel* and other venues. *Tel Quel* published partial French translations of *Finnegans Wake* as early as the 1960s. *Tel Quel*, 30 (1967) featured Philippe Lavergne's translation of "Shem the Penman," and in 1973, *Tel Quel* included translated portions of Book IV. Critical essays on Joyce, translations of Joyce's "dirty letters" to his wife Nora, even a rather incidental essay Joyce wrote ("L'influence universelle de la Renaissance") in order to obtain certification to teach at a Berlitz school in Trieste, populated the pages of *Tel Quel* until its final issue in 1983.
34. Joyce, *Finnegans Wake*, 185.6.
35. Stephen Heath writes in *Tel Quel* that Sollers's project is admittedly not a translation but a "brutal, risky transformation" (quoted in Lernout, *The French Joyce*, p. 125).
36. The essay was originally published in French as "Le Temps des femmes," in *Trente Quatre/Quarante Quatre. Cahiers de recherche des sciences des textes et documents*, 5 (Winter 1979): 5–19. The end of the article lists the date of the essay as "Juin 1978" (19). It was subsequently published in English in *Signs*, 7 (1981): 13–35; reprinted in N. O. Keohane, M. Z. Rosaldo, and B. C. Gelpi (eds), *Feminist Theory: A Critique of Ideology* (Chicago: Chicago University Press, 1982), and in *The Kristeva Reader*, pp. 187–213, to which the page references in the text refer. As its publication history indicates, the essay has been widely received as an important articulation of Kristeva's feminist theory.
37. The implicit reading of "species" as "space" occurs in the French as well. The French includes the supposed quotation in English and then takes from it the concepts of "espace" and "temps": " 'Father's time, mother's species,' disait Joyce et c'est en effet à l'*espace* générant en formant notre espèce humaine que l'on pense en évoquant le nom et le destin des femmes, advantage qu'au *temps*, au devenir ou à l'histoire" ("Le Temps des femmes," 6; emphasis Kristeva's).
38. Lernout catalogues a number of these references in *The French Joyce*, pp. 131–4. Indeed, Lernout's textual detective work first alerted me, indirectly, to the wayward reference in "Women's Time."
39. M. A. Macciocchi, *Deux mille ans de bonheur*, trans. Jean-Noël Schifano (Paris: Grasset, 1983).
40. *James Joyce: The Augmented Ninth: Proceedings of the Ninth International James Joyce Symposium*, ed. Bernard Benstock (Syracuse, NY: Syracuse University Press, 1988).
41. Jean-Louis Houdebine and Philippe Sollers, "La Trinité de Joyce I," *Tel Quel* 83 (1980): 36.
42. Longinus, "On Sublimity," *The Norton Anthology of Theory and Criticism*, ed. Vincent B. Leitch (New York: W. W. Norton, 2001), p. 414.
43. As Kristeva points out, Freud always discussed transference love in terms of a female patient and a male analyst (10). A number of Kristeva's own examples, where she was herself the analyst, indicate, of course, that the dynamic occurs in every permutation of genders.
44. For reasons that exceed the scope of this summary, Kristeva further explains the earliest delineations of these amorous identifications by using the term "narcissism" (or more precisely, "primary narcissism"). A number of critics – Neil Hertz and Cynthia

Chase, to name only two examples – have put Kristeva's commentary on this topic to use in particularly suggestive literary analyses, stressing the link she makes between signification (the dynamics of signifiers, signifieds, and shifting reference) and identification. See the "Afterword" to Hertz's *The End of the Line*, and Chase's reading of Hertz's reading of Kristeva in "Primary Narcissism and the Giving of Figure," in *Abjection, Melancholia, and Love* (see the Annotated Bibliography).

45. See Leslie Hill ("Julia Kristeva: Theorizing the Avant-Garde?"), who similarly observes the thematic tendencies in Kristeva's recent literary analyses: "Arguably what takes place [. . .] in a number of readings of specific texts in Kristeva's work (for instance in *Polylogue*, or the more recent *Histoires d'amour*, or *Soleil Noir*) is that the thematic dimension is privileged and comes, increasingly, to predominate. However brilliantly executed, Kristeva's method of reading literary texts becomes, as her work proceeds, less and less easy to distinguish from the psychoanalytic interpretation of themes" (*Abjection, Melancholia, and Love*, p. 149)
46. *The Sirens' Song: Selected Essays by Maurice Blanchot*, ed. Gabriel Josipovici, trans. Sacha Rabinovitch (Bloomington: Indiana University Press, 1982).

5 Wordsworth's Tales of Love

1. Paul de Man, *The Rhetoric of Romanticism* (New York: Columbia University Press, 1984), p. 87.
2. Paul de Man, "Time and History in Wordsworth," *Romanticism and Contemporary Criticism: The Gauss Seminar and Other Papers*, ed. E. S. Burt, Kevin Newmark, and Adrzej Warminski (Baltimore: Johns Hopkins University Press, 1993), p. 89.
3. *Deconstruction and Criticism*, ed. Harold Bloom, Paul de Man, Jacques Derrida, Geoffrey Hartman, and J. Hillis Miller (New York: Continuum, 1979), p. ix.
4. See chapter 3, "The Notion of Blockage in the Literature of the Sublime" (40–60), for this reading of Wordsworth.
5. William Wordsworth, *The Prelude: 1799, 1805, 1850*, ed. Jonathan Wordsworth, M. H. Abrams, and Stephen Gill (New York: W. W. Norton, 1979). Hertz here cites the 1850 version of this passage, though he more regularly refers to the 1805 *Prelude*. All of my own subsequent citations refer to the 1805 *Prelude*, unless otherwise noted.
6. Hertz does not mention these lines, though they certainly further support his argument. I consider this final line, especially in light of a series of other episodes in Books IV and VII of *The Prelude*, in " 'Sole Author I, Sole Cause': Wordsworth and the Poetics of Importance," *Modern Language Notes*, 113 (1998): 993–1021.
7. What Hertz does not mention is the unbearably sad story that accompanies Weiskel's publication, and the aura of sublime potential that seems to surround it: it would be his only book, written during his sabbatical from the Department of English at Yale. He drowned while skating with his daughter in 1974.
8. We can see this argument in "Freud and Love: Treatment and Its Discontents," in *Tales of Love*. It is a revised version of "L'abjet d'amour." Here, Kristeva seeks to "emphasize this notion of emptiness which is at the root of the human psyche" through explicit analogy to "the Saussurian sign," which has been "placed in front of a bar, or even an emptiness, that constitutes the referent/signified/signifier relationship." Kristeva argues that we need to theorize this emptiness and its genesis

beyond Lacan's understanding of it as merely the "*gaping hole* of the mirror stage" (23; emphasis Kristeva's).

9. He originally published "The Notion of Blockage in Literature of the Sublime" in *Psychoanalysis and the Question of the Text*, ed. Geoffrey Hartman (Baltimore: Johns Hopkins University Press, 1978).
10. "Lurid Figures," *Reading de Man Reading*, ed. Lindsay Waters and Wlad Godzich (Minneapolis: University of Minnesota Press, 1989), pp. 82–104. "More Lurid Figures," *diacritics* 20.3 (1990): 2–27.
11. In *Abjection, Melancholia, and Love: The Work of Julia Kristeva*, ed. John Fletcher and Andrew Benjamin (London: Routledge, 1990), pp. 124–35
12. Echoing another of our own central claims in this book, Chase justifies the de Man/Hertz/Wordsworth/Kristeva debate over the "enigma" of signification by pointing out Kristeva's own grounding as a *literary* theorist: "Both Hertz [. . .] and de Man [...] draw their answers from literature; doesn't Kristeva, as well, if from more distant reading? – Mallarmé and Lautréamont, before Céline, or Ovid" (128). For this very reason, de Man and Hertz and Wordsworth help us to read Kristeva just as much as the reverse. As Chase somewhat acrobatically puts it: "The critical texts on the romantic texts provide an interpretation of the effects in Kristeva's essay, of how as it differentiates the indicating from the indication, the difference blurs" (128).

Annotated Bibliography

Books by Julia Kristeva

***About Chinese Women*, trans. Anita Barrow. New York: Urizen, 1977**

This text represents the first major, book-length work by Kristeva available in English, which arguably makes it significant in itself. Its focus on women and its identification of a marginal(ized) discourse that potentially threatens the security of the paternal symbolic structure helped to secure Kristeva as an important voice of "French feminism." But the timing of the publication, coming years before Kristeva's earliest, most definitive theoretical statements (*Séméiotiké, Le Texte du roman, La Révolution du langage poétique*) makes Kristeva's English debut a peculiar one. Her profoundly rigorous thesis text, which Kristeva surely considered a more fitting representative of her theoretical position, would only become available in English – and then at only one-third its original length – in 1984. *About Chinese Women*, by contrast, has been widely criticized for its extreme ethnocentrism, where Chinese women seem a self-serving prop for Kristeva's musings on matrilineal vs. patrilineal culture, Nietzsche's Apollonian and Dionysian opposition, the semiotic and the symbolic. On the other hand, its highly personalized, often theoretically penetrating speculations signal that Kristeva was already a provocative voice in post-structuralist discourse, not to be ignored.

In April and May of 1942, Kristeva took a trip to China with the Tel Quel group, as a kind of research mission cum pilgrimage, for the group was deeply committed to Maoism as a viable strategy of political intervention. Tel Quel would come to move away from this position, and Kristeva in particular expresses her ambivalence and eventual rejection of such sympathies in subsequent works and interviews. However, the trip did make a deep impression and presented to Kristeva an opportunity to work out some of her own theoretical premises, which she committed to paper during her stay. A French feminist press, Éditions des Femmes, secured a contract to publish those musings, which Kristeva claims she was reluctant to do. In fact, in the book's prefatory "Note," she curiously disavows the project. She writes: "These notes do not make up a book. They are simply a journal of facts and inquiries inspired by a trip I was able to take to the People's Republic of China [...] This work leaves something to be desired."

***Black Sun: Depression and Melancholia*, trans. Léon S. Roudiez. New York: Columbia University Press, 1989**

Kristeva's final work in the "trilogy" also containing *Powers of Horror* and *Tales of Love*, *Black Sun* considers the "borderline discourse" of melancholia from a highly psychoanalytic point of view. Kristeva identifies melancholia not with a failure to correspond to its object of desire, but with a lack of the object as such. In the face of this lack, the subject in melancholia experiences only a vague, shapeless "Thing," an unrepresentable "black sun" intimately connected to a stunted or undeveloped primary narcissism. Similarly, this "black sun" corresponds to a lack of language, the inability of the symbolic to represent its own experience. As Kristeva argues, an interesting consequence of pain is a kind of pain-for-pain's-sake; there is no meaning in pain other than pain's very presence as a (pre-)condition of psychic experience.

As she does in *Tales of Love*, Kristeva punctuates her theoretical discourse in the early chapters of the book with lyrically narrated case studies drawn from her own analytic practice. Later chapters of the book deal more exclusively with art and literature – such as the painting of Hans Holbein, the novels of Dostoevsky and Marguerite Duras, and the poetry of Gérard de Nerval. Her analysis of Holbein's chilling 1522 painting *The Corpse of Christ in the Tomb* is especially powerful. Despite the darkness of her subject matter and her examples, Kristeva's analysis is emphatically optimistic, aiming to provide a "counter-depressant" (rather than an anaesthetizing anti-depressant) to the subjective crises it examines.

***Desire in Language: A Semiotic Approach to Literature and Art*, ed. Léon S. Roudiez, trans. Thomas Gora, Alice Jardine and Léon S. Roudiez. New York: Columbia University Press, 1980**

Roudiez selects these essays, written over a period of ten years, which include some of Kristeva's most important discussions of language, literature and semiotics, from two largely untranslated and highly significant works, *Polylogue* and *Séméiotiké*. "The Bounded Text" and "Word, Dialogue, and Novel," both from *Séméiotiké*, remain two crucial sources for the appearance of dialogic theory in European culture. Both published in 1969, the two essays introduced Bakhtin's work, largely unknown at the time, to a wide intellectual audience. Many of the eight essays from *Polylogue*, which include "How Does One Speak to Literature?" and "The Novel as Polylogue," appeared in that work as reprinted essays. Kristeva originally delivered "From One Identity to an Other," for example, as a paper at a seminar at the Collége de France in 1975; *Tel Quel* published the essay later the same year. An essential collection for any reader, the text offers extensive notes, including an explanation of Kristeva's terminology, and a fine introduction by Roudiez.

***Julia Kristeva Interviews*, ed. Ross Guberman. New York: Columbia University Press, 1996**

Consisting of twenty-two individual interviews with Julia Kristeva and her 1992 essay "Memories of Sofia" for *Le Nouvel Observateur*, this collection, divided thematically into seven sections, offers the reader an intimate examination of Kristeva's thinking. The first section, "Profiles," presents a general encounter with Kristeva's thought, from the philosophical roots of her theory to her groundbreaking distinction between the semiotic and the symbolic. The next two sections, "Psychoanalysis" and "Women," include musings on ethics and love, Kristeva's treatment of melancholy in *Black Sun*, the dynamic between psychoanalysis and feminism, and Kristeva's view on "sexual effacement" in the literary institution. Subsequent sections confront Kristeva's work in semiotics and literary criticism (the interview by Jacques Henric on Céline is especially compelling), and call attention to Kristeva's thoughts on culture, intertextuality, the avant-garde and writing fiction. Several of these interviews were published previously in various magazines and journals; but Guberman's book is the first to collect these into a coherent whole.

The Kristeva Reader, ed. Toril Moi, trans. Sean Hand and Léon S. Roudiez. New York: Columbia University Press, 1986

Editor Toril Moi organizes this collection into two parts: "Linguistics, Semiotics, Textuality" and "Women, Psychoanalysis, Politics." The ostensible parallelism well reflects continuity between the two sections; Moi's editorial arrangement highlights a strong correspondence between Kristeva's analyses of language and literature and her critiques of culture and psychoanalysis. Moi draws the individual essays from a wide range of sources, including *Le Texte du roman, About Chinese Women,* and *Folle vérité*; a significant portion of Kristeva's *Revolution in Poetic Language* appears, as well as "Stabat Mater," a stylistically experimental work (printed with dual margins) that first appeared in *Tel Quel,* 74 (1977) as "Hérethique de l'amour" and was later included in *Tales of Love.* The text also includes essays more difficult to locate, such as "Women's Time," "Why the United States?" and "A New Type of Intellectual: the Dissident," which stand alongside such classics as "The System and the Speaking Subject." Moi supplements each essay with a substantial introduction. Perhaps the most influential Kristeva commentator writing in English, Moi's masterful editorial introductions (as well as her overview essay at the beginning of the volume) guide the reader through the arguments, influences, context, and significance of each selection.

The Portable Kristeva, ed. Kelly Oliver. New York: Columbia University Press, 1997

Along with Moi, Oliver is a leading voice in Kristeva criticism, and in many ways, her collection seems to stand as a second volume to Moi's *Reader.* All-encompassing, this edition incorporates diverse material by Kristeva written over a period of twenty years, spanning from *Revolution in Poetic Language* (1974) to *Time and Sense* (1994). Part one, of seven, contains an autobiographical essay composed for the *New York Times Literary Forum* entitled "My Memory's Hyperbole"; significantly, this essay quite candidly contextualizes Kristeva's intellectual positions throughout a dynamic career. Parts 2 and 3 consider the subject's role in signification, time, sensation, and emotional language; composed of extracts from *Desire in Language, Tales of Love, New Maladies of the Soul,* and several other key texts, these two sections of Oliver's anthology provide a momentous overview of several core concepts. Parts 4 and 5, "Individual and National Identity" and "Maternity, Feminism, and Female Sexuality," include portions of *Strangers to Ourselves, Black Sun,* and other works. Oliver's introduction usefully reflects on the critical and theoretical impact of Kristeva's work; and this introduction, combined with Oliver's selection of texts, illustrates precisely and perceptively the spacious arc of Kristeva's writing.

Powers of Horror: An Essay on Abjection, trans. Léon S. Roudiez. New York: Columbia University Press, 1982

The first work in what many critics regard as a trilogy, *Powers of Horror* remains one of Kristeva's most inviting and captivating excursions into the nature of identity. Marking a turn toward the psychoanalytic in her intellectual trajectory, this text reflects on the radical consequences of boundary as such, and what happens when the idea of boundary breaks down. Abjection, in Kristeva's use of the term, consists of both an immediate, temporally specific crisis in the subject's integrity as a subject, and an enduring structure that organizes psychic experience throughout life – indeed, throughout culture. Moreover, Kristeva links this tension with a process through which the drives render the pre-symbolic mother abject. Instances of post-maternal abjection, Kristeva asserts, involve the unnameable, or that which cannot be represented or symbolized. The abject is intimately tied to language; for that which exists beyond linguistic representation yields back to the primal drives so causally responsible for abjection itself. The book's first five chapters suggest a strong Bakhtinian influence; carnivalesque notions such as the unclean and the improper, along with Kristeva's generally dialogic notion of the subject-in-crisis, compel some comparison with Bakhtin's writings on Rabelais. But her expressly psychoanalytic approach sets her study apart. The second half of the book presents a study of Louis-Ferdinand Céline's literary *oeuvre*. Through Céline's explosive, highly performative, style – more than in his lurid themes and shocking positions – abjection speaks.

***Revolution in Poetic Language*, trans. Margaret Waller. New York: Columbia University Press, 1984**

Perhaps her most influential and far-reaching work, Kristeva's *La Révolution du langage poétique*, a six hundred and forty-six page doctoral thesis delivered in 1973 in Paris, establishes much of the theoretical foundation upon which Kristeva's later work relies. The French edition, published in 1974 by Seuil, presents Kristeva's effort in full; the English translation presents only a third of the massive text, leaving the majority of the work, a comprehensive study of the French poets Mallarmé and Lautréamont, unavailable to an English-speaking audience. Nevertheless, Kristeva's project in *La Révolution du langage poétique* is readily apparent, even in the reduced English version. *Revoution* considers such monumental concepts as the *chora* (the semiotic, non-symbolic space inhabited by primal drives, which cannot be represented); intertextuality; the dynamic processes of *signifiance* (polysemy within the symbolic); the geno-textual/pheno-textual dimensions of language; and the wide-ranging social, political, and philosophical implications of a decentered subject. Although the theoretical language and exposition of Kristeva's project often appears unnecessarily difficult and opaque, its challenge to traditional academic notions of literature, perception, linguistics and philosophy has had an indelible impact on literary theory.

***The Samurai: A Novel*, trans. Barbara Bray. New York: Columbia University Press, 1992**

To date, Kristeva has written three novels. Her first novel, *The Samurai*, is a fictional autobiography concerning the intellectual and political life in late-sixties Paris. Its title suggests a parallel with Simone de Beauvoir's *The Mandarins* (1954), an exploration of the previous generation's intellectual culture, but Kristeva has disavowed an express connection between the two. A salacious and occasionally scathing *roman à clef*, *The Samurai* provides a rich tableau for understanding the context in which Kristeva's theoretical ideas were formed. It features a cast of characters that includes many of the most important European theorists of the twentieth century – Barthes, Althusser, Lacan, Derrida, Emile Benveniste, Lévi-Strauss, Hélène Cixous, and others. Kristeva's alter-ego in *The Samurai* is Olga Morena, newly arrived from her Eastern-bloc homeland and quickly adopted into the intense, influential circuit of Paris intellectuals, bound by their shared passion for and commitment to "words and texts" (18). A separate, first-person narrative records the story of a tangential figure, a psychoanalyst named Joëlle Cabarus, whose reflections distinctly echo a number of Kristeva's own theoretical claims. "There are no more tales of love," she records in her first entry, recalling Kristeva's book of that name. The dual narrative device also underscores one of Kristeva's major theses: that identity is always divided, subjectivity split.

Strangers to Ourselves, trans. Léon S. Roudiez. New York: Columbia University Press, 1991

Many critics have cited the 1988 publication of *Étrangers à nous-mêmes* as another moment of epochal shift in Kristeva's career. The work seems to signal a renewed, or newly explicit, psychoanalytically-informed political engagement with the rise of nationalisms and newly virulent xenophobia expressed in many European contexts. Subsequent works explore these and other current political conditions, such as *Lettre ouverte à Harlem Désir* (1990) (translated into English by Léon Roudiez as *Nations Without Nationalism* in 1993), *Contre la dépression nationale* (1998), and a compelling interview on "Forgiveness" published in *PMLA* (2002). This book considers the notion of the stranger – both culturally or nationally (from without) and metaphysically or psychologically (from within). Her study deploys a broad historical perspective – from the Hellenistic world through Augustine and Paul, to the Renaissance and the Enlightenment – in order to situate the problem of the being-as-stranger within the discourse of the "exile" throughout time. In the cosmopolitan spirit of her topic, Kristeva draws simultaneously from history, literature (an inventive reading of Camus's Meursault appears in the first chapter) and philosophy, including an astounding redefinition of Kant's principle of universality in the book's closing pages. True to her psychoanalytic background, Kristeva reflects on the unconscious elements of being-as-stranger (including an analysis of Freud's "uncanny"). The discrepancies among external identity, internal identity and unconscious identity factor largely in Kristeva's approach to the problem of the self. Abstract concepts, however, are well supplemented by concrete examples from Aeschylus, the Bible, Diderot and Thomas Paine. Kristeva also explores the legal rights (and legal complications) of the exile and "the foreigner."

Tales of Love, trans. Léon S. Roudiez. New York: Columbia University Press, 1987

The second installment in Kristeva's trilogy on horror, love, and melancholy, *Tales of Love* argues that love is fundamentally connected to a feeling of loss precipitated by the ego's separation from its mother; according to Kristeva, the love which results from a separation from the mother enables the ego to achieve narcissism, through which psychic space develops a sense of identity. The book takes as its theoretical basis Freud's work on the phenomenon of "transference love" or "amatory identification" in the psychoanalytic doctor/patient relationship, and indeed draws directly from Kristeva's own case studies. Through a complex anatomy of "tales" dealing with love, from Plato's *Symposium* and the Bible's Song of Songs to the poetry of Shakespeare and Baudelaire, Kristeva argues that narcissism is a necessary condition for love; the sense of loss resulting from the ego's separation from its mother lies at the heart of the ego's movement toward the father, and an identity *vis-à-vis* narcissism. Because this turn toward the father requires an ideal "Other" to resolve narcissism's need for self-identification, a threat of failure always underlies such emotional dynamics. In her discussion of Bataille, Kristeva asserts an analogy between art and love: psychic space, as the ego strives to coalesce with its object of desire, realizes the importance of change in the apprehension of life; and the semiotic function of art, its cultivation of polysemy, affects just such an apprehension.

Time and Sense, trans. Ross Guberman. New York: Columbia University Press, 1996

This vast study, derived in part from four lectures Kristeva delivered in 1992 at the T. S. Eliot Memorial Lectures in Canterbury and published in 1993 as *Proust and the Sense of Time*. *Time and Sense* uses Proust's *Remembrance of Things Past* as a focus for analyzing force in the analysis of time, metaphor, memory, and sensation, with particular emphasis on how such phenomena relate to the experience of literature. Clearly, Kristeva consciously writes this text in light of – and in contrast to – *Narrative Discourse: An Essay on Method* (1980), Gerard Genette's influential "structuralist" study of Proust's major work. Although Kristeva's initial concern appears to be how Proust's style and content suspend the sense of death, the text quickly subordinates that theme to a broader exploration of time and sensation in themselves, using Proust's work more as a heuristic device than as an object to be explicated (a method Genette famously admits, and worries about, in his "Preface" to *Narrative Discourse*). The work divides into three major sections: "The Characters Regained," as one might expect, examines the notion of the fictional character as it relates to identity and memory; "When Saying is Perceiving" considers the dynamic between sensation and metaphor and language as they occur in time; "The Imaginary; or, Geometry in Time" focuses on the distinctiveness and nature of the "Proustian sentence," and how such stylization affects time and perception.

Books by Other Authors

Allen, Graham, *Intertextuality*. London: Routledge, 2000

A lucid introduction to both the development and reception of the concept in critical literature and its theoretical complications, Allen's exploration of intertextuality serves simultaneously as an overview and a case study. The first chapter, for example, traces the origins of intertextuality as a socio-philosophical phenomenon in the works of Bakhtin. Kristeva's subsequent revisions of, and observations into, intertextuality, juxtaposed with Bakhtin's own foundational studies, present a well-rounded view of the concept's movement through the twentieth century. Allen supplements this historical perspective with a synopsis of Roland Barthes's pioneering work regarding super-textual dynamics; Barthes's complex reading of *S/Z* is particularly well represented by Allen. The book's final three chapters contrast structuralist examinations of intertextuality with the term's eventual handling by Harold Bloom, postmodernism, and non-literary arts. Perhaps most remarkably, Allen's striking condensation of Riffaterre's difficult theory proves astoundingly clear and useful, a heroic feat given the notorious complexity of Riffaterre's textual readings.

Attridge, Derek and Daniel Ferrer, *The Post-structuralist Joyce*. Cambridge: Cambridge University Press, 1984

Editors Attridge and Ferrer, compiling essays from seven of the most important theorists studying Joyce, provide a wide range of critical material ranging from reflections on lexical meaning and signification to the very problem of reading Joyce as such. Ferrer's own essay offers a unique interpretation of textual continuity in the "Circe" chapter of Joyce's *Ulysses*. Critical readings by Jacques Derrida and Jacques Aubert, conversely, focus on individual Joycean words (in the case of the former, two, in the latter, one). André Topia's essay, contrasting the work of Joyce to that of Faulkner or Woolf, seeks to demonstrate a fundamental polyphony in *Ulysses*, arguing that Joyce's novel rejects dialectical synthesis as a response to duality. Although some essays may strike the Anglo-American ear as unnecessarily impish or coy (the editors' introduction itself is rather eccentric), the selection provides a vast resource largely unnoticed or neglected by those foreign to French studies.

Bakhtin, Mikhail, *The Dialogic Imagination: Four Essays*, trans. Caryl Emerson and Michael Holquist, ed. Michael Holquist. Austin: University of Texas Press, 1981

A collection of four essays originally published, along with two others, as *Voprosy literatury i estetiki: Issledovaniia raznykh let* (Moscow, 1965). Of the four essays, "Discourse in the Novel" ("Slov v Romane") has proven to be the most influential both for Kirsteva's concept of intertextuality and for literary theory in general. In this essay, Bakhtin considers the genre of the novel as an intersection of refracted, and refracting, zones, which constitute a number of author–character dynamics. Such emphasis on "heteroglossia," the presence of multiple voices within one text or narrative, stimulates Bakhtin's notion of dialogism, allowing him to found a revolutionary principle of interpretation: became all utterances possess a unique social and historical dimension, those utterances become dialogized, or "double voiced." This concept relies upon Bakhtin's distinction between centripetal and centrifugal forces in language, in which the former seeks to centralize or homogenize any given linguistic mode and the latter seeks to decentralize or disperse such modes. This distinction highlights heteroglossia as the general condition of language governing the interaction between centripetal and centrifugal forces. Similarly, dialogism exposes the multiplicity of the linguistic utterance. For social and historical conditions, or heteroglossia, are simply too complex to be repressed by monologism; and as such, the refraction of meanings exists as a wholly pluralistic network of voices. More problematic, however, is Bakhtin's insistence that the novel exhibits fundamentally greater dialogism than other genres, such as poetry or the epic. Prose tropes, Bakhtin asserts, demonstrate a high degree of centrifugal force, and so act as heterogeneous coincidences of utterance; in contrast, poetry strives to unify a single voice, while the epic mythologizes a distant past. Both examples argue in favor of a hierarchy of discourses, which Bakhtin rejects.

Bakhtin, Mikhail, *Problems of Dostoevsky's Poetics*, trans. Caryl Emerson. Minneapolis: University of Minnesota Press, 1984

Originally published in 1929 as *Problemy tvorchestva Dostoevskogo* (reprinted in 1963 as *Problemy poetiki Dostoevskogo*), this classic text examines dialogism within the works of Fyodor Dostoevsky, whom Bakhtin credits with creating the "polyphonic" novel. Polyphony, Bakhtin argues, occurs when several narrative voices coexist within one narrative. It should be noted that this particular form of dialogism does not occur as a result merely of different characters maintaining peculiar author–character functions; rather, polyphony requires an entirely heterogeneous arc of voices that deny synthesis by an authoritative narrator. Such a diffuse form of discourse, almost a kind of debris manifest through stratification, encourages pluralism, not monism. Accordingly, this phenomenon cultivates a preference for what Bakhtin christens the "open" text, one in which the textual dialogism repudiates "closed" or fixed modes of discourse. Consequently, the open text acts, again, as centrifugal rather than centripetal; and as such polyphony works to threaten or dissolve those modes of discourse responsible for unity or static definition.

Barthes, Roland, *Image – Music – Text*, trans. Stephen Heath. New York: Noonday, 1977

In this text, Barthes considers the nature of signification within such distinct arts as photography, film, music, and literature. Most appropriate to Kristevan studies are the two essays "The Death of the Author" and "From Work to Text." Intimately tied to one another, both essays examine the concept of intertextuality: "We know now that a text is not a line of words releasing a single 'theological' meaning [. . .] but a multi-dimensional space in which a variety of writings, none of them original, blend and clash." Furthermore, "[t]he text is a tissue of quotations drawn from the innumerable centres of culture." One readily detects the presence of Bakhtin in such a definition of the text; and the distance from Barthes's "multi-dimensional space" to Kristeva's "intertextuality" is one of degree rather than kind. Though Barthes, especially in "From Work to Text," proposes understanding the text as a linguistic event in its own right (as opposed to a medium through which communication travels from intention to expression, or "addresser" to "addressee"), Kristeva expands this notion to encompass the entire scope of psychological experience, a kaleidoscopic range Barthes seems hesitant to adopt. In "The Death of the Author" Barthes cites Mallarmé's poetic accomplishment as an auspicious example of this pre-existent, authorless "tissue of quotations." Perhaps the two most important qualifications come from Barthes's two essays respectively: "Once the author is removed, the claim to decipher a text becomes quite futile"; "the Text does not stop at [. . .] Literature." Here, Barthes flamboyantly paves the way for Derrida's consequent, "Il n'y a pas d'hors-texte." Barthes likewise explores Kristeva's notion of *signifiance*, albeit compactly and with great haste, in "From Work to Text." Much material in these essays derives from or points to external distinctions already made, either by Barthes himself or by those theoretically aligned with him. In fact, a great deal of *Image – Music – Text* restates positions delineated in *S/Z*.

Barthes, Roland, *The Pleasure of the Text*, trans. Richard Miller. London: Cape, 1976

Published in 1975, *Le Plaisir du texte* has had an enormous influence on Kristeva's treatment of psychoanalysis and literature. In this work, Barthes distinguishes between two kinds of pleasure derived from the process of reading: *plaisir* and *jouissance. Plaisir*, usually translated simply as "pleasure," involves a general sort of lackadaisical enjoyment in, and of, the orderly principles of perception and interpretation, processes which largely inhere in our cultural and individual identities. Barthes connects this specific response to what he calls the "readerly" text, which emphasizes the imposition of structural constraint on the linguistic or semiological play of language in – and for – itself. Again, an analogy may be drawn between Bakhtin's centrifugal/centripetal distinction and Barthes's attention to the binary nature of discourse. The subsequent term, often translated as "bliss," occurs in what Barthes calls the "writerly" text, involving ruptures or breakdowns in the semiological process. As order and structure relate to *plaisir*, communicative gaps and subversions relate to *jouissance*; and it is imperative not to overlook the sexual undertones in Barthes's terminology, which conceptualizes *jouissance* as a near orgasmic delight in the open-ended play of language processes, or *signifiance*.

Barthes, Roland, *S/Z*, trans. Richard Miller. London: Cape, 1975

Perhaps Barthes's most ambitious and esteemed work, *S/Z* argues that literature falls into two general classes: that which privileges the writer, assigning to language the transitive role of medium; and that which privileges the reader, imploring him or her to participate actively in the construction of meaning. Whereas the "readerly" text (accentuating the passive, subordinated role of the reader) renders the reader complicit, auxiliary, or even redundant, the "writerly" text (accentuating the active, participatory role of the reader) invites that person, in effect, to co-author the text. Here, Barthes further divides the *lisible* and the *scriptible* along the lines of *lisibilité* and *illisibilité*, or readability and unreadability; the latter he associates with that which is *scriptible*, and the former with that which is *lisible*. Here, we should notice Barthes's insistence on meaning as a process, rather than meaning as a system. The very unreadability of the writerly text, which stimulates *jouissance* by both initiating the reader into a process and subverting his or her cultural identity, indicates the unfinished, ever-changing nature of the "Text" (as opposed to the "Work"). Similarly, dismantling the autonomous text that attempts to correspond signifiers with stable signifieds, redirects *signifiance* and allows signifiers a level of free play among themselves.

At this point, Barthes begins his famous analysis of Balzac's *Sarrasine*, a story Barthes identifies as "readerly." Deploying five separate codes (the hermeneutic, semic, symbolic, proairetic, and cultural), Barthes separates *Sarrasine* into 561 "lexias," or signifying units. Although Barthes's explanation of these five codes often appears opaque (they deal, respectively, with narrative functions, connotative functions, grouping or gestalt functions, action functions, and referential/vocative functions), his intention is to access these codes, through which the readerly, bourgeois *Sarrasine* becomes a writerly, avant-garde textual space, in order to dissolve the apparent realism of Balzac's story. In doing so, he aims of expose the dynamic processes upon which signification rests. Consequently, there can be no single, unified meaning to any text; and as such the signifiers act more as proto-signifiers, pointing only to other signifiers rather than to signifieds, generating a complex interplay of signs. And these sign-processes must be codified, decodified and recodified by interpreters, those who partake of and perceive the immanent reality of a sign-driven existence.

Barthes, Roland, *Writing Degree Zero*, trans. Annette Lavers and Colin Smith. London: Jonathan Cape, 1967

Barthes's first book, published by Seuil in 1953, *Le Degré zero de l'écriture* largely concerns itself with the historical and textual complications of style, particularly the *écriture classique*, or classical French style, established in the seventeenth century and exemplified by Racine. Challenges to the classical style, Barthes argues, did not occur until the nineteenth century when realist novelists, such as Flaubert and Zola, sought to appropriate the entire concept of style.

Barthes's argument in *Writing Degree Zero* organizes itself into a twofold strategy. First, Barthes seeks to demonstrate that it was in the nineteenth century that the classical style began to consider itself an artificial, encoded means of signification, not a transparent or inevitable objectivity through which one may discern the real. The *écriture classique*, Barthes contends, attempted to reflect without consequence a transcendent reality composed of stable, natural meanings. In an especially pointed barb, Barthes characterizes this tendency as bourgeois, a maneuver reminiscent of Bakhtin. Of course, with the challenge to *l'écriture classique* comes an ambition to shape a new style more appropriate to modern discourse; as the old style died, writers yearned for one to take its place. Hence the emergence of the exquisitely wrought sentences of Flaubert, which eventually gave way to the *style blanc*, or white-writing, of Camus, in which style is deliberately effaced.

At this point, Barthes's second major point becomes apparent: just as there can be no objective style, likewise there can be no writing without style; writing, in essence, is composed entirely and solely of *style*. (This proves particularly important for Kristeva's analysis of Céline in *Powers of Horror*.) And as such, all writing is duplicitous in the sense that it simultaneously expresses or signifies some point and comments upon or complicates the code in which it involves itself. These codes generate meaning in the way they enact signification; they do not simply reflect things "as they are." It is this latter point with which Barthes indicts the *style blanc*.

Benjamin, Andrew and John Fletcher (eds), *Abjection, Melancholia and Love: The Work of Julia Kristeva*. London: Routledge, 1990

A superb collection bringing together eleven essays on Kristeva's key concepts of "borderline discourse," this volume concentrates on problems surrounding sexuality, identity, and the subject with respect to literature. The collection begins with Kristeva's own essay "The Adolescent Novel," in which she identifies novelistic fiction through synecdoche, with adolescence itself: "[novelistic writing] would be, from this point of view, the work of a perpetual subject-adolescent"; however, Kristeva considers adolescence as "less an age category than an open psychic structure." From these premises Kristeva develops a provocative theory of the novel both as genre and identity.

Victor Burgin's "Geometry and Abjection" first considers the spatial implications of Kristeva's theory (and Lacan's as well), specifically their understanding of unconscious "space" in terms similar to "non-Euclidean geometries." He goes on to put Kristeva in the exciting context of the aesthetics of the sublime – exciting because it has, improbably, been so rarely done – by showing suprising similarities between Plotinus' "intellectual beauty" and Kristeva's abjection. Cynthia Chase's essay, "Primary Narcissism and the Giving Figure," examines, in relation to Kristeva, the observation by Neil Hertz that " 'a drama of subjectivity' [. . .] must occur 'within a discourse [. . .] which is committed to questioning its privilege as an interpretive category.' " Chase combines a deconstructive rhetorical reading with Hertz's statement in order to explore primary narcissism, with respect to Kristeva, as "a figure, not simply an instance, of the uncertain agency of language." Likewise, performance and action as textual events, two concepts often neglected in Kristeva studies, find full attention in Chase's essay. Those interested in intersections between rhetorical deconstruction and psychoanalysis may find this volume, and Chase's addition in particular, especially enlightening.

Another remarkable feature of this collection is its effort to draw Kristeva's work into discussions of English literature. Specifically, it moves her theory thus, outside the domain of the literary authors Kristeva herself privileges. Sophisticated essays by Mikiko Minow-Pinkney and Maud Ellmann bring her work into conversation with Virginia Woolf and T. S. Eliot, in ways that carefully transcend mere thematic application. Indeed Leslie Hill's "Julia Kristeva: Theorizing the Avant-Garde?" deftly critiques Kristeva's own approach to avant-garde literature. She even tentatively suggests that Kristeva herself, in discussing psychoanalytic concepts and literary texts together, has a tendency in "a number of readings of specific texts" to fall back into thematic analysis.

Benveniste, Emile, *Problems in General Linguistics*, trans. Mary Elizabeth Meek. Miami: Miami University Press, 1971

Second in importance perhaps only to Saussure's comparable study, Benveniste's meticulous critique of linguistics has proven invaluable to subsequent theory, both literary and semiological. Three observations in particular have had a lasting impact on literary theory: distinctions between relations, the hierarchical nature of signifying systems, and the identification of *discours* and *histoire*. Concerning relations between units in a linguistic system, Benveniste isolates and opposes two: distributional, which displays the relation between units of the same level; and integrative, which displays the relation between units on different levels. From this, Benveniste theorizes that the assimilation of lower-level linguistic constituents determines or constitutes the form of a unit; conversely, integration of higher-level linguistic constituents determines the meaning of the unit. Naturally, this presumes a specific hierarchy within language, from which any constituent partakes of pattern; in other words, any conceivable unit derives both its form and meaning from how it contributes to a larger whole.

Such a critical point has had an enormous influence on the study of narrative, as Culler indicates. In essence, Benveniste makes spatial what in Saussure had been limited to abstract simultaneity. Most compelling, perhaps, is Benveniste's discrimination between story and discourse, the latter referring to forms in which the text refers to the subject or situation of an utterance or enunciation. Barthes expands this point in order to analyze the impersonal *récit,* demonstrating the traditional tendency in narrative to depersonalize and make eternal that which is, in fact, an enunciation relating to a specific set of constructed conditions.

Culler, Jonathan, *The Pursuit of Signs: Semiotics, Literature, Deconstruction.* Ithaca: Cornell University Press, 1981

This concise critique examines exactly what is at stake in semiotic theory both as a scientific poetics and as a literary adjunct or method. It is divided into three sections, of which the first describes the general parameters and boundaries of semiotic interpretation. Section 2 offers an inquiry into theoretical principles and trends, such as Riffaterre's strategies in explicating poetry, and the reader-oriented theory of Stanley Fish. Section 3 considers some complications of semiotic reading as relating to apostrophe, metaphor, and narrative. Always an astute and shrewd theorist, Culler juxtaposes the principles of semiotics with the consequences such principles provoke within the boundaries of their own context.

Most immediately relevant to Kristeva, however, is Culler's fifth chapter, "Presupposition and Intertextuality"; here, Culler offers a critique of a concept that has received only cursory consideration: "The concept of intertexuality is thus central to any structuralist or semiotic description of literary signification, but it proves somewhat difficult to work with." Culler wonders whether there is a relatively unexamined discrepancy between the *theory* of intextuality (as an abstract process in language) and the readerly *practice* of critics who identify its workings in literary texts. In support, he probes two main examples: Laurent Jenny, who rejects allusion as participating in "intertexuality proper"; and Julia Kristeva, who, while investigating Lautréamont's *Poésies* both in *Séméiotiké* and in *La Révolution du langage poétique,* reduces Barthes's pre-existent "tissue of quotations" to a simple case of allusion. Such elegant readings characterize much of Culler's expository style; his handling of presupposition as an *a priori* condition for legibility at once complicates and clarifies the immense obscurity surrounding much discussion of intertextuality.

Culler, Jonathan, *Structuralist Poetics.* Ithaca: Cornell University Press, 1975

This text represents one of the most influential efforts to bring vibrant and complex debates about structuralism (and the poststructuralism it posited beyond structuralism) to an English-speaking audience. Because Culler spends so much time considering the work of Roland Barthes in particular, his study provides a helpful context for understanding the grounds of literary theory from which Kristeva first worked, and how her theory complemented that of Barthes (and in some cases, probably influenced it in turn). Culler directly assesses Kristeva's early treatments of intertextuality, somewhat critically – a critique he expands in *The Pursuit of Signs*.

Published six years before *The Pursuit of Signs*, this text, like its successor, divides into three general sections. The first of these, "Structuralism and Linguistic Models," examines the foundations of structuralism in linguistics, anthropology, and literature: specifically, he traces the structuralist "method" from Saussure to Lévi-Strauss and on to Jakobson and Greimas. Section 2, "Poetics," maybe the most illuminating of the book, examines the concepts of linguistic competence, convention and naturalization in both the poetic lyric and the novel. "Poetics of the Lyric," an especially illuminating chapter in this section, confronts four "convention[s] or expectation[s] governing the lyric," although one might qualify such a statement by indicating Culler's sensitivity to the process of reading itself, not just the dynamics of lyricism. In fact, much of section 2 considers genres such as "the lyric" or "the novel" as strategies of reading rather than inherent principles of textuality. Section 3, "Perspectives," falls into two chapters, both of which explore the limitations of Culler's own discourse and the consequent challenges to structuralism per se. The first chapter in section 3, " 'Beyond' Structuralism: Tel Quel," offers a brief examination of Derrida and Kristeva within the context of the structuralist project.

One might assess Culler's overall position as an attempt to establish a set of conditions accounting for *how* we read rather than to propose a taxonomy of *what* we read. In this way, he both contrasts and compares with those structuralists to whom he directs his critical attention.

Derrida, Jacques, *Dissemination*, trans. Barbara Johnson. Chicago: University of Chicago Press, 1981

Dissemination, a careful and subtle work originally published in *Tel Quel* in 1969, divides into four sections: "Outwork, Prefacing," "Plato's Pharmacy," "The Double Session," and "Dissemination." Each section in its turn develops the concept of the "supplement" as appropriate to that section; supplements act as additions to pre-existing bodies or to obscure a gap or sense of lack. In this sense, writing acts as a supplement to speech, according to Plato. However, the supplement is also conceived as menacing since it has the agency to challenge conventionalized meanings or structures. In "Plato's Pharmacy," for example, the *pharmakon*, which at once offers a cure and a poison, comes to represent the supplementation of writing onto speech.

Derrida analyzes this Platonic view of writing in order to attack Plato's denigration of writing according to the presence/absence hierarchy. The "metaphysics of presence," exemplified by Plato's *pharmakon*, presupposes a problematic and inaccurate concept of writing as supplement. "The Double Session," a highly sophisticated and influential reading of Mallarmé's "Un coup de dés," focuses on the consequences of typography and syntax on the letter (i.e., writing), thereby exploring such effects in terms of *différance*, or the process or condition of language by which signification at once differs and defers. The final section of the book, from which the title comes, openly calls into question notions of textual boundary, in terms both of the supplement and of *différance*. It is interesting to note that Kristeva had already been participating actively in *Tel Quel* by the time *Dissemination* was published.

ffrench, Patrick and Roland-François Lack (eds), *The Tel Quel Reader*. London: Routledge, 1998

The first of its kind, this text translates into English a number of substantial essays written by those in collaboration with the French publication over a period of twenty years, from 1960 to 1982. The worth of this collection lies principally in its introduction to an Anglo-American audience formerly untranslated essays, many of great importance, by theorists largely inaccessible to the non-French-speaking world. Editors Lack and ffrench organize the material into four distinct sections: "Science," "Literature" (in which Michel Foucault's astute "Distance, Aspect, Origin," an analysis of several works by Robbe-Grillet, appears), "Art" and "Dissemination."

Two essays by Julia Kristeva, "Towards a Semiology of Paragrams" and "The Subject in Process," appear in "Science" and "Literature" respectively. The first essay, a formidable excursion into Saussure's "Anagrams," posits a critique of two separate formalist methodologies: mathematics (or meta-mathematical sign notation) and generative linguistics. From this follows the " 'paragrammatic' conception of poetic language," a tripartite thesis asserting a few basic observations concerning Saussure's paragram: "Poetic language is the only infinite code"; "The literary text is double: writing–reading"; and "The literary text is a network of connections." These three statements allow Kristeva to use poetic discourse as a starting point for examining the paragrammatic aspect of all language. Although the purpose of such exposition is to reveal the underlying processes responsible for signification itself, Kristeva proposes an initial investigation into poetic language because at that level paragrammaticism is "more easily described." Paragrams, then, contain two dimensions: the phonetic, directed toward the physicality of language as such, and the semic, directed toward communication as a function. This duplicity in poetic language generates a totality, or syntagmatic "writing-gram," wherein the relationship between part and whole is one of equivalence rather than constitution: the textual infinite. Whereas the grammatic is monologic, the paragrammatic is dialogic; and as such, this poetic unity renders language the "only real infinity."

Kristeva's second essay, "The Subject in Process," originally conceived as a paper for the 1972 conference "Artaud/Bataille: Towards a Cultural Revolution," considers the subjective consequences of the signifying process. Although much of the essay recalls Kristeva's premises in *Revolution in Poetic Language*, some important innovations set the essay apart. The "chora" and drives receive due attention, in addition to the subject's role in meaning-production; however, Kristeva also draws upon a twofold description of negation advanced by Gottlob Frege (an unlikely influence, to say the least) which proves vital to Kristeva's subsequent treatment of Freud. Kristeva identifies in the work of Antonin Artaud a desire for "an exteriority of language [...] in conflict and thus in dialectic with himself"; this exteriority differs remarkably from Hegel's idea of the exterior, which involves self-suppression: Artaud sees in exteriority that which discloses the process of "things itself." Essentially, Kristeva's analysis of Artaud allows her to situate the subject as the focus around which signification gravitates, and repels: a subject in process.

Hertz, Neil, *The End of the Line: Essays on Psychoanalysis and the Sublime*. New York: Columbia University Press, 1985

It would be inaccurate to say that Hertz's text provides a "Kristevan" reading of literary or aesthetic discourse. But it does, like so many of Kristeva's theoretical efforts, aim to develop a distinctly pre-Oedipal, post-Freudian approach to them. In a number of exciting, if underdeveloped, moments in Hertz's discussions, he invokes Kristeva's concepts of abjection and primary narcissism as compelling models for describing the "end of the line" rhetorical dynamics he sees in, for instance, the poetry of William Wordsworth. While direct references to Kristeva are tantalizing but sparse, Hertz's approach to Longinus' "On Sublimity," the logic of "Medusan" male hysteria, his reading of an astonishing painting by Corot, and other analyses, suggest that a more sustained conjunction between Hertz's and Kristeva's theory could be quite fruitful (as Cynthia Chase has noticed – see Benjamin/Fletcher annotation). In its own right, Hertz's book warrants reading simply because it represents such an elegant and sophisticated example of what the theoretical intersection of psychoanalytic theory and careful literary analysis can look like, attentive to the level of the letter as Kristeva herself advocates.

Kaplan, Alice Yaeger, *Reproductions of Banality: Fascism, Literature, and French Intellectual Life*, Theory and History of Literature, vol. 36. Minneapolis: University of Minnesota Press, 1986

Kaplan provides an excellent historical and rhetorical analysis of fascism in France in the middle of the twentieth century. In one illuminating chapter on Céline ("Bodies and Landscapes") Kaplan contends with Kristeva's formidable impact on Céline studies following the publication of *Powers of Horror*, while offering a persuasive reading of her own. Acknowledging that Kristeva's reading quickly became essentially "authoritative," Kaplan nevertheless proves willing to give a penetrating critique of Kristeva's argument, in particular evaluating the way in which Kristeva decides to navigate the two dominant "poles" of Célinian analyses: those that ignore his politics in favor of his revolutionary "style," and those who do the opposite. Kaplan deems Kristeva the critic perhaps most successfully to negotiate both readings (though she acknowledges that Kristeva ultimately privileges the radicality of his style over the reprehensibility of his politics).

More than a reading of Kristeva, however, Kaplan's discussion is a brilliant reading of Céline's narrative and linguistic style in its own right. Highlighting the remarkable biographical fact that Céline was practicing medical doctor, she draws suggestive parallels between his medical interests and his literary pursuits. Just as Kristeva so often talks about literary discourse as a kind of "cure," Kaplan invokes that trope as well. But Kaplan gives it concrete grounding by pointing out the significance of Céline's dissertation, a highly idiosyncratic study of Philip Semmelweis, who discovered that puerperal fever (the "childbed disease") was actually caused by unsanitary birthing processes, most provocatively by doctors who carried contamination by moving quickly from autopsies to deliveries. Céline drew rich symbolic force from this discovery, this notion of death literally infecting life at its inception.

Kaplan points out what a formidable influence this medical insight would have upon Céline's work, both thematically and stylistically. As Kristeva does, Kaplan argues that Céline's writing insistently "lets the body talk," in all its visceral intensity. But, more so than Kristeva (though Kristeva also notes the aptness of puerperal fever as a figure for abjection), Kaplan stresses the continuity between the doctor and the writer, who saw both pursuits at finding a kind of "cure." She regards his gruesome discourses on death, shit, decay, blood, guts, and disease as part of a deliberate rhetorical strategy she suggestively calls "tripe talk." Despite the gore, misanthropy, and pessimism that pervade Céline's writings, Kaplan ultimately assesses his project positively. She concludes that reading him, even historicizing his project, we should proceed by "recognizing that along with all the death and excrement in Céline's novels, something is being built."

Kaplan, Alice and Philippe Roussin (eds), *Céline USA: South Atlantic Quarterly* 93, no. 2 (1994)

This special issue of *South Atlantic Quarterly*, devoted entirely to the French writer Louis-Ferdinand Céline, features a host of essays by diverse scholars. The issue follows from the colloquium, "Céline: His American Presence," which took place at Duke University from October 31 through November 2, 1992. The essays and roundtable discussions included variously consider Céline's relevance to and context within, the American literary tradition: issues of translation; Céline's influence on American writers; Céline's reception among American readers; the belated American awareness of Céline's fascism and anti-Semitism; and the significant role of America in the "Célinian imagination." Ample attention is given to Céline's place within European modernism and the avant-garde as well.

Lechte, John, *Julia Kristeva*. New York: Routledge, 1990

A lucid survey of Kristeva's major contributions to theory from the 1960s through the 1980s, Lechte's introductory text both contextualizes Kristeva within a larger European intellectual climate and explores the nuances of a critical body of work spanning three decades. Divided into two major parts, "Context and Influences" and "A Reading of Kristeva's Oeuvre," the text first establishes Kristeva's influences (the second chapter deals largely with Lacan), and then demonstrates the idiosyncratic manner in which Kristeva elaborates upon those influences in order to produce a diverse and sophisticated critical legacy. Part 2's three chapters examine Kristeva's theoretical projects in each of the three decades respectively, revealing both continuities and divergences in the corpus. Lechte supplements this material with a thoughtful conclusion reflecting on Kristeva's importance to, and effect upon, both feminism and postmodernism, and the political and economic subtleties embedded deep within analysis as a perceptual institution. Though brief and necessarily selective, Lechte's study offers a concise digest of complex material. Invaluable for students.

Leitch, Vincent B. (ed.), *The Norton Anthology of Theory and Criticism*. New York: W. W. Norton, 2001

An immense resource, this rich compilation of writings from ancient Greece to the present explores the notion of literary theory from a variety of perspectives. Although most readings are excerpted from larger works, the selections offer an unusually representative introduction both to the larger context of the period considered and to the broader philosophical concerns of the text in question. Because Kristeva's arguments are themselves so often in conversation with the long, dense history of literary criticism and theory (with formalism and the New Criticism, with structuralist linguistics, with her fellow Parisian poststructuralists, with the ancient philosophers, theological scholars and so on), the *Norton Anthology* serves as an indispensable companion text to understanding her work.

The anthology begins with a miscellany of foundational works from the Hellenistic and Roman eras, including Plato's *Republic*, Aristotle's *Poetics* and *Rhetoric*, Longinus' "On Sublimity" and Quintilian's *Institutio Oratoria*. Examples from the Medieval, Renaissance and Augustan periods follow. Romantic literary theory, more generously represented, includes pieces from Schiller, Hegel, Coleridge, Shelley, and Emerson. Perhaps most fruitful, however, is the collection of modern theorists; readings from Eichenbaum, Jakobson, Wimsatt, and many others, provide a concentrated acquaintance with both the New Criticism and its origins in the formalist method. Impressively, the anthology juxtaposes thinkers as diverse as J. L. Austin, Louis Althusser, and Jürgen Habermas, stimulating a multidimensional rather than uniform idea of what constitutes theory as such. In addition, the anthology presents ample material from such difficult texts as Jacques Derrida's "Pharmacy" section in *Dissemination* and Michel Foucault's *History of Sexuality*. The text also contains two useful pedagogical tools: a Selected Bibliography and alternate Tables of Content in which the teacher may organize readings according to theme, critical approach, or historical period.

Lernout, Geert, *The French Joyce*. Ann Arbor: University of Michigan Press, 1990

Lernout's book pursues the convergence of Joyce's writings with French theorists in the 1960s, 1970s, and 1980s. In a self-reflexive introduction, Lernout notably says that he set out, in this project, "to do for Joyceans what Jonathan Culler, in *Structuralist Poetics* [...] had done for American theoreticians of literature" (4). In other words, he sought to bridge the divide between Anglo-American Joyce studies and those emerging, largely in the name of poststructuralism, in France. One of the principal strengths of this work is Lernout's unflinching evaluation, not mere regurgitation, of the peculiar reception of Joyce within French culture and criticism; Lernout offers a critique, in the fullest sense of the word, of French poststructuralism and its capacity to confront and digest the scope of Joyce's material. Rather than simply present a history of Joyce in French theory, Lernout provides a judicious, if controversial, assessment of nearly forty years of Franco-Joycean studies. This is not to suggest that Lernout's analysis is ultimately unfavorable; such academic simplification, as Lernout himself implies, is not so easily tenable. Instead, this study identifies key phenomena, and problems, within the French reception of Joyce's work: a tendency to deal less with the actual text than with widely-cited half-quotations; a preference for abstraction rather than close reading; and a laxity in regarding what Lernout argues to be a very real gulf between cultures. Lernout's chapter on foundational readings by Derrida, Cixous, and Lacan establishes a paradigm against which to consider later French readings of Joyce. This comparison gives a much needed context to what has become a remarkable celebrity Joyce now enjoys among French theorists.

Moi, Toril, *Sexual/Textual Politics: Feminist Literary Theory*. London: Routledge, 1985

As the annotation to *The Kristeva Reader* suggests, Moi is a formidable authority on Kristeva, and deservedly so. In this widely read text, she provides an indispensable introduction to feminist poststructuralist theory and Julia Kristeva's precise, if ambivalent and sometimes misunderstood, place within it. Moi situates Kristeva in a lineage of French feminism that was inaugurated by Simone de Beauvoir. By choosing Kristeva as one of three contemporary theorists who represent contemporary French feminism, Moi has arguably contributed to a triumvirate – Cixous, Kristeva, Irigaray – that critics often treat as monolithically unified. Nevertheless, in the process of providing an elegantly lucid overview of Kristeva's key theoretical propositions, she also makes a persuasive case for Kristeva's originality and importance. Moi maps out Kristeva's roots in linguistics and her characteristic gestures – in her theories of poetic language, femininity, sexual difference, and decentered subjectivity – that make her work distinctly poststructuralist interventions. Moi's work can be usefully read alongside some of the other clearest and best informed Kristevan commentators writing in English, such as Alice Jardine and Jacqueline Rose.

Oliver, Kelly (ed.), *Ethics, Politics, and Difference in Julia Kristeva's Writing*. London: Routledge, 1993

As Kelly Oliver states in her introduction, "The essays in this collection attempt to delineate both those aspects of Kristeva's theories that hinder the possibility for an ethics of difference and those aspects of her work that provide the starting points for an ethics of difference." Three seminal essays in this collection explore with unusual ingenuity these concepts of theoretical and ethical tension: Alice Jardine's "Opaque Texts and Transparent Contexts," Jacqueline Rose's "Julia Kristeva – Take Two," and Judith Butler's "The Body Politics of Julia Kristeva." Butler's essay in particular takes issue with Kristeva's treatment of the semiotic as a seditious force in the locus of maternity. According to Oliver, "Kristeva proposes an ethics that is not a question of morals or submission to the law. Rather it is a question of the boundaries of the law – what is on the other side of the law." This distinction becomes especially important in essays like those by Butler and Jardine, which "[push] Kristeva's theories to their limits"; such rigor, effectively fulfilled in arguments like Butler's, not only accomplishes this expansion, but also serves simultaneously to contextualize and critique a theoretical position both embodied by Kristeva and in excess of her.

Oliver, Kelly, *Reading Kristeva: Unraveling the Double-bind*. Indianapolis: Indiana University Press, 1993

Oliver's text, a remarkably clear investigation into some of Kristeva's most opaque work, attempts to explicate Kristeva's dialectical treatment of the body as a locus for signification. The tensions that arise from the body-as-subject (as well as the subject-as-body) play an important role in Oliver's concept of the "double-bind": an oscillation between that which, on the one hand, dispels subjectivity and that which, on the other, consolidates it. Oliver gives a rigorous assessment of Kristeva's emphasis on abjection as an integral part of this meaning-process. Similarly, Oliver lucidly explains Kristeva's rather baroque 'semanalysis' as simultaneously an extension and a critique of formalism, one in which an attempt to procure a place for the body in such structuralism meets with the consequences of Lacan and, especially, Freud. Herethics and the semiotic/symbolic distinction both play a significant part in Oliver's evaluation of Kristeva; but most interesting, perhaps, is the emphasis placed upon maternity and the "marginal woman" in Oliver's readings of *Powers of Horror*, *Tales of Love* and *Black Sun*. Readers interested in Kristeva's role in, and thoughts on, feminism may find the last two chapters, "Politics in an Age of Propoganda" and "Importing 'The French Feminists' and Their Desires," of particular importance. A sustained and learned analysis of Kristeva's *oeuvre*, this text does an excellent job of both situating Kristeva's work within feminism and dealing explicitly with the consequences of Kristeva's intellectual legacy.

Payne, Michael, *Reading Theory: An Introduction to Lacan, Derrida, and Kristeva*. Oxford: Blackwell, 1993

Possibly the most impressively crystalline introduction to key texts by these three authors available to students, Payne's text disassembles, in order to reconstruct, Lacan's *Écrits*,

Derrida's *Of Grammatology*, and Kristeva's *Revolution in Poetic Language*. Each work, with an entire chapter devoted to its nuances and intricacies, receives substantial elucidation; and Payne's elegant introductory first chapter provides the broader intellectual context of each theorist's work – their relation to existing philosophical debates and to one another.

Though the indebtedness to Lacan of Kristeva's *Revolution in Poetic Language* remains fairly transparent, Payne displays the far less evident dynamic between Derrida and Kristeva by identifying in the works of both theorists an emphasis on polysemy and an uncompromising rejection of closure. However, as Payne himself is quick to declare, a certain respect for former theorists attends this radical redefinition, especially in Derrida's work, as it draws heavily from both Heidegger and Nietzsche. In Derrida's case, Payne closely observes several key, yet often overlooked, features of "deconstruction": that deconstructive agency resides solely within the text itself; that deconstruction is not ahistorical, but rather regards history as a form of text; and that it is not a method, but rather a manner of revealing what textuality itself performs. These conditions allow Payne then to link Derrida's observation of writing as a process with Kristeva's concept of poetic language: both destabilize logocentrism; both may be conceived as simultaneously an arrival and a departure; and both work to characterize textuality as open-ended and dynamic rather than closed and static.

Saussure, Ferdinand de, *Course in General Linguistics*, trans. Wade Baskin, ed. Charles Bally and Albert Sechehaye. New York: McGraw-Hill, 1966

Arguably the most influential book for critical theory in the twentieth and twenty-first centuries, Saussure's foundational text, first published posthumously in 1916, derives from a series of lectures delivered from 1906 to 1911. Saussure establishes a revolutionary set of oppositions intended to reorient the linguistic project away from historical scholarship towards the science of signs, in which relations between units of meaning come to qualify meaning proper. Saussure conceived of language as a unified and self-contained, albeit abstract, system where two basic ideas coexist in mutual support. *Langue*, or the basic principle of competence, acts as a generative force, making possible through its determining conditions all possible real variations. *Parole*, on the other hand, represents the concrete, individual, social act of utterance through which *langue* comes to be. The relationship between *langue* and *parole* can be thought of as dialectical; as *parole* would not be possible without the governing conventions of *langue*, *langue* would not exist in time and space without the realization of its principles in *parole*.

Saussure succinctly declares the proper object of linguistic study the synchronic investigation of *langue*, rather than the diachronic investigation of *parole*. In order to demonstrate this idea, Saussure devotes the first chapters of the *Course* to a phonological study demonstrating the *differential* mechanisms by which words come to mean. That is to say, linguistic meaning operates by structural or relational principles; an object only means something by differing from some other object. Consequently, a phoneme achieves meaning not in its own properties of articulation but in the phonological differences been that phoneme and some other phoneme. A great deal of subsequent phonology has dealt with this principle in identifying a distinction between phonetic or actual difference, and phonemic or perceived difference, in order to emphasize the fact that such a difference indicates the structural, and structuring, nature of language.

As such, language is a system, Saussure famously contends, "without positive terms"; and the differences responsible for generating meaning within that system function as signs. Each linguistic sign contains a signifier (a sound-image) and a signified (a concept); the linguistic sign is both arbitrary and "unmotivated" in that nothing naturally or necessarily connects signifier with signified other than convention. A last set of oppositions inherited from Saussure's *Course* is the distinction between the sign's syntagmatic and paradigmatic axes. The syntagm organizes units into "horizontal" relations of linear sequence in which temporal quantity factors prominently. The paradigm, on the other hand, organizes units into "vertical" relations of simultaneous association in which semantic quality factors prominently. Subsequent linguists and literary theorists, notably Roman Jakobson, have expanded Saussure's opposition on the model of metaphor and metonymy identifying selection as the primary instrument in the paradigm and combination as the primary instrument in the syntagm.

Solomon, Philip H., *Understanding Céline.* Columbia: University of South Carolina Press, 1992

Solomon's analysis of Céline, one of the few of its kind in English, focuses largely on emergent themes common throughout Céline's career. Each chapter, excluding the first, explores the idiosyncratic presentation of these themes in a work, or in several works with a common origin. As Solomon notes, "All of Céline's protagonist's [. . .] are engaged in the apprenticeship of life." Consequently, as these protagonists become more educated in the grotesque reality envisioned by the author, Céline "dissects the human condition, exposing its malignancies, but he offers no treatments or cures." The study begins with Céline's first novel, *Journey to the End of the Night,* and concludes with the infamous *Conversations with Professor Y,* a fictional interview in which Céline rather abrasively descants on his stylistic nuance and innovation. Solomon observes, "Céline's dislocated language forms the rails upon which his subway will run. Those rails, he reminds us, must be distorted." Solomon, thus, structures his text according to developmental principles, whereby Céline's regularly recurring motifs may be scrutinized within a larger context of authorship. As such, the work's main interest is in unifying the disparate works that litter Céline's *oeuvre*; those interested in Céline's style may wish to focus on the book's final chapter.

Bibliography

Works by Julia Kristeva

Kristeva, Julia, *About Chinese Women*, trans. Anita Burrows. New York: Urizen, 1977.

——, "Actualité de Céline." *Tel Quel*, 71–3 (1977): 45–52.

——, "L'Autre langue, ou traduire le sensible." *L'Infini*, 57 (1997): 15–28.

——, *L'Avenir d'une révolte*. Paris: Calmann-Levy, 1998.

——, "Bakhtin, le mot, le dialogue et le roman." *Critique*, 23 (1967): 438–65.

——, "Bataille, l'expérience et la pratique." *Bataille: Actes du Colloque de Cerisy-la-Salle*. Paris: Union Générale d'Éditions, 1973.

——, *Black Sun: Depression and Melancholia*, trans. Léon S. Roudiez. New York: Columbia University Press, 1989.

——, "Bulgarie, ma souffrance." *L'Infini*, 51 (1995): 42–52.

——, "Céline le moderne." *Trente Quatre/Quarante Quatre. Cahiers de Recherche des Sciences des Textes et Documents*, 1 (1976): 16–22.

—— and Philippe Petit, *Contre la dépression nationale: Entretien avec Philippe Petit*. Paris: Textuel, 1998.

——, *Desire in Language: A Semiotic Approach to Literature and Art*, trans. Thomas Gora, Alice Jardine, and Léon S. Roudiez, ed. Léon S. Roudiez. New York: Columbia University Press, 1980.

——, "Distance et représentation." *Tel Quel*, 32 (1968): 132–49.

——, "Étrangers." *L'Infini*, 23 (1988): 13–20.

——, "Événement et révélation." *L'Infini*, 5 (1984): 3–14.

——, *The Feminine and the Sacred*, trans. Jane Marie Todd. New York: Columbia University Press, 2001.

——, "La Femme tristesse." *L'Infini*, 17 (1987): 5–9.

——, "La Fille au sanglot: du temps hystérique." *L'Infini*, 54 (1996): 27–47.

——, "Four Types of Signifying Practices." *Semiotext(e)*, 1 (1973): 25–39.

——, Jack Cowart, and Juan Hamilton, *Georgia O'Keefe*. Paris: Adam Biro, 1989.

——, *Hannah Arendt*, trans. Ross Guberman. New York: Columbia University Press, 2001.

——, "Hannah Arendt's Concept of 'Life,' " trans. Louise Burchill. *Common Knowledge*, 6 (1997): 159–69.

——, *Hannah Arendt: Life is a Narrative*, Alexander Lecture Series. Toronto: University of Toronto Press, 2000.

——, "Il n'y a pas de maître à langage." *Nouvelle Revue de Psychanalyse*, 20 (1979): 119–40.

——, "De l'imaginaire mélancolique." *Le Genre Humain*, 13 (1986): 65–81.

——, "Inclure ou exclure?" *Le Monde*, 14361 (1991): 21.

——, *In the Beginning was Love: Psychoanalysis and Faith*, trans. Arthur Goldhamer. New York: Columbia University Press, 1987.

——, *Julia Kristeva: Interviews*, ed. Ross Guberman. New York: Columbia University Press, 1996.
——, *The Kristeva Reader*, trans. Sean Hand and Léon S. Roudiez, ed. Toril Moi. New York: Columbia University Press, 1986.
——, *Language, the Unknown: An Initiation into Linguistics*, trans. Anne M. Menke. New York: Columbia University Press, 1989.
——, Jean Claude Milner, and Nicolas Ruwet (eds), *Langue, discours, société*. Paris: Seuil, 1975.
——, "Linguistique et sémiologie aujourd'hui en U.R.S.S." *Tel Quel*, 35 (1968): 3–8.
——, "Littérature et révolution." *Tel Quel*, 48–9 (1972): 66–71.
——, "Narration et transformation." *Semiotica*, 1 (1969): 422–48.
——, *Nations without Nationalism*, trans. Léon S. Roudiez. New York: Columbia University Press, 1993.
——, "Ne dis rien." *Tel Quel*, 91 (1982): 33–44.
——, *New Maladies of the Soul*, trans. Ross Guberman. New York: Columbia University Press, 1995.
——, "Noms de lieu." *Tel Quel*, 68 (1976).
——, "Le Nouveau monde solitaire." *Le Genre Humain*, 11 (1984–5): 207–14.
——, "L'Objet, complément, dialectique." *Critique*, 28 (1971): 99–131.
——, *The Old Man and the Wolves*, trans. Barbara Bray. New York: Columbia University Press, 1994.
——, "On Yuri Lotman." *PMLA*, 109 (1994): 375–84.
——, *Polylogue*. Paris: Seuil, 1977.
——, *The Portable Kristeva*, ed. Kelly Oliver. New York: Columbia University Press, 1997.
——, *Possessions: A Novel*, trans. Barbara Bray. New York: Columbia University Press, 1998.
——, *Powers of Horror: An Essay on Abjection*, trans. Léon S. Roudiez. New York: Columbia University Press, 1982.
——, "A propos de l'idéologie scientifique." *Promesse*, 27 (1969): 53–77.
——, *Proust and the Sense of Time*, trans. Stephen Bann. New York: Columbia University Press, 1993.
——, "Psychoanalysis and the Polis." *Critical Inquiry*, 9:1 (1982): 77–92.
——, "Quelques particularités du discours dépressif." *Information psychiatrique*, 68:3 (1992): 239–50.
——, "La Révolution du language poétique." *Tel Quel*, 56 (1973): 36–59.
——, *Revolution in Poetic Language*, trans. Margaret Waller. New York: Columbia University Press, 1984.
——, "Les Samouraïs tel quels." *L'Infini*, 49/50 (1995): 57–61.
——, *The Samurai: A Novel*, trans. Barbara Bray. New York: Columbia University Press, 1992.
——, *Séméiotiké: Recherches pour une sémanalyse*. Paris: Seuil, 1969.
——, "La Sémiologie comme science des idéologies." *Semiotica*, 1 (1969): 196–204.
——, "The Semiotic Activity." *Screen*, 14:1–2 (1973): 25–39.
——, "La Sensation est-elle un langage?" *Nouvelle Revue de Psychanalyse*, 3 (1992): 9–30.
——, *The Sense and Nonsense of Revolt*, trans. Jeanine Herman. New York: Columbia University Press, 2000.
——, "The Speaking Subject." *On Signs*, ed. Marshall Blonsky. Baltimore: Johns Hopkins University Press, 1985.
——, *Strangers to Ourselves*, trans. Léon S. Roudiez. New York: Columbia University Press, 1991.

Kristeva, Julia, "The Subject in Signifying Practice." *Semiotext(e)*, 1:3 (1975): 19–26.
——, "Sujet dans le langage et pratique politique." *Tel Quel*, 58 (1974): 22–7.
——, *Tales of Love*, trans. Léon S. Roudiez. New York: Columbia University Press, 1987.
——, "Le Temps des femmes." *Trente Quatre/Quarante Quatre. Cahiers de recherche des sciences des textes et documents*, 5 (1979): 5–19.
——, *Le Texte du roman: Approches sémiologique d'une structure discursive transformationnelle*. The Hague: Mouton de Gruyter, 1970.
——, *Time and Sense*, trans. Ross Guberman. New York: Columbia University Press, 1996.
——, "D'une identité à l'autre." *Tel Quel*, 62 (1975).
——, "La Vierge de Freud." *L'Infini*, 18 (1987): 22–33.
——, *Visions capitales*. Paris: Réunion des Musées Nationaux, 1998.
——, "La Voix de Barthes." *Communications*, 36 (1982): 119–23.
——, "What of Tomorrow's Nation?" *Alphabet City*, 2 (1992): 32, 34.
——, "Within the Microcosm of the 'Talking Cure,' " trans. T. Gora and M. Waller. *Psychiatry and the Humanities*, eds. William Kerrigan and Joseph Smith, vol. 6. New Haven, CT: Yale University Press, 1983.
——, "Word, Dialogue, and Novel." *The Kristeva Reader*, trans. Sean Hand and Léon S. Roudiez, ed. Toril Moi. New York: Columbia University Press, 1986.

Other Works

Abrams, M. H., *Glossary of Literary Terms*. Fort Worth: Harcourt, 1993.
Allen, Graham, *Intertextuality*. London: Routledge, 2000.
Attridge, Derek, *Peculiar Language: Literature as Difference from the Renaissance to James Joyce*. Ithaca: Cornell University Press, 1988.
——, *Joyce Effects: On Language, History, and Theory*. New York: Cambridge University Press, 2000.
—— and Daniel Ferrer, *The Post-structuralist Joyce*. Cambridge: Cambridge University Press, 1984.
Austin, J. L., *How to Do Things with Words*. Cambridge: Harvard University Press, 1962.
Bakhtin, M. M., *The Formal Method in Literary Scholarship: A Critical Introduction to Sociological Poetics*, trans. A. J. Wehrle. Baltimore: Johns Hopkins University Press, 1978.
——, *The Dialogic Imagination: Four Essays*, trans. Caryl Emerson and Michael Holquist, ed. Michael Holquist. Austin: University of Texas Press, 1981.
——, *Problems of Dostoevsky's Poetics*, trans. Caryl Emerson. Minneapolis: University of Minnesota Press, 1984.
——, *Rabelais and His World*, trans. H. Iswolsky. Bloomington: Indiana University Press, 1984.
——, *Speech Genres and Other Late Essays*, trans. Vern W. McGee, eds. Caryl Emerson and Michael Holquist. Austin: University of Texas Press, 1986.
——, *Art and Answerability: Early Philosophical Essays*, trans. V. Liapunov, eds. M. Holquist and V. Liapunov. Austin: University of Texas Press, 1990.
Balakian, Anna, *The Symbolist Movement*. New York: New York University Press, 1977.
——, *The Fiction of the Poet*. Princeton, NJ: Princeton University Press, 1992.
Barthes, Roland, *Writing Degree Zero*, trans. Annette Lavers and Colin Smith. London: Cape, 1967.

——, *S/Z*, trans. Richard Miller. London: Cape, 1975.

——, *The Pleasure of the Text*, trans. Richard Miller. London: Cape, 1976.

——, *Image – Music – Text*, trans. Stephen Heath. New York: Noonday, 1977.

Bataille, Georges, *The Bataille Reader*, ed. Fred Botting and Scott Wilson. Oxford: Blackwell, 1997.

——, *Essential Writings*, ed. Michael Richardson. London: Sage, 1998.

Beardsley, Monroe C. and W. K. Wimsatt, Jr, "The Intentional Fallacy." *The Verbal Icon: Studies in Meaning of Poetry*. Lexington: University of Kentucky Press, 1954.

Becker-Leckrone, Megan, " 'Sole Author I, Sole Cause': Wordsworth and the Poetics of Importance," *Modern Language Notes*, 113 (1998): 993–1021.

Benjamin, Andrew and John Fletcher (eds), *Abjection, Melancholia and Love: The Work of Julia Kristeva*. London: Routledge, 1990.

Benstock, Bernard (ed.), *James Joyce: The Augmented Ninth*. Syracuse, NY: Syracuse University Press, 1988.

Benveniste, Emile, *Problems in General Linguistics*, trans. Mary Elizabeth Meek. Miami: Miami University Press, 1971.

Birkett, Jennifer, "French Feminists and Anglo-Irish Modernists: Cixous, Kristeva, Beckett and Joyce." *Miscelánea: A Journal of English and American Studies*, 18 (1997): 1–19.

Blanchot, Maurice, *Le livre à venir*. Paris: Gallimard, 1959.

——, *The Gaze of Orpheus and Other Literary Essays*, ed. P. Adams Sitney, trans. Lydia Davis. New York: Station Hill Press, 1981.

——, "Where Now? Who Now?" *The Siren's Song: Selected Essays by Maurice Blanchot*, ed. Gabriel Josipivici, trans. Sacha Rabinovitch (Bloomington: Indiana University Press, 1982), pp. 192–8.

——, *Faux Pas*, trans. Charlotte Mandell. Stanford: Stanford University Press, 2001.

Bloom, Harold, Paul de Man, Jacques Derrida, Geoffrey Hartman, and J. Hillis Miller (eds), *Deconstruction and Criticism*. New York: Continuum, 1979.

Blunden, Edmund, *Undertones of War*. London: Penguin, 1928.

Booth, Wayne C., *The Rhetoric of Fiction*. Chicago: University of Chicago Press, 1961.

Bowie, Malcolm, *Mallarmé and the Art of Being Difficult*. Cambridge: Cambridge University Press, 1978.

Brogan, T. V. F. and Alex Preminger (eds), *The New Princeton Encyclopedia of Poetry and Poetics*. Princeton, NJ: Princeton University Press, 1993.

Brownstein, Marilyn L., "The Preservation of Tenderness: A Confusion of Tongues in *Ulysses* and *Finnegans Wake*." *Joyce: The Return of the RePed*, ed. Susan Stanford Friedman. Ithaca, NY: Cornell University Press, 1993, pp. 225–56.

Carpenter, William, " 'Le Livre' of Mallarmé and James Joyce's *Ulysses*." *Mallarmé in the Twentieth Century*, ed. Robert Greer Cohn. London: Associated University Press, 1998, pp. 187–202.

Céline, Louis-Ferdinand, *Journey to the End of the Night*, trans. John H. P. Marks. Boston: Little, Brown, 1934.

——, *Journey to the End of the Night*, trans. Ralph Manheim. New York: New Directions, 1938.

——, *Death on the Installment Plan*, trans. Ralph Manheim. New York: New Directions, 1966.

——, *Castle to Castle*, trans. Ralph Manheim. New York: Delacorte, 1968.

——, *Rigadoon*, trans. Ralph Manheim. New York: Dell, 1974.

——, "Louis-Ferdinand Céline vous parle." *Romans*, vol. II. Paris: Gallimard, 1974.

——, *Conversations with Professor Y*, trans. Stanford Luce. Hanover: University Press of New England, 1986.

Clayton, Jay and Eric Rothstein (eds), *Influence and Intertextuality in Literary History*. Madison: University of Wisconsin Press, 1991.

Cornell, Kenneth, *The Symbolist Movement*. New Haven, CT: Yale University Press, 1951.

Culler, Jonathan, *Structuralist Poetics*. Ithaca, NY: Cornell University Press, 1975.

——, *The Pursuit of Signs: Semiotics, Literature, Deconstruction*. Ithaca, NY: Cornell University Press, 1981.

——, *Ferdinand de Saussure*. Ithaca, NY: Cornell University Press, 1985.

——, *Literary Theory: A Very Short Introduction*. Oxford: Oxford University Press, 1997.

Davis, Robert Con and Patrick O'Connell (eds), *Intertextuality and Contemporary American Fiction*. Baltimore, MD: Johns Hopkins University Press, 1989.

de Lauretis, Teresa, *Technologies of Gender: Essays on Theory, Film, and Fiction*. Bloomington: Indiana University Press, 1987.

De Man, Paul, *Romanticism and Contemporary Criticism: The Gauss Seminar and Other Papers*, ed. E. S. Burt, Kevin Newmark, and Adrzej Warminski. Baltimore, MD: Johns Hopkins University Press, 1993.

——, *The Resistance to Theory*. Minneapolis: University of Minnesota Press, 1986.

——, *The Rhetoric of Romanticism*. New York: Columbia University Press, 1984.

Deleuze, Gilles and Félix Guattari, *Anti-Oedipus: Capitalism and Schizophrenia*. Minneapolis: University of Minnesota Press, 1972.

Derrida, Jacques, *Of Grammatology*, trans. Gayatri Chakravorty Spivak. Baltimore, MD: Johns Hopkins University Press, 1974.

——, *Dissemination*, trans. Barbara Johnson. Chicago: University of Chicago Press, 1981.

Eichenbaum, Boris, "The Theory of the 'Formal Method'." *Russian Formalist Criticism*, trans. Lee T. Lemon and Marion J. Reis. Lincoln: University of Nebraska Press, 1965.

Felman, Shoshana, "Introduction." *Literature and Psychoanalysis: The Question of Reading: Otherwise*, ed. Shoshana Felman. Baltimore, MD: Johns Hopkins University Press, 1982.

ffrench, Patrick, *The Time of Theory: A History of Tel Quel (1960–1983)*. New York: Oxford University Press, 1995.

—— and Roland-François Lack (eds), *The Tel Quel Reader*. London: Routledge, 1998.

Fletcher, Angus, *Allegory: The Theory of a Symbolic Mode*. Ithaca, NY: Cornell University Press, 1964.

Fonágy, Ivan, "The Functions of Vocal Style." *Literary Style: A Symposium*, ed. Seymour Chatman. London: Oxford University Press, 1971, pp. 159–74.

——, "Prélangage et régressions syntaxiques." *Lingua*, 36 (1975): 163–208.

——, "L'Accent français: Accent probabilitaire (dynamique d'un changement prosodique)." *L'Accent en français contemporain*, ed. Ivan Fonágy and Pierre Léon. Ottawa: Didier, 1979, pp. 123–233.

——, *La Vive Voix: Essais de psychopoétique*. Paris: Payot, 1983.

Fowlie, Wallace. *Mallarmé*. Chicago: University of Chicago Press, 1953.

Freud, Sigmund, *Beyond the Pleasure Principle*, trans. James Strachey. New York: W.W. Norton, 1961.

——, *Civilization and its Discontents*, trans. and ed. James Strachey. New York: W.W. Norton, 1961.

——, *The Interpretation of Dreams*, trans. and ed. James Strachey. New York: Avon, 1965.

Frey, Hans-Jost, *Studies in Poetic Discourse*, trans. William Whobrey. Stanford, CA: Stanford University Press, 1996.

Genette, Gérard, *Figures III*. Paris: Seuil, 1977.
——, *Narrative Discourse: An Essay in Method*, trans. Jane E. Lewin. Ithaca, NY: Cornell University Press, 1980.
——, *Figures of Literary Discourse*, trans. Alan Sheridan. New York: Columbia University Press, 1982.
Graves, Robert, *Good-Bye to All That*. Garden City: Doubleday, 1957.
Gregory, Shelley, "Rewaking the Mother Tongue in *Finnegans Wake*: A Kristevan Approach." *English Language Notes*, 34:1 (1996): 63–76.
Hartman, Geoffrey, *The Unremarkable Wordsworth*. Minneapolis: University of Minnesota Press, 1987.
—— (ed.), *Psychoanalysis and the Question of the Text*. Baltimore: Johns Hopkins University Press, 1978.
Hertz, Neil, *The End of the Line: Essays on Psychoanalysis and the Sublime*. New York: Columbia University Press, 1985.
——, "Lurid Figures." *Reading de Man Reading*, ed. Lindsay Waters and Wlad Godzich. Minneapolis: University of Minnesota Press, 1989, pp. 82–104.
——, "More Lurid Figures." *Diacritics*, 20:3 (1990): 2–27.
Holdcroft, David, *Saussure: Signs, Systems, and Arbitrariness*. Cambridge: Cambridge University Press, 1991.
Houdebine, Jean-Louis and Philippe Sollers, "La Trinité de Joyce I." *Tel Quel*, 83 (1980): 36–62.
——, "La Trinité de Joyce II." *Tel Quel*, 83 (1980): 63–85.
Joyce, James, *Finnegans Wake*. New York: Penguin, 1967.
——, *A Portrait of the Artist as a Young Man*. New York: Penguin, 1968.
Kaplan, Alice Yaeger and Philippe Roussin (eds), *Céline USA*. *South Atlantic Quarterly*, 93:2 (1994).
Kaplan, Alice Yaeger, *Reproductions of Banality: Fascism, Literature, and French Intellectual Life*, Theory and History of Literature, vol. 36. Minneapolis: University of Minnesota Press, 1986.
Lacan, Jacques, "The Agency of the Letter in the Unconscious, or Reason since Freud." *Écrits*, trans. Alan Sheridan. New York: W.W. Norton, 1977.
——, "The Freudian Thing, or the Meaning of the Return to Freud in Psychoanalysis." *Écrits*, trans. Alan Sheridan. New York: W.W. Norton, 1977.
——, "Aggressivity in Psychoanalysis." *Écrits*, trans. Alan Sheridan. New York: W.W. Norton, 1977.
——, "The Mirror Stage as Formative of the Function of the I as Revealed in Psychoanalytic Experience." *Écrits*, trans. Alan Sheridan. New York: W.W. Norton, 1977.
——, "Tuché and Automaton." *Four Fundamental Concepts of Psychoanalysis*, trans. Alan Sheridan, ed. Jacques-Allain Miller. New York: W.W. Norton, 1978.
——, *Feminine Sexuality: Jacques Lacan and the "ecde Freudienne,"* ed. Juliet Mitchell and Jacqueline Rose. New York: W. W. Norton, 1982.
Ladd, D. Robert, *Intonational Phonology*. Cambridge: Cambridge University Press, 1996.
Lawler, James, *The Language of French Symbolism*. Princeton, NJ: Princeton University Press, 1969.
Lechte, John, *Julia Kristeva*. New York: Routledge, 1990.
—— and Mary Zournazi (eds), *The Kristeva Critical Reader*. Edinburgh: Edinburgh University Press, 2003.

Leitch, Vincent B. (ed.), *The Norton Anthology of Theory and Criticism*. New York: W.W. Norton, 2001.

Lernout, Geert, *The French Joyce*. Ann Arbor: University of Michigan Press, 1990.

Lewis, Philip, "Revolutionary Semiotics." *Diacritics*, 4:3 (1974): 28–32.

Macciocchi, Maria-Antonietta, *Deux mille ans de bonheur*, trans. Jean-Noël Schifano. Paris: Grasset, 1983.

MacMahon, Barbara, "The Effects of Word Substitution in Slips of the Tongue, *Finnegans Wake* and *The Third Policeman*." *English Studies: A Journal of Language and Literature*, 82:3 (2001): 231–46.

Meschonnic, Henri, *Critique du Rythme*. Lagrasse: Verdier, 1982.

Metzer, François, "Unconscious." *Critical Terms for Literary Study*, ed. Frank Lentricchia and Thomas McLaughlin. Chicago: University of Chicago Press, 1995.

Moi, Toril, *Sexual/Textual Politics: Feminist Literary Theory*. London: Routledge, 1985.

Nietzsche, Friedrich, *The Birth of Tragedy and Other Writings*, trans. Ronald Spiers, ed. Raymond Guess and Ronald Spiers. Cambridge: Cambridge University Press, 1999.

O'Brien, Tim, "How to Tell a True War Story." *The Things I Carried*. New York: Broadway Books, 1990.

Oliver, Kelly (ed.), *Ethics, Politics, and Difference in Julia Kristeva's Writing*. London: Routledge, 1993.

——, *Reading Kristeva: Unraveling the Double-bind*. Indianapolis: Indiana University Press, 1993.

Payne, Michael, *Reading Theory: An Introduction to Lacan, Derrida, and Kristeva*. Oxford: Blackwell, 1993.

Pearson, Roger, *Unfolding Mallarmé*. Oxford: Clarendon, 1996.

Porter, Laurence, *The Crisis of French Symbolism*. Ithaca, NY: Cornell University Press, 1990.

Rabaté, Jean-Michel, *Jacques Lacan: Psychoanalysis and the Subject of Literature*. New York: Palgrave, 2001.

Ransom, John Crowe, *The World's Body*. Baton Rouge: Louisiana University Press, 1968.

Rosenberg, Isaac, *The Collected Works of Isaac Rosenberg*, ed. Ian Parsons. New York: Oxford University Press, 1979.

Roudinesco, Elisabeth, *Jacques Lacan & Co.: A History of Psychoanalysis in France, 1925–1985*, trans. Jeffrey Mehlman. Chicago: University of Chicago Press, 1990.

Saussure, Ferdinand de, *Course in General Linguistics*, trans. Wade Baskin, ed. Charles Bally and Albert Sechehaye. New York: McGraw-Hill, 1966.

Schloss, Carol, "Teaching Joyce Teaching Kristeva: Estrangement in the Modern World." *Pedagogy, Praxis, Ulysses: Using Joyce's Text to Transform the Classroom*, ed. Robert Newman. Ann Arbor: University of Michigan Press, 1996, pp. 47–61.

Scott, Clive, *A Question of Syllables: Essays in Nineteenth-Century French Verse*. Cambridge: Cambridge University Press, 1986.

——, *Vers Libre: The Emergence of Free Verse in France, 1886–1914*. Oxford: Clarendon Press, 1990.

——, *The Poetics of French Verse*. Oxford: Oxford University Press, 1998.

Smith, Anna, *Julia Kristeva: Readings of Exile and Estrangement*. New York: St. Martin's Press, 1996.

Sollers, Philippe, *Lois*. Paris: Seuil, 1972.

——, *Women*, trans. Barbara Bray. New York: Columbia University Press, 1990.

Solomon, Philip H., "Céline's *Death on the Installment Plan*: the Intoxication of Delirium." *Yale French Studies*, 50 (1974): 190–203.

——, *Understanding Céline*. Columbia: University of South Carolina Press, 1992.

Thiher, Alan, *Céline: The Novel as Delirium*. New Brunswick: Rutgers University Press, 1972.

Virgil, *The Aeneid*, trans. Robert Fitzgerald. New York: Vintage, 1990.

Volosinov, V. N., *Marxism and the Philosophy of Language*, trans. L. Matejka and I. R. Titunik. Cambridge, MA: Harvard University Press, 1986.

Weber, Samuel, *The Return to Freud: Jacques Lacan's Dislocation of Psychoanalysis*, trans. Michael Levine. Cambridge: Cambridge University Press, 1991.

——, *The Legend of Freud*. Minneapolis: University of Minnesota Press, 1982; reissued Stanford, CA: Stanford University Press, 2000.

Weinberg, Bernard, *The Limits of Symbolism*. Chicago: University of Chicago Press, 1966.

Wordsworth, William, *The Prelude: 1799, 1805, 1850*, ed. Jonathan Wordsworth, M. H. Abrams, and Stephen Gill. New York: W.W. Norton, 1979.

Index